PHL

5406000134634

D1581512

WITHDRAWN

THE
PAUL HAMLYN
LIBRARY

DONATED BY

ENGLISH HERITAGE LIBRARY

TO THE

BRITISH MUSEUM

opened December 2000

ENGLISH HERITAGE
CENTRAL ARCHAEOLOGY SERVICE
FORT CUMBERLAND
FORT CUMBERLAND ROAD
EASTNEY, PORTSMOUTH
HANTS.
PO4 9LD
WITHDRAWN FROM
ENGLISH HERITAGE
LIBRARY

WITHDRAWN

Navio

The fort and *vicus* at Brough-on-Noe, Derbyshire

Edited by

Martin J. Dearne

TEMPVS REPARATVM

BAR British Series 234
1993

936.251 DEA

B.A.R.

All volumes available from:

Hadrian Books Ltd, 122 Banbury Road, Oxford OX2 7BP, England

The current BAR catalogue, with details of all titles in print, post-free prices and means of payment, is available free from the above address.

All volumes are distributed by Hadrian Books Ltd.

BAR 234

Dearne M J (Ed) 1993
Navio: The fort and vicus at Brough-on-Noe, Derbyshire

© The individual authors 1993

ISBN 0 86054 759 0

Tempvs Reparatvm Volume Editor: David P Davison

British Archaeological Reports are published by

TEMPVS REPARATVM
Archaeological and Historical Associates Limited

All enquiries regarding the submission of manuscripts for future publication should be addressed to:

David P Davison MA MPhil DPhil
General Editor BAR
Tempvs Reparatvm
29 Beaumont Street   Tel: 0865 311046
Oxford OX1 2NP   Fax: 0865 311047

To my parents, John and Sylvia Dearne

Contents

List of Contributors

J.E. Bartlett — The Old Stables, Youlgreave, Derbyshire

M.C. Bishop — 36 Simpson St., Crookhill, Ryton, Tyne and Wear

K. Branigan — Dept. of Archaeology and Prehistory, University of Sheffield

M.J. Dearne — Dept. of Archaeology and Prehistory, University of Sheffield

C. Drage — 29 Golden Valley, Riddings, Derbyshire

J.F. Drinkwater — Department of Classical and Archaeological Studies, University of Nottingham

C.R. Hart — Arbeia Roman Fort Museum, South Shields

J.A. Lloyd — Institute of Archaeology, 36 Beaumont St., Oxford

List of Figures

List of Plates

Preface

The presence of a Roman fort at Brough-on-Noe in the Derbyshire Peak District has been recognised for a long time and the first excavations occurred nearly ninety years ago. The existence of a *vicus* outside it has only more recently been confirmed. Both elements of the site have been the subject of several pieces of archaeological work but the interpretation of the site has been somewhat handicapped by the fact that for various reasons a number of these pieces of work have not been fully published. The completion of six years of research and rescue work in the *vicus* in 1986 underlined the need for a period of evaluation and publication of results, as indeed had been called for with respect to the fort by Jones and Wild sixteen years earlier (Jones and Wild 1970, 106). Thus the present volume has the dual aims of publishing as fully as possible those pieces of work on the fort and *vicus* which remain unpublished and of presenting some unified account and interpretation of both elements of the site.

The editor would like to record his thanks to all those who have contributed papers to this volume and especially Prof. Keith Branigan, Clive Hart and Dr. John Lloyd who encouraged his interest in the site and discussed aspects of it with him over many years. Thanks are also offered to Mr. Fred Coupland who as well as acting as site supervisor in 1986 accompanied the editor to the site many times and maintained an intermittent watch on minor roadworks, etc., in the vicinity. The editor is also grateful to the Committee for the Ashmolean Library, Oxford for permission to publish the report by the late Sir Ian Richmond and J.P. Gillam, and to the Haverfield Fund, the Peak Park Planning Board and the Kiln Trust for financial assistance in the preparation of the volume. The text was processed and typeset by Russ Adams of the Department of Archaeology and Prehistory, University of Sheffield, and Clive Hart and Jean Parkes assisted greatly in the checking of bibliographical references.

M.J. Dearne
August 1993

1. Brough-on-Noe: The Background and Context of the Site

Martin J. Dearne

The Site and its Historical Context

The fort at Brough-on-Noe (SK 181827) lies on a low spur of land at 170m (545 ft) OD, in a bend of the R. Noe a short distance north west of its confluence with a tributary, the Bradwell Brook. A second smaller and unnamed tributary, today occupying a steep sided valley enters the Noe to the north of the fort. The *vicus* lies on sloping land south east of the fort either side of the Bradwell Brook as far as a high steep hill with another small area on sloping land south west of the fort (Figure 1:1). The site lies on Limestone Shale immediately north of the boundary of the carboniferous Limestone dome of the Peak District, and its subsoil is formed chiefly by clayey sub-glacial deposits and the Limestone Shale.

Brough-on-Noe lies in an important strategic position at the widest part of the Hope Valley, which represents a natural corridor of lowland between the Limestone uplands of the White Peak to the south and the high Gritstone moors to the north (Figure 1:2). The importance of this valley in pre-Roman times is reflected by the large Iron Age hillfort of Mam Tor which lies at the head of the valley, and in Medieval times by the nearby Peveril Castle. The Hope Valley provided a routeway for part of the Roman road system in the peak and the fort at Brough doubtless played a role in its supervision, at least four roads meeting at or passing through the site (see further Dearne, this volume).

The nature of the area in the late pre-Roman Iron Age is obscure. It may have formed part of the tribal territory of the Brigantes but the most southerly place listed by Ptolemy (*Geography* II, 3,10) as within their orbit was either Slack (Rivet and Smith 1981, 295) or Castleshaw (Hartley and Fitts 1988, 4). An alternative attribution of the area to the Corieltavi (now known to be the correct name for the tribe formerly called the Cornovii; *Britannia* (1983, 349 ff)) is possible (e.g. Rivet 1964, 142). However, there is little on which to decide the matter (Dearne 1990, 21–23). In either event there is almost no evidence at present for late Iron Age activity in the Peak District (Dearne 1990, 29 ff). Mam Tor appears to have gone out of use by the sixth century B.C. (Coombs 1977; Hart 1981, 73) and no significant Iron Age material has been recovered from elsewhere in the Hope Valley or adjacent areas. Indeed, excepting a few finds mainly in caves in the south of the Peak District there is no indication of permanent late Iron Age settlement throughout the majority of the upland south Pennines.

No Roman military activity is likely to have occurred in the Peak District before the governorship of Q. Petilius Cerialis in the early 70s. Rather the south Pennines probably formed at least *de facto* part of the buffer client state of Brigantia. Dynastic struggles between its queen, Cartimandua, and her consort Venutius recorded by Tacitus (*Annales* xii, 40; *Historia* iii, 45), though their exact details are disputed (Frere 1987, 82; Hanson and Campbell 1986, 77–9), probably led to the establishment of a defensive cordon around the area from the 50s on (Figure 1:3). The cordon on the east probably included Templeborough founded under Didius Gallus (May 1922, 6; Simpson 1973, 84); Strutt's Park, Derby in the early 50s (Dool 1985, 25); and perhaps Chesterfield, although the most recent assessment of its foundation suggests a date no earlier than the 60s (Ellis 1989, 124). Such a cordon may have run west from Derby to include Rocester where there are two pre-Flavian forts (Cleary and Ferris 1988), Trent Vale and temporary camps at Astbury and Hogg (Jones 1968, 2 ff). Indeed Wroe (1982) has suggested that a road and fort remain to be discovered between Chesterton (the successor to Trent Vale) and Manchester. The cordon might have stretched as far as Chester (Hanson and Campbell 1986, 82) but much work is required to clarify the situation west of the Pennines (*cf.* also Carrington 1986). To the east of the Pennines a number of pre-Flavian vexilation fortresses, whose exact relationship remains uncertain, may also have played a role. Hanson and Campbell (1986, 80 ff) suggest that those at Osmanthorpe, Broxtowe and Newton-on-Trent represent a line set up to watch over Brigantia with Rossington Bridge as an advanced post.

It is clear from Tacitus (*Agricola* 17) that Cerialis conquered much of Brigantia following the rescue of Cartimandua from anti-Roman elements amongst the tribe in 69. Exactly what this entailed is uncertain but it seems clear that he was enclosing the southern Pennines in a pincer movement and activity across the Stainmore Pass, and at Malton, York, Carlisle and Hayton may be attributable to him (Frere 1987, 84; Salway 1981, 136). Whether he was active in areas such as the Peak District is unknown but the area must be essentially considered as conquered by *c*.73. Conventionally the consolidation of the conquest and notably the construction of roads and forts such as Brough-on-Noe is assigned to the governorship of Julius Agricola (78 or 79 to 84).

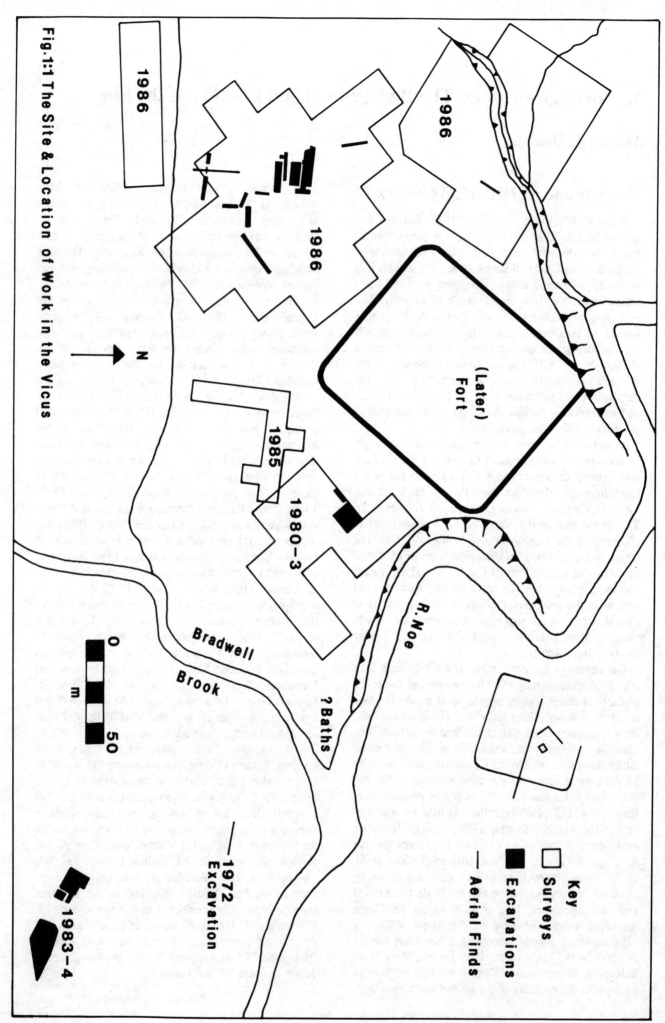

Fig. 1:1 The Site & Location of Work in the Vicus

N

0 50
m

Key
☐ Surveys
■ Excavations
— Aerial Finds

1986

1986

1986

(Later) Fort

1985

1980-3

1972 Excavation

?Baths

R. Noe

Bradwell Brook

1983-4

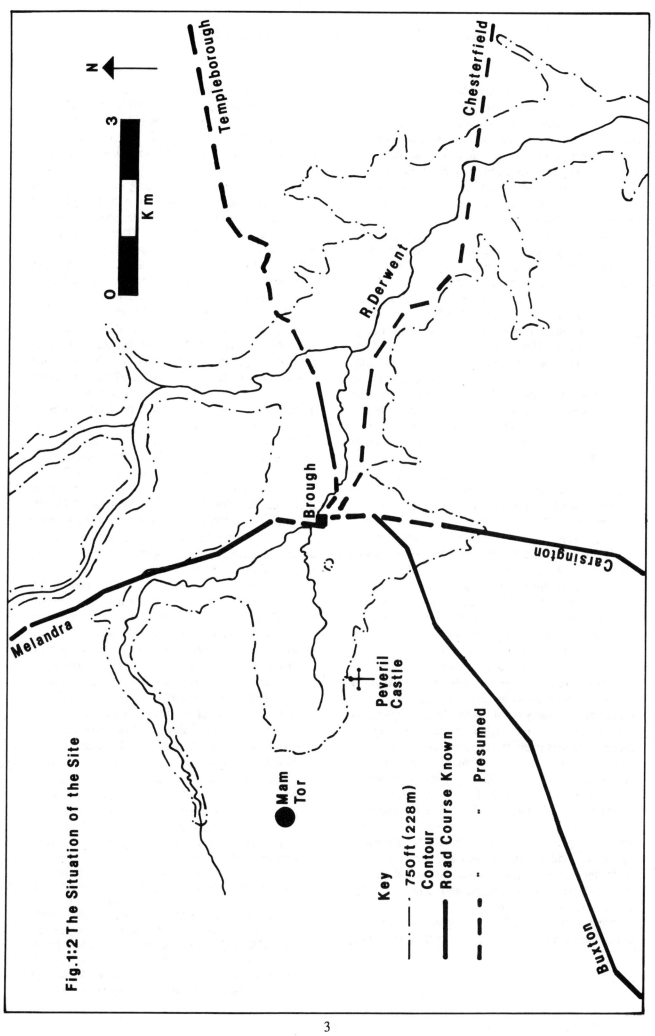

Fig.1:2 The Situation of the Site

Key

750ft (228m) Contour
Road Course Known
" " Presumed

Templeborough

Chesterfield

R.Derwent

Carsington

Brough

Melandra

Mam Tor

Peveril Castle

Buxton

N

0   Km   3

3

However, given the considerable problems with the placing of his campaigns and the probable bias of our main literary source, the *Agricola* written by his son-in-law Tacitus some caution is required in assessing Agricola's role in conquest and consolidation. The assigning of the consolidation of much of northern England to just six or seven years during which much campaigning also occurred must be questionable. Indeed, as Hanson and Campbell (1986, 89) and Hanson (1987, 64) point out if all the forts at present regarded as Agricolan foundations are such then there is a problem in terms of the size of the campaigning force that he would have had at his disposal. Rather it seems probable that some consolidation occurred under Agricola's predecessor, Julius Frontinius, or his successors. Unfortunately archaeological evidence is often unable to differentiate between foundation dates in the mid- and late-70s but at least one site, Castleford, now seems to have been a Frontinian foundation (Abramson 1988, 44). As Jones (1968, 6) has pointed out, Brough-on-Noe is on strategic grounds as likely a candidate as any for a Frontinian rather than Agricolan origin, but this must remain speculative.

Whatever the precise date of the garrisoning of the south Pennines it is clear that a network of forts existed in the later-first century both around its edge (Manchester; Rocester; Little Chester, Derby; probably Pentrich; Chesterfield; ?Templeborough; and Castleford) and in the uplands proper (Slack; Castleshaw; Melandra; Brough). Whether further forts existed at Buxton (e.g. Hart 1981, 87; Burnham and Wacher 1990, 176 ff) and Carsington (Ling and Courtney 1981; Ling *et al.* 1990; Dearne, Anderson and Branigan forthcoming) remains speculative.

Little is known of the subsequent history of the area. Indeed, whether it became part of a *civitas* (and if so which) or at some point partly or totally attained another status such as an Imperial estate due to its lead mining industry is not known. Buxton is likely to have developed into a religious spa, and any military presence there is likely to have been short lived, while the settlement at Carsington may possibly be identified with *Lutudarum*, the presumed administrative centre of the lead industry (Ling and Courtney 1981; Ling *et al.* 1990; Dearne, Anderson and Branigan forthcoming). At most of the known forts *vici* grew up but only at Derby, Rocester, Castleford, and perhaps Manchester can a case be made out for their survival or later re-foundation as civil settlements not dependent on the forts (Dearne 1991; Abramson 1988, 48).

Rather most of the forts and their military *vici* closed during the course of the first half of the second century, Brough itself probably closing *c*.120.[1] The removal of these garrisons probably in two waves, *c*.120/30 and *c*.140, was presumably connected to the garrisoning of Hadrian's Wall and the subsequent move to the Antonine Wall. Immediately before the middle of the second century only the fort at Little Chester, Derby would seem likely to have been in commission. However, two sites were re-garrisoned early in the second half of the second century. Manchester was re-occupied *c*.160 and continued to be so into at least the late-fourth century (Walker 1986, 141 ff) and Brough was re-occupied from *c*.155/8 until the mid-fourth century. The reason for this is unclear. Various pieces of evidence have been cited for a Brigantian revolt *c*.154 leading to such re-occupations, though at least some of the evidence may alternatively relate to A. Pius's seizure of lowland Scotland (e.g. Frere 1987, 135 ff). Whatever the reason for the re-occupations (and for the south Pennines the reason could be as simple as a desire for a police force at a time when lead production is likely to have been important and concern over the security of the road network) the pattern of military garrisons in the area had been fixed. The fort at Derby closed either *c*.200 or *c*.330 (Wheeler 1985, 302) and Templeborough was re-occupied between the later-third and ?mid-fourth centuries (Simpson 1973, 89) but these were the only changes. Essentially after 155/8 Brough stood alone as a military base in the upland south Pennines supported only by an occasional fort on the Pennine edges.

Little is known of other aspects of the area in the Roman period. The lead industry was clearly important at least into Hadrianic times and some lead production continued in the fourth century, but many details of its chronology and organisation remain uncertain (see further Dearne, this volume). A considerable influx of rural settlers, perhaps primarily in the early-second century, seems likely and may have been connected to the development of this industry (Hodges and Wildgoose 1981; Hodges 1991, 70–91). However, work on such rural settlements is as yet limited and little beyond the broad pattern of their

---

1 Templeborough: probably occupied to the late-70s or early-80s (Simpson 1973, 84 and 89) and again at some point until late-Antonine times (May 1922, 62ff). Chesterfield: closed *c*.120/150 (Ellis 1989, 126). Pentrich: only late-first century material known (Smithard 1911) though very little investigation has occurred. Rocester: closed by the mid-second century (*Britannia* 18 (1987), 323; Cleary and Ferris 1988). Manchester: closed *c*.110/25 (Walker 1986, 141ff). Castleshaw: reduced to a fortlet *c*.100 and closed *c*.120 (Start 1985, 13; Mcneil, Start and Walker 1989). Slack: reduced in size 122/5 and closed *c*.140/60 (Hunter, Manby and Spaul 1967/70, 80). Melandra: closed *c*.140 (Conway 1906, 126; Petch 1949, 1-40 and 49-63).

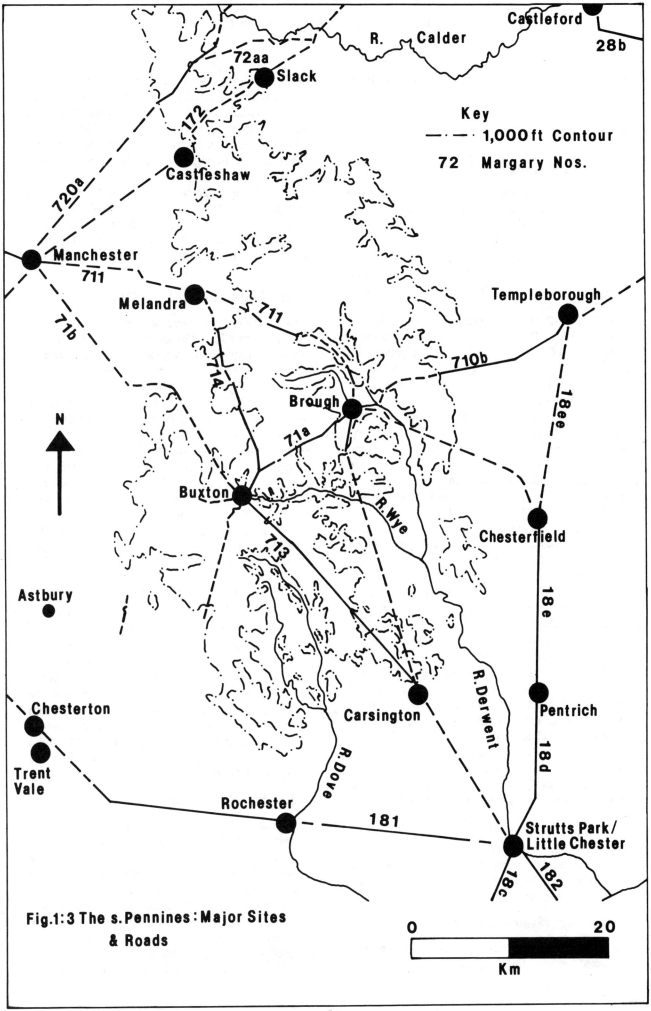

Key
- —·—·— 1,000 ft Contour
- **72** Margary Nos.

R. Calder

Castleford
28b

72aa Slack
172
720a
Castleshaw

N

Manchester
711
71b
Melandra
711
714

Templeborough
710b
18ee

Brough
71a
R. Wye

Chesterfield
18e

Buxton
713
R. Derwent

Astbury

Carsington
R. Dove

Pentrich
18d

Chesterton

Trent Vale

Rochester
181

Strutts Park/
Little Chester
18c   182

Fig.1:3 The s.Pennines: Major Sites
& Roads

0   20
Km

5

distribution is known in detail (Makepeace 1985; Dearne 1990, 167 ff).

The History of Work at the Site

a) Records Prior to 1903

The existence of the fort (or at least of a Roman site of some sort) at Brough-on-Noe was recognised by Pegge in 1761 if not before and between then and 1885 a number of finds and features were noted (conveniently summarised by Thompson-Watkin 1885, 80-5). Most notable are records of an oblong stone building, apparently with ?*opus signinum* ?floors and associated with bricks and tiles including one stamped COH[, at the confluence of the R. Noe and the Bradwell Brook. At the same location a "double row of pillars" is recorded and, together with more recent evidence, these suggest that this was the site of the baths (Dearne 1986, 98ff.). Other ?*opus signinum* floors may have been found elsewhere and Bateman suggests that some foundations were still visible in the middle of the nineteenth century. However, most traces had disappeared by 1885 and their removal by ploughing, noted by all modern excavators within the fort and represented by prominent ridge and furrow over most of the site, was clearly in train by 1761.

Two sculptures, both lost, are recorded. The first seen in 1761 was said to be a rude bust of Apollo and another deity. The second, recorded in 1767, was apparently a half length female figure within a rebated panel with her hands crossed on her breast and wearing a large "peaked bonnet". Other finds included a gold coin of Vespasian (3rd consulate; A.D. 71); further tiles with partial COH stamps; an urn apparently with an inscription probably to be read VITA/VIV/TR; three urns full of ashes; and three column or moulding fragments (of which one still remains built into the wall surrounding the mill at the site). Only one of these finds may be exactly located, though the coin clearly came from the area of the mill at the Noe/Bradwell confluence. The urns are probably those marked on O.S. maps (e.g. Garstang 1904, plate 1) at the Brough lead works south of the known *vicus* and provide the only hint to date of the location of a cemetery. An altar (*R.I.B.* 278; No.5 below) was also found in the grounds of Haddon Hall near Bakewell before 1695 and its reference to *Cohors I Aquitanorum* suggests that it may originally have come from Brough. No further discoveries are recorded between 1885 and 1903.

b) The Excavations of 1903

The first archaeological excavations at the site were conducted in the fort by John Garstang for the Derbyshire Archaeological and Natural History Society in 1903 (Garstang 1904). His work identified the fort wall at a number of points, examined the west angle tower and the north west gate. However, the most important discoveries were that of the stone headquarters building, much of the external wall of which he traced, and the stone cellar within it. A few other building fragments, drains and stretches of roadway were also recovered. The finds from this work are almost all lost or divorced from their provenances except for a number of altars, inscriptions etc. at Buxton Museum (Foster-Smith 1984).

c) The Excavations of 1938/9

Further excavations were undertaken by Sir Ian Richmond and John Gillam in 1938/9. An interim report (Richmond 1938) appeared on the first season's work but the final report remained unpublished until it was included in this volume. The work demonstrated for the first time the existence of the earlier fort by revealing its defensive ditches at the west corner and on the south west side. It also examined the later fort's defences in these areas, recovered the majority of the plan of the later *principia*, fragments of buildings to the north west and south east of it and part of the south west gate. Again the finds from the work are lost or divorced from their provenance (Foster-Smith 1984, 9–11) but Gillam's assessment of the pottery gave the first basic chronology for the site.

d) The Excavations of 1958/9

The most important outstanding problem with the fort, at least in its later phases, after 1938/9 was the position of the south east defences. J.E. Bartlett's work in 1958/9 established their details, examined the south angle tower and found the ditches of the earlier fort below it. However, an important feature of the work was the discovery of a late Roman ?cavalry exit inserted through the south east fort wall. Interim reports appeared on the work (Bartlett 1959; 1960) and a full report appears in this volume. The finds are in Sheffield Museum.

e) The Excavations of 1965–9

Five seasons of work on the fort by Manchester University from 1965 to 1969 were directed by Prof. G. D. B. Jones, Dr. J. P. Wild and others. The work examined the north west and north east defences but was principally concerned with the interior of the earlier and later forts. It located and recovered parts of the plans of the earlier fort's granary, ?*praetorium* and probably *principia*, thus demonstrating the orientation of the fort. Much of the plan of one building, at least in the fort's third phase a stables, and fragments of others in the later fort's *praetentura* were uncovered together with details of the phase 2A and 2B granaries and phase 3 ?*praetorium*. Other miscellaneous building fragments were also noted and the late changes to access on the south east were re-examined. However, the most important result of the work was the confirmation and refinement of a three phase chronology for the fort. Five interim reports appeared (Jones and Thompson 1965; Jones, Thompson and Wild 1966; Jones 1967; Jones and Wild 1968; 1970). The finds and archives from the work are held in the Department of Archaeology, Manchester University.

f) The Excavations of 1971/2

Limited rescue work directed by Mr. H. Lane seems likely to have re-located the ?baths building noted by antiquarians at the Noe/Bradwell confluence and to have revealed for the first time part of the *vicus* adjacent to the modern road through the village. A brief note of the work appeared (Lane 1973) but no further details are available and the fate of the finds and any records is unknown.

g) Finds in 1979/80

In addition to casual finds of pottery etc. Mr. J. Eyre recovered two altars (Nos. 6 and 8 below) in 1979/80 during construction work at his farm on the future site of the 1983/4 excavations (Figure 1:1).

h) The Survey and Excavations of 1980–83

A large geophysical survey and excavations for the University of Sheffield were directed by Dr. J. A. Lloyd and Dr. J. F. Drinkwater in 1980–83 and concentrated on the area of the *vicus* immediately south east of the fort. The main results of the work were the location and examination of two roads leaving the south east fort gate with traces of presumably *vicanal* activity and metal working between them. The work is published in the present volume and the finds are in Sheffield Museum.

i) The Excavations of 1983/4

A watching brief on building work in the vicinity of the altar finds by members of Sheffield University revealed in 1983 further traces of the *vicus*. A rescue excavation was conducted under the direction of Dr. D. Kennedy of Sheffield University. Subsequently C. Drage of the Trent and Peak Archaeological Trust directed a more extensive excavation in 1984 immediately south east of this revealing a terraced road and a number of phases of *vicanal* activity at the edge of the settlement. A full report on this work appears in this volume and the finds are in the Sheffield Museum.

j) The Surveys and Excavations of 1985/6

A small geophysical survey directed by the present author in 1985 covered an area of the presumed *vicus* south east of the fort not covered by the survey of 1980–83 (Figure 1:1). It is published herein along with the work in 1980–3. Subsequently the intention of the landowners to afforest large areas to the west and south west of the fort led to another large geophysical survey in 1986 directed by the present author which revealed possible archaeological features in the threatened area. Trial trenching in the same year confirmed these findings and led to more extensive excavations directed by Prof. K. Branigan and the present author. This work identified a possibly isolated area of *vicanal* activity to the south west of the fort as well as other features. A full report appears in the present volume and the finds are in Sheffield Museum.

k) Aerial Reconnaissance in 1988

Aerial photographs taken by Dr. D Riley in 1988 revealed a possible rectangular ?military enclosure across the R. Noe from the fort and details of the road network south east of the fort. This work appears in this volume.

l) Miscellaneous Work

Numbers of casual finds, chiefly of pottery, have occurred both by local farmers and archaeologists over many years (*cf.* Foster-Smith 1984, 20–3; author's records), most of the material remaining in private hands. However, it is clear that further excavations at Brough have gone largely unrecorded. Small collections of material in Sheffield Museum donated by the late R. W. P. Cockerton and J. P. Heathcote (both of whom were long associated with the site, the former having been a prime mover in the work of 1938/9) seem to relate to such work (*cf.* Foster-Smith 1984, 20–1). It appears that at least some of this work probably occurred in 1945–52, 1962 and perhaps the 1970s. One excavation in 1948 appears to have confirmed the site of the baths and recovered part of a tile stamped CE ?A (*Journal of Roman Studies* 39 (1949), 114 No.4). Others, probably in 1962, seem to have sectioned the roads leaving the fort gates to judge from published inscribed amphora sherds (*Journal of Roman Studies* 53 (1963), 166 No.50; No. 10 below). A copy of a sketch plan held by the author (through the good offices of C. R. Hart and P. Wroe) indicates the broad outlines of this work, however Hart (pers. comm.) examined Heathcote's archives (now presumed lost) and found that they revealed little more about the work. The amphora fragments appear to be in the Cockerton collection in Sheffield Museum. A decorated copper alloy strip in Buxton Museum also seems to derive from some part of this work.

The Inscriptions and Altars From the Site

The following inscriptions and uninscribed altars are known from the site. Stamped tiles and bricks are excluded (for these see above and Branigan and Dearne, this volume; Jones and Wild, 1970, 106).

No. 1 *R.I.B.* 283; Garstang (1904), 197–201
Four fragments of an inscribed tablet 142 X 76 cm with moulded border in Millstone Grit found re-used in the *principia* cellar in 1903 and now in Buxton Museum:
IMP.CAESARI.T.[AEL.HADR]/[AN]TONIN O.AV[G.PIO.P.P]/COH.I.AQVITAN[NORVM]/SVB.IVLIO.V[ERO.LEG.]AVG/PR.PR.INS T[ANTE]/[C]APITONI[O.]SCO.PRAE
(For the) Emperor Caesar Titus Aelius Hadrianus Antoninus Augustus Pius, Father of his Country, (Built by) the First Cohort of Aquitanians Under Julius Verus, Emperor's Propraetorian Legate, Under the Charge of Capitonius...scus, Prefect.

No.2 *Journal of Roman Studies* 53 (1963), 160
Fragment of a Gritstone ?imperial statue base 22 X 15 cm reused as a walling stone and retaining a wedge shaped slot. Found in 1962 on the edge of the fort. Present location unknown:
[I]MP.CAES[
Emperor Caesar...

No.3 *R.I.B.* 281; Garstang (1904), 194
Square Gritstone altar 50 x 30 cm with focus and bolsters on upper face, the inscription within a wreath. Found in the *principia* cellar in 1903 and now in Buxton Museum;
DEAE/ARNOMECTE/AEL.MOTIO/V.S.L.L. M.
(To the) Goddess Arnomecta, Aelius Motio Gladly, Willingly and Deservedly Fullfilled his vow.

No.4 *R.I.B.* 282; Garstang (1904), 194
Top of a Gritstone altar 25 X 20 cm with highly moulded sides and top with an inscription below the moulding. Found in the *principia* cellar in 1903 and now in Buxton Museum:
DEO.MARTI[
(To the) God Mars...

No.5 *R.I.B.* 278
Gritstone altar 122 X 48 cm with bolsters on upper face found in the grounds of Haddon Hall, near Bakewell before 1695, having

probably been removed from Brough in post-Roman times and still at Haddon Hall:
DEO/MARTI/BRACIACAE/Q.SITTIVS/CAE CILIAN/PRAEF.COH/I.AQUITANO/V.S.
(To the) God Mars Braciaca, Quintus Sittius Caecilianus, Prefect of the First Cohort of Aquitanians Fulfilled his Vow.

No.6 *Britannia* 10 (1980), 404 No.3; Drage (this volume)
Gritstone altar 109 X 48 cm with bolsters on upper face, the first line of the inscription on an ansate panel below the focus and large leaf stops in the inscription. Found in 1979/80 on the site excavated in the *vicus* in 1984 and now on loan to Sheffield Museum:
HERCVLI.[AV]G/[OB]RESTITVTIONEM.PS /ACAEP.ASC[ ]/[ ]/PROCVLVS/PRAEF.POSVIT/IDEM QVE.DEDICA/VIT
(To) Hercules Augustus.......Proculus the Prefect set this up and Dedicated it Because of his Restoration of....

No.7 Garstang (1904), 194
Gritstone altar with moulded base and top, probably originally inscribed. Found at Hope in 1903 having presumably been removed from Brough in post Roman times.

No.8 (*cf.* No.6)
Small altar found near to No.6 at the same time and uninscribed.

No.9 *Britannia* 16 (1985), 326 No.16; Drage (this volume)
Millstone Grit upper quern stone originally 39 cm in diameter found on the 1984 site in the *vicus* and now in Sheffield Museum:
SATVRNINI
(Property of) Saturninus

No.10 *Journal of Roman Studies* 53 (1963), 166 No.50; Davies (1971), 131 note 64
Base of globular amphora found in 1962 in a roadside ditch in the *vicus*. A graffito cut before firing:
J.R.S.:ILITRIIB[ ]/LIII.FRV[ ]/[ ]I[ ]
Davies (to be preferred):
ILITRIIB/LIII.PRVN[A]/[ ]I[ ]
(?From) Ilitreb, 53 Prunes...
(Ilitreb = ? unmatched Spanish place name)

No.11 Thompson-Watkin (1885), 80–5
Urn. Only recorded by antiquarians and now lost:
VITA/VIV/TR
Expansion uncertain

The Name of the Site

The Roman name of Brough-on-Noe is established as *Navio* (Rivet and Smith 1981, 423 ff). It appears as

Navione and *Nanione* in Ravenna but *R.I.B.* 2243, the lower part of a milestone found at Buxton, confirms the name giving A NAVIONE M P XI (from *Navio* 11 Miles). Rivet and Smith (1981, 423 ff) note the probable derivation from a river name meaning 'fast flowing water'.

It is not clear whether the notional third declension nominative *Navio* derived by Rivet and Smith from the sources was actually in use, nor whether the whole site would have simply been known as *Navio* or whether both or either the fort and *vicus* would have been known by the name with appropriate prefixes (*cf.* Sommer 1984, 25 ff).

Unstratified Coins from the Site

Unstratified Coins

The following coins were recovered unstratified from the environs of the fort and *vicus* including the banks and bed of the River Noe and the field north east of and across the river from the fort by Mr G. Fletcher using a metal detector between 1979 and 1982. The identifications are by Wendy Huddle, formerly of Sheffield Museum, to whom the author is grateful for details.

1. *As* (Di.27mm)
   Obverse: Lauriate head to r.
   Reverse: Female figure seated to l. with staff in crook of l.arm.
   Incomplete. A. Pius/M. Aurelius/Commodus (139–192). Die axis 180°. R. Noe '400 yards north west of fort'.

2. *Antoninianus* (Di. 22m)
   Obverse: Radiate head to r. GALLIENVS AVG
   Reverse: Capricorn r. NEPTVMO CONS AVG. Retrograde lower central field N.
   Complete. Gallienus (sole reign) (260–8). *R.I.C.* v(i)245. Die axis 0°. Rome mint. Field north east of the fort across the R. Noe.

3. *Antoninianus* (Di. 20mm)
   Obverse: Radiate, draped bust r. [IMP C VICT] ORINVS PF AVG
   Reverse: Sol walking r., r. hand raised, l. hand holding whip INVICTUS. Star upper left field.
   Complete. Victorinus (268–70). *R.I.C.* v(ii)114. Die axis 0°. Cologne mint. Ridge south of 1986 site.

4. *Follis* (Di. 30mm)
   Obverse: Lauriate, curiassed bust r. in low relief IMP MA [XIMIAN] VS AVG
   Reverse: Genius standing l. holding *patera* and cornucopia, wearing *modus* and *chalmys* draped over l. arm. GENIO POP IVLI ROMANI

Incomplete. Maximianus (303–5). *?R.I.C. vi* 28b. Die axis 180°. ?London mint. East corner of field north east of fort across the R. Noe.

5. *Aes* (Di. 20mm)
   Obverse: Lauriate, draped bust l. holding victory in r. hand and *mappa* in l. CONSTANTINVS [IVN] NOE C.
   Reverse: Globe on altar with three stars above and VO/TIS/[XX] on altar. BCATA TRAN/QUILLITAS.
   Complete. Constantine II as Caesar (321–3). *R.I.C. vii* 420. Die axis 180°. Trier mint. River Noe '200 yards north west of fort'.

6. *Aes* (Di. 17mm)
   Obverse: Lauriate bust wearing imperial cloak with reversed spear CONSTAN/TINOPOLIS.
   Reverse: Victory standing l. on prow of ship with spear and shield TRP in lower field.
   Complete. House of Constantine (330–1). *R.I.C. vii* 530. Die axis 180°. Trier mint. River Noe '200 yards north west of fort'.

7. *Aes* (Di. 18.5mm)
   Obverse: Helmeted bust l. VRBS ROMA.
   Reverse: She-wolf standing l. suckling twins with two stars above SMKS in lower field.
   Complete. House of Constantine (333–4). *R.I.C. vii* 90. Die axis 180°. Cyzicus mint. River Noe.

8. *Aes* (Di. 19mm)
   Obverse: Helmeted bust to l. VRBS ROMA.
   Reverse: She-wolf standing l. suckling twins with two stars above.
   Complete. House of Constantine (333–5). As *R.I.C. vii* 349. Die axis 180°. Rome mint. River Noe near Bradwell.

9. *Aes* (Di. 16.5mm)
   Obverse: Lauriate and curiassed bust r. CONSTANTINVS NOB C.
   Reverse: Two soldiers standing looking at each other, reversed spear in outer hand, other resting on shield on ground. Between two standards AQP below +.
   Complete. Constantine II as Caesar (334–5). *R.I.C. vii* 125. Die axis 0°. Aquilea mint. River Noe.

10. *Aes* III (Di. 17mm)
    Obverse: Draped, curiassed, pearl diademed bust r. DN VALEN/S PF AVG.
    Reverse: Victory advancing l. holding wreath and palm. OF upper left field.
    Incomplete and struck off centre. Valens (364–75). As *R.I.C. ix* 12 or as *R.I.C. ix* 2 or 17b. Die axis 180°. Lyons or Arles mint. ?North east side of field north east of fort across River Noe.

11. *Aes* (Ae 3/4) (Di. 17.5mm)
Obverse: ?Lauriate, ?draped and ?curiassed bust r. [ ]STA[ ]/VS PF AVG.
Reverse: ?Figure standing [ ] REPVBLICE.
Incomplete. ?House of Constantine (fourth century). Die axis 180⁰. River Noe north west of the fort.

These coin finds, entirely random and far too small a sample to be statistically significant, make a total of 17 coins recorded from the site. The preponderance of fourth century coinage is not surprising and only No. 10 seems to be at variance with the proposed dating of the site. Its provenance makes it likely that it is related to activity along the line of the road to Templeborough which probably crossed the field north east of the fort and not necessarily to the fort and *vicus* itself.

2. The Roman Fort at Brough-On-Noe, Derbyshire (1938/9)

the late Sir I. A. Richmond and J. P. Gillam
with editorial notes by M. J. Dearne

Editor's Preface

This paper, with the exception of these introductory remarks, the footnotes and some further comments at the end, was compiled in ?1955 by the late Sir Ian Richmond and John Gillam as the final report on the work at the fort at Brough in 1938/9. It is published here with the kind permission of the Committee for the Ashmolean Library, Oxford who hold the original typescript, its earlier drafts and the site books, plans and photographs extant from the work. The editor would like to thank Brian McGregor and Graham Piddock of the Ashmolean Library for their help in making these available.

The work was curtailed by the outbreak of war in 1939, though the results of the first season had already been published in interim form.[1] This interim covered the work on the later and earlier fort defences, west angle tower, *principia* and a few other internal features. However, the assessment of these features contained herein is more detailed and differs in some details. Moreover it records details of other features excavated in 1939 and J. P. Gillam's assessment of the pottery.

In editing the paper the intention has been as far as possible to leave the text unchanged, though the pottery has been separated from the main text. Therefore footnotes have been used for bibliographical references (which have been amended to reflect the progress of work since 1955) in the main text and for editorial comment. Regrettably, except for Gillam's notes on the pottery, almost no records of the finds exist and the finds themselves are either lost or divorced form their provenance (perhaps excepting a few sherds at Manchester).[2] Even more regrettably the drawings of the numbered vessels described by Gillam cannot now be located amongst the Richmond papers. The only extant pottery drawings are those of five samian sherds which, as Gillam notes, were not worth illustrating. The figures accompanying the article are based on the plans and site book in the Ashmolean Library or are taken from the 1938 interim report.

Introduction

The Roman fort of Brough, Derbyshire, lies at the junction of the Bradwell Brook and the River Noe, some two miles downstream from Castleton, the medieval administrative centre of Peak Forest. It lay, as did so many Roman forts, not only at a river crossing but at a junction in the strategic network of roads by which it was the Roman practice to dominate restive tribal territories. Here a road from Templeborough to Buxton crossed the Noe and cordoned off the wildest hills in the Peak District, including the Iron Age hill fort of Mam Tor. It was joined by a road from the north, skilfully driven through the Doctor Gate pass from the fort of Melandra Castle, near Glossop, and it is likely that this route continued southwards down the valley to Matlock and towards Littlechester, though this supposition remains to be proved.[3] That the river crossing , however, was uppermost in the minds of those who chose the fort-site is suggested by the name chosen by the Romans for the place. This was *Navio*, formed from a river name *Nava*, in the same fashion as *Derventio*, *Cunetio*, and other Romano-British place names. The name occurs in the geographical work known as the *Ravenna cosmography*, derived from an Imperial road map. It is also found in the ablative case, on the Buxton milestone, in the phrase *a Navione*.[4]

Excavations took place here in 1903 and in 1938–1939.[5] Shortly after the first excavation the site was fully discussed in the Victoria County History by Haverfield, with a full bibliography to which reference may be made for earlier writers.[6] The concern of this article is with the second excavation and its results.

The Earlier Fort (Figure 2:1)

The remains of this fort were first discovered in 1938, below the NW and SW defences of its successor. They comprised a close set double ditch, laid out almost on

---

1 Richmond (1938).

2 Foster-Smith (1984, 9–11).

3 This has now been shown to be the case. For this and the road system generally see Wroe (1982); Wroe and Mellor (1971); Dearne (1990, 67 ff).

4 Rivet and Smith (1981, 423 ff).

5 Garstang (1904); Richmond (1938).

6 Haverfield (1905).

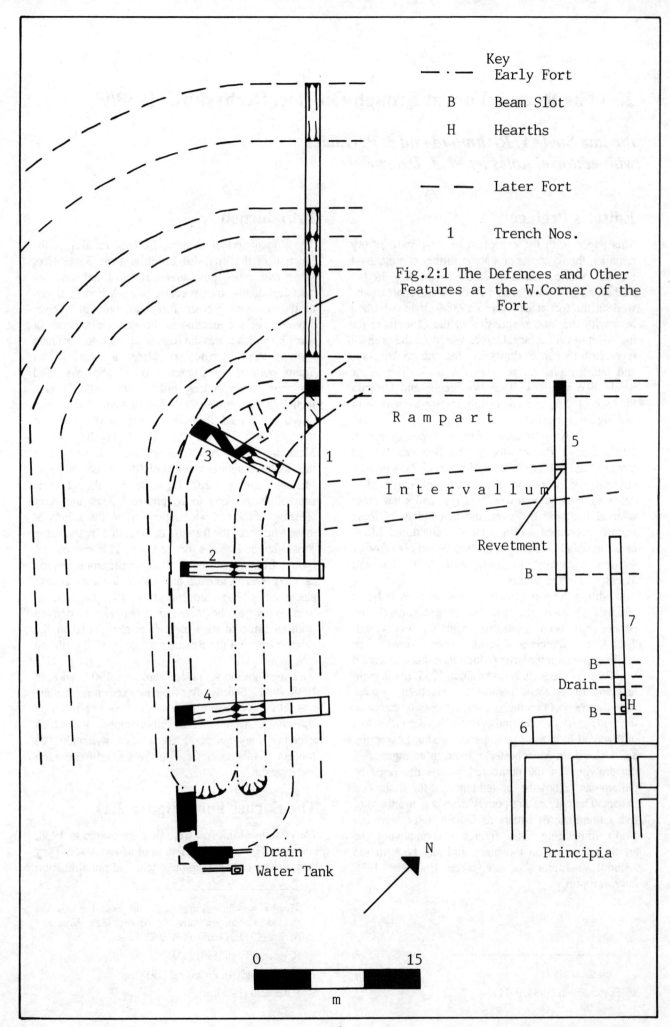

Key
— · — · — Early Fort
B Beam Slot
H Hearths

— — — Later Fort

1 Trench Nos.

Fig.2:1 The Defences and Other Features at the W.Corner of the Fort

Rampart

Intervallum

Revetment

B

Drain
Water Tank

N

Principia

0   15
                m

the same orientation as the later works, with its western angle below the later west angle tower.[7] The early south west gate, however, lay slightly north of the later *porta decumana*, and so little space is left between it and the north west front of the early fort as to establish that the gate cannot have been, as in the later fort, the *porta decumana*: it must be regarded rather as the *porta principalis sinistra* of a fort facing northwestwards up the valley and thus laid out along the ridge instead of across it.[8] But while excavation has thus established the existence and position of the earlier fort, it has not yet fixed its limits, which may be expected to have extended beyond those of the later fort on the south east.[9] The north east front, on the other hand, probably coincided closely with that of the later fort, the breadth of the one being equivalent to the length of the other.[10] It is evident that the *praetentura* of this early fort was very small, a feature in planning which it shares with Oakwood (Selkirkshire).[11]

Little is known of the early internal buildings. The excavations of 1938 revealed in the early *praetentura* trenches for sleeper beams, two cooking hearths and a V-shaped open drain of thin slabs, all suggestive of a barrack veranda.[12] In the area south east of the early *via pricipalis*[13] primary sleeper trenches were also discovered, but the opportunity to recover their plan in detail did not present itself. One suggestive grouping was provided by two trenches set close

together, at right angles to a third.[14] These might well be part of a timber built granary lying parallel with the *via principalis* and north east of the position normally reserved for the headquarters building.[15] It should be remarked that the very thorough pillaging for stone to which the upper levels have been subjected would render further excavation to recover the earliest plan comparatively easy, under skilled direction. It may also be noted that, at the lowest level, the entire area of the early fort seems to have been deliberately sealed by a spread of clay from nine inches to one foot (0.23–0.30 m) thick, probably derived from the demolition of its rampart. This operation is comparable with the covering of the early fort at Ambleside by a thick layer of sammel, or firm sand.[16] The general date of the early level thus sealed is not in doubt, as is shown by associated pottery (below).

The Later Fort (Figures 2:1 and 2:4)

The defences of the later fort comprise four ditches and a stone wall, backed by the usual earth bank.[17] The ditch system clearly includes two distinct and successive schemes. The innermost ditch, 18.5 ft (5.6 m) wide and 5.5 ft (1.7 m) deep, was kept open and tidy until it was finally abandoned, whereupon it silted up, becoming choked with fallen stones and masonry as the abandoned fort wall fell into ruin or was robbed and being ultimately filled up by

---

7 The inner ditch seen in trenches 1–4 (Figure 2:1 and 2:4) 8 ft (2.4 m) wide and 2 ft (0.6 m) deep of V-shaped profile with a rectangular slot at its base. The outer seen in trenches 2–4 but only just over half of it available for excavation at any point, 21 ft (6.4m) to 24 ft (7.3 m) wide, 5 ft (1.5 m) deep and of V-shaped profile. Both were filled with stripped turf, *Cf.* Richmond (1938, 55 ff and Appendix 1).

8 Subsequent work in the 1960s by Manchester University in fact established that the fort faced south west (Jones and Wild 1968, 90) and that this was in fact the *porta praetoria*.

9 For the position of these defences see Bartlett and Dearne this volume.

10 These defences have not been found but Richmond's conclusion remains valid.

11 Despite the misidentification of the gate later work has confirmed that the *praetentura* was small. For Oakwood *cf.* Steer (1951/2, fig. 3).

12 The drain was V-shaped and formed of angled slabs; the two hearths took the form of small square pits; the sleeper trench was 9 inches (0.2 m) square.

13 The *via principalis* in fact seems to have lain on the same line as its later successor. The area referred to here is in fact the centre and south east of the early *raetentura*.

14 It is not clear which of the building fragments marked on the archive plan were allocated to this phase and which to the later fort's stone buildings. However, the features marked on Figure 2:2 as belonging to the first fort do not seem to tally with the larger stretches of certainly later stone walls found by Richmond (below). The group of three adjacent trenches certainly belong to the first fort but they do not seem to relate clearly to the other fragments. A single photograph in the archives probably relates to features belonging to the first fort in this area. It shows two parallel trenches about a foot (0.3 m) apart with two rectangular features to one side. These do not seem to agree with features on the archive plan and suggest that more building fragments were recovered than shown on Figure 2:2.

15 Later excavations (*cf.* note 8) have now shown the building fragments to lie along the north east side of the *via principalis* roughly in the centre of the *raetentura*. The position would normally suggest the *principia*, though proof is as yet lacking and the fragments make little sense.

16 Ambleside: Collingwood (1916, 59 ff.).

17 Only trench 1 examined the ditches and later work indicates that there were a number of variations at other points (Jones and Thompson 1965; Jones and Wild 1970, 105; Bartlett and Dearne this volume).

agriculture.[18] The three outer ditches,[19] on the other hand, were allowed to silt up early and rubbish thrown from the fort wall found its own way into them. This rubbish comprises pottery dated to the later-second century, including No.9 below, and no later material. It is therefore evident that the outer ditches were not retained in the later reorganisation of the fort. Their design suggests that they belong to the type disclosed at Newstead III, in which the ditches were filled with twisted branch obstacles, the Roman equivalent of barbed wire entanglement;[20] and it may be commented that the presence of such obstacles would encourage casual throwing down of rubbish among them. The object of such an arrangement was to embarrass and pin down the enemy within killing range of missiles thrown from the rampart. The later ditch, on the other hand, belongs to the type of dry open moat, close to the wall; and this was the more common type of defence, designed to prevent assault upon the wall with scaling ladders or primitive rams.

The wall, like those of many Roman forts in the earthwork tradition, is to be considered less as a wall than as a fire proof vertical revetment for the rampart. It was 4 ft 9 inches (1.4 m) wide,[21] sufficiently thick to carry a sentry walk which could be used as a firing step for those actually defending its crenellated top, while the rampart walk proper, a cobbled path crowning the rampart bank, would facilitate the movement of men and supplies or the removal of

casualties. There is no need to suppose that the sentry walk was higher than fifteen feet (4.6 m); the bank behind it, 22 ft (6.7 m) wide, would conveniently cease about 5 ft (1.5 m) lower, as at York, where the arrangement survives intact.[22] Behind the wall came a 25 ft (7.6 m) intervallum, clearly defined on all sides but the north east, where it cannot have differed much, if at all.[23]

The explorations of 1903 disclosed enough of the fort wall to enable an estimate to be made of the overall dimensions of the fort. It measured, over its wall, 313 ft (95 m) from north west to south east and 346 ft (105.5 m) from north east to south west.[24] The axis of the *via principalis* lies at 175 ft (53 m) behind the north east front. The *viae praetoria* and *decumana*, on the other hand, are not axial, a misplacement probably due to a desire to take advantage of the existing causeways of the *portae principales* of the earlier fort.[25] Allowing, then, for the 53 ft (16.1 m) strip occupied by wall, rampart and intervallum, there are two blocks, 110 ft (33.5 m) by 80 ft (24.4 m) and 110 ft (33.5 m) square respectively, available in the *praetentura* for the barracks, while in the *raetentura*, when the main range is subtracted (below) there are two blocks approximately 20 ft (6 m) by 85 ft (25.9 m) and 20 ft

---

18 The ditch was dug on a slight slope 7–8 ft (2.1–2.4 m) in front of the fort wall. Richmond (1938,54) gives the width of the ditch as 22 ft (6.7 m) though on the accompanying plan and section it is shown as 23–24 ft (*c*. 7.3 m) wide and the archive plan and site book section suggest a width of 25 ft (7.6 m). Its depth is given as 8 ft (2.4 m) by Richmond (1938, 54) and the accompanying section and that in the site book indicate that this reflects a 7–9 ft (2.1–2.7 m) depth depending on where on the slope it is measured. The width variation is also because of the slope since it is difficult to say where the actual cut starts.

19 The middle ditch was of W-profile and was not separated by a gap from the inner. Its full width appears to be 18–20 ft (5.5–6 m), slight variations being due to where exactly it is considered to end. The first element was 3 ft (0.9 m) deep and the second element was 2.5 ft (0.8 m) deep. There followed a 20 ft (6 m) gap and then an outer ditch around 16–17 ft (4.9–5.2 m) wide but at the point examined widening to join a natural gully. The ditch again lay on a slight slope but the published and site book sections give its depth as 2–4 ft (0.6–1.2 m). An upcast bank was visible beyond this (Richmond 1938, 54 ff).

20 *Cf*. Johnson (1983, 53–5).

21 Richmond (1938, 54) says 5.5 ft (1.7 m) wide but all other records seem to concur on 5 ft (1.5 m) or just under. 1 ft 6 in (0.45 m) of the inner face was just of rubble and unfaced (Richmond 1938, 54).

22 There is considerable variation in the rampart width in different published and unpublished sources. For the north west rampart sectioned by trench 1 most of the sources are agreed on a figure from 24–26 ft (7.3–7.9 m) except for the archive plan (28 ft (8.5 m)) and Richmond (1938, fig. 1) (39 ft (11.9 m)). Nearer to the north west gate trench 5 sectioned the rampart and, if a revetment marked on a plan in the site book represents its edge, it was 21 ft (6.4 m) wide and a section cut in this vicinity in 1965 (Jones and Thompson 1965) also showed a rather narrow rampart. The south west rampart is 25 ft (7.6 m) wide in most sources but 27–28 ft (8.2–8.5 m) on the archive plan and Richmond (1938, Figs. 1 and 2). On balance a figure of 25 ft (7.6 m) is acceptable but there may have been variations in original width and in preservation. Certainly a width of 39 ft (11.9 m) seems unlikely. York: Miller (1928, 63).

23 The archive plan shows it roughly this wide but site book plans and Richmond (1938, fig. 1) differ notably, giving a width of around 14 ft (4.3 m). Variations in the rampart width (note 22) may have had some effect on the intervallum road width but it seems very unlikely that the road was in fact this wide given the wall fragments found in trench 5 and later work in the area (Jones and Thompson 1965). An intervallum road *c*. 14 ft (4.3m) wide would however seem to fit other evidence.

24 Although Garstang's (1904, plate 3) plan is unreliable in some particulars the figures are of the right order (see further Dearne this volume).

25 In fact the *portae praetoria* and *decumana* of the earlier fort.

(6 m) by 110 ft (33.5 m).[26] It can thus be said at once that the later fort is of abnormal type, since nowhere within it are there building plots large enough to contain the usual barrack block measuring approximately 150 by 30 ft (45.7 by 9.1 m), which is the most typical standard building in any normal auxiliary fort.[27] The total area available will not contain more than the equivalent of 3 *centuriae*, or half a quingenary cohort.

The gates have been heavily robbed. The north west gate was examined, without very clear result, in 1903 and only the *porta decumana* was available for excavation in 1939. The north west side was defined as a massive wall, 5 ft (1.5 m) thick capable of supporting a tower over the passage. There was no guard chamber, and the gate manifestly belongs to the simple type used for the north gates of milecastles of Hadrian's wall or for the *porta decumana* of Hardknott.[28] To judge from the record of 1903 the north west gate was of the same type, since the passage walls, 16 ft (4.9 m) apart, lie too close together for a double portal. There is thus room for a more ambitious design only at the *porta praetoria*, on the river front, though it is not in fact known that any such elaboration obtained.

The main range of internal buildings was partly explored in 1903, when the notable strongroom was discovered below the shrine of the standards at the back of the headquarters building, together with part of the building itself. The work was insufficient, however, to define the plan of the headquarters, and this was achieved in 1939. It has already been noted in general, particulars being given below, that the later garrison of *Navio* does not attain even to a small cohort, but is of approximately half that size. It is not therefore surprising to find the plan of the headquarters building (Figure 2:2) abnormal also. The main deviation consists in the lack of the front courtyard, invariably provided in standard types, its place being taken by four rooms, disposed in pairs on either side of a closed central passage.[29] Only the

northward pair of rooms were uncovered in 1939, when enough was done to show that the foundations, which alone remained, were of one build with the main outer wall of the building. It may therefore be assumed that these rooms are not additions, but part of the original plan. Next follows a shallow hall, 17 by 77 ft (5.2 by 23.5 m) internally.

In the rooms at the back of the building the *sacellum*, or shrine of the standards, occupies, as always, the central position. While its underground strongroom was successfully delimited in 1903, the shrine itself was only discovered in 1938, when the northwest half of the room was fully excavated. It was a large room, of which the back, askew to the rest of the building, was occupied by a low re-entrant semi-circular dais (*suggestus*), strengthened in the middle of its front wall by a massive foundation intended for a heavy object, which analogy would suggest to have been an imperial statue.[30] In front of the dais a boarded floor will have covered the strongroom, which was not re-excavated in 1938, though the tops of its walls were disclosed in order to relate it to the shrine. It was found that the steps leading down into it were so placed as to occupy the axis of the room and to ensure that the trap door by which they were reached lay in a central position at its front. The military savings kept in such strongrooms are described in papyri as deposited *ad signa* and such an example as this brings home the literal truth of the

---

26 The wall/rampart/intervallum strip in fact seems more likely to be *c*. 44 ft (13.4 m); see notes 21–23.

27 Johnson (1983, 166 ff.).

28 The gate's north west side narrowed to about 2 ft 4 in (0.7 m) at its inner end. An archive photograph indicates that it survived in places to several courses but that on its south east edge only a single course remained. On gates generally *cf.* Jonson (1983). Hardknot: Collingwood (1928, 326).

29 Conflation of Richmond's archive and site book plans and Garstang (1904, plate 3) does not fully confirm this. The dividing wall between the two postulated southern rooms is suggested on Richmond's archive plan to have lain some 9.5 ft (2.9 m) north west of the south east external wall. Garstang's plan shows some

form of projection from the north east outer wall here but it is far from clear if it was a wall fragment, especially since Garstang (1904, 186) refers to only three transverse walls. Rather its width at *c*. 6 ft (1.8 m) may suggest the base of an internal feature. A dividing wall could have lain further north west where Garstang did not excavate and would produce more symmetrical rooms but it must be possible that there was a large undivided room at the south east end of the front range. It is not certain whether Richmond re-excavated the north east external wall.

The *principia* walls were founded on clay and cobble packed trenches, and that was all that remained of the *sacellum* walls. However, Richmond (1938, Figs. 5 and 8) indicates that the external walls survived above foundation level and were of solid masonry construction. The dividing wall between the cross hall and north western office also survived above the foundations but had facing stones retaining a rubble core. Note that the gap in the north west wall observed by Garstang was found to be an illusion resulting from stone robbing. The archive plan records a ?drain running north east from the centre of the room at the north corner of the *principia*. Another is marked on this and the site book plan running north west from the north west side of the *sacellum*.

30 Johnson (1983, 112).

statement.[31] Hallowed by the most reverend objects that the regiment possessed, the savings and their safe keeping became a sacred trust. There is, however, no doubt that the strongroom is a later insertion. Built into its staircase wall were fragments of a fine inscribed tablet, commemorating building activity under the governor Iulius Verus by the First Cohort of Aquitanians and their commanding officer.[32] This tablet may be taken to belong to the original period of the stone built fort now being described and its re-use as building material for the strongroom fits well the general fact that these large underground strongrooms normally belong to the third century.[33] The *sacellum* is flanked on the north west by a very wide office, now forming one single room, though a perishable partition may once have divided it into two. On the south east there was a deeper and more equally proportioned room, separated from the *sacellum*, according to the plan of 1903, by a narrow compartment like a lobby. Since the back of this part of the range exactly coincides with the point at which the skew plan of the *sacellum* would place it, the arrangement would appear to be original and intentional and not the result of later rebuilding. The two rooms together form an office with lavatory attached, as not infrequently in the later arrangement of headquarters buildings.[34] The accommodation is designed for a group of military clerks quartered in their office.

The whole building is of distinctly abnormal type. It differs from the normal headquarters building in the absence of a front courtyard, and the range of rooms substituted for it. Without these, it would be strikingly like the two third century headquarters buildings of the legionary detachments at Corbridge, particularly the eastern example.[35] The resemblance is the more interesting since the force at *Navio* is plainly a detachment also, much smaller in size than a cohort. Here the numerous nodules of stream-gathered lead ore with which this part of the site abounded must be taken into account.[36] The site lies in close proximity to the ore bearing districts of Derbyshire and its later existence must be connected with the lead mines. If the task of the detachment was to police the lead mines, while its station served as a collecting depot for stream washed ore, then the curtailed headquarters building and the extra row of offices or stores on its front are explained. The fort begins to assume a close relation to the special economic status of the country round it.

To the south east of the headquarters building the excavators of 1903 discovered part of a sizeable rectangular building. This is almost certainly the commandant's house, which cannot have differed much from the normal size of such dwellings.[37] To the northwest of the building might normally be expected the granaries of the fort and it is possible that the 3 ft (0.9 m) thick walls identified in this position in fact belong to a granary. But only further excavation could demonstrate this point.[38]

many of his more generalised conclusions may be challengeable.

37 Richmond's speculations on its size are omitted here since the building is now known to have been the phase 2B granary (Jones and Wild 1970; Bartlett and Dearne this volume).

38 Since the phase 2B (and 2A) granaries were south east of the *principia* (note 37) the features to the north west of it presumably belonged to the *praetorium*, though the granaries may have lain here in phase 3. For an interpretive discussion see Dearne, this volume. Trenches 5, 6 and 7 crossed a number of features in this area and the site book and archive plan provide far more information than Richmond (1938, fig. 1). However, the nature of some features remain uncertain. As Figure 2:3 shows five north east – south west stone walls, four of them parallel and one on a different alignment or with an unexcavated offset, were found. The site book suggests that these walls, from south east to north west were 2 ft 5 in (0.7m), 2 ft 10 in (0.86 m), 2 ft (0.6 m), 2 ft 9 in (0.84 m) and 2–3 ft (0.6–0.9 m) wide. North west of these walls was a 6 in (0.15 m) wide drain, presumably that of the intervallum road (which does not seem to have been found here; above) though a revetment (note 22), presumably connected to the rampart, further north west would suggest that the intervallum road was only *c.* 8 ft (2.4 m) wide here. Another 6 in (0.15 m) wide drain lay a short distance south east of the most north westerly wall and a feature between the north west *principia* wall and the most south easterly wall found in trenches 6 and 7, though not identified in the site book, lay in a position where one would expect another drain. The third wall north west and the adjacent drain were also found by Garstang (1904, plate 3). Two further fragments of a wall were found immediately north east of the intervallum road along the south west defences in trenches 2 and 4 (Figure 2:3). The wall was 2 ft 9 in (0.8 m) thick and is likely to have belonged to a barracks/stable.

31 The small and regular deductions *ad signa* are mentioned in papyri such as *P. Gen. Lat* recto part 1 (=Fink 1971 No. 68). According to Vegetius (*epitoma rei militaris* II, 19) half of every imperial donative was also deposited *ad signa*. On the interpretation of the papyri see e.g. Fink (1971) and Spiedel (1973).

32 *R. I. B.* 283; Garstang (1904).

33 They become increasingly common from the mid-second century on; Johnson (1983, 113 ff).

34 Johnson (1983, 132).

35 Corbridge: Richmond & Birley (1940); Richmond (1943).

36 See further Richmond (1938, 61–5) for Smythe's analysis of seven unstratified samples, two of which had been heated to the point of chemical change; though

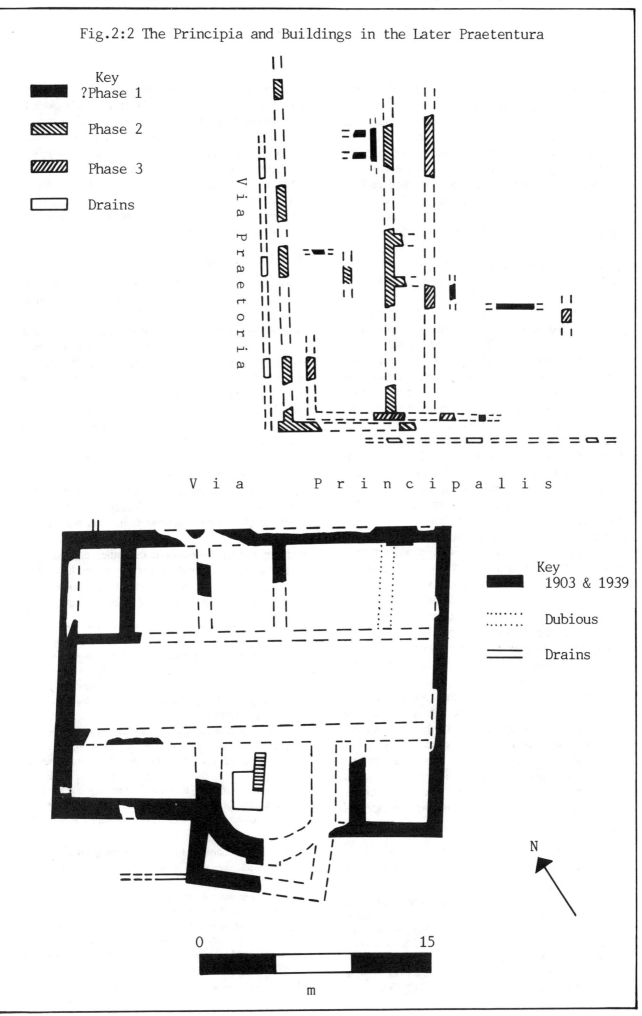

Fig.2:2 The Principia and Buildings in the Later Praetentura

Key
?Phase 1

Phase 2

Phase 3

Drains

Via Praetoria

Via Principalis

Key
1903 & 1939

Dubious

Drains

N

0   15

m

Buildings in the *praetentura* were carefully sought, in the exception that when the upper part of the slope, occupied by the main range of principal buildings was left behind deeper cover, better preserved buildings and, in particular, stratified floors would come to light. The hope was not fulfilled. As the buildings descended the slope towards the river their remains grew no better, floors having been totally removed. To recover a detailed plan of the walling was not part of the programme of 1939, and, as war drew near, it seemed right to cease excavation which appeared so unlikely to yield the desired stratification.

Meanwhile, however, it had proved possible to recover details about the structure and planning of the buildings in the *praetentura* which offered proof of sequence and were in themselves of considerable intrinsic interest (Figure 2:3). The timber buildings of the earliest fort have already been noted. Their characteristic construction was in sleeper trenches, of which the soft filling of frittered shale argued sleepers removed and empty trenches gradually filling with material eroded from their sides. These buildings, of somewhat slight construction, were succeeded by the first buildings related to the later fort, which, as disclosed in the south eastern half of the *praetentura*, comprised a small double block divided by a medial wall but devoid of recognizable cross divisions. The main and medial walls were carried by timber uprights set at intervals in a continuous trench packed tight with blue river cobbles. This cobbling was only eighteen inches (0.5 m) wide and was not packed in clay, as the foundation of a sill wall would have been, but tightly filled the trench to the very bottom, thus excluding the existence of sleeper beams. Such filling was plainly used at Brough in preference to the loose shaley clay, obtainable on the site, which breaks down into spongy mud when beaten or rammed: and the method is matched in comparable subsoil at Melandra.[39] If it is asked why the uprights were not bedded in separated post holes, it may be observed that it is easier to prepare a site by digging trenches, since this does not involve the exact setting out of each individual post hole, and permits a working gang to concentrate steadily upon an unbroken piece of work. The slight extra labour is amply compensated by the gain in convenience of organization.[40]

In due course the timber block was rebuilt in stone; not on quite the same lines, but sufficiently close to them to show that the builders were intending to erect the same kind of building in more durable materials. These foundations were of pitched stone set in yellow clay, comparable with, but considerably less well laid than, those of the headquarters building. This is perhaps not surprising, since the headquarters is contemporary with the timber building marked by cobble packed trenches.[41]

The Water Supply

During the excavation of the *porta decumana* in 1939 attention was early directed to a covered channel running through the gateway along the north western side of the passage. Since the conduit falls towards the fort, like the general slope from the south west, it could not have served as an outfall drain, like the one which occurs, sloping in the other direction, close beside it.[42] On the contrary, it was clearly a duct bringing water into the fort, like those which feed through the north gates at Chester, Birrens and the north east gate at Caernarvon.[43] Immediately inside the gateway the duct was linked with a feature which put its purpose beyond all doubt. It ran into a stone trough or tank, internally 2 ft 8 in (0.8 m) long, 1 ft 8 in (0.5 m) wide and 1 ft (0.3 m) deep, carved out of a single block of fine Millstone Grit. This served as a small *castellum aquae*, or distributing tank. Its outer end was fed by the conduit; the inner end had two outlets, towards its south corner a stone built conduit, towards its north corner a round hole, to which a lead pipe, now removed, must originally have been

---

one running north west – south east along the north east edge of the *via principalis* and one running south west – north east along, presumably, the south east edge of the *via praetoria* were also traced intermittently. The former at least probably related to this and the subsequent phase.

41 Again the features are only known from the archive plan and there is a possibility that some features marked as of phase 1 on Figure 2:2 in fact belong to this phase (note 14). However it seems most likely that the walls belonging to phase 3, representing a double barracks/stables, are as shown, and probably represent the reconstruction of the earlier buildings at a greater width.

42 Part of the course of this drain, curving north towards the ?*praetorium* north west of the *principia* was found by Garstang (1904, plate 3). The drain ran under the main structure of the north west side of the *porta decumana* and was wider than the inflow conduit, but similarly constructed of roughly squared masonry. No slab covers appear to have been found *in situ*. The inflow conduit was similarly constructed but slighter with one cover slab *in situ*.

43 On water supplies see Johnson (1983, 202 ff).

---

39 Melandra: Petch (1943, 55 ff). Though the construction is not entirely clear from this.

40 These features appear only on the archive plan, from which, however, it is clear that they were traced intermittently for a distance of 78 ft (23.8 m), the width of the block, which seems likely to have been a barracks/stables, being about 23.5 ft (7.2 m). Two small fragments of walls at right angles to the block seem to have been found along its south east wall. Two drains,

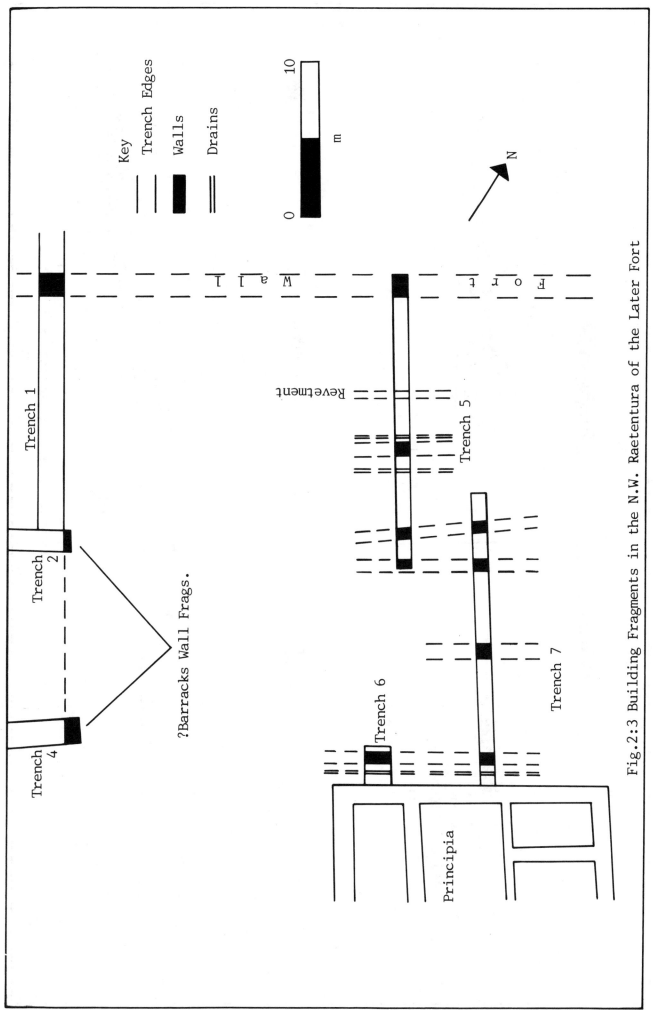

Fig.2:3 Building Fragments in the N.W. Raetentura of the Later Fort

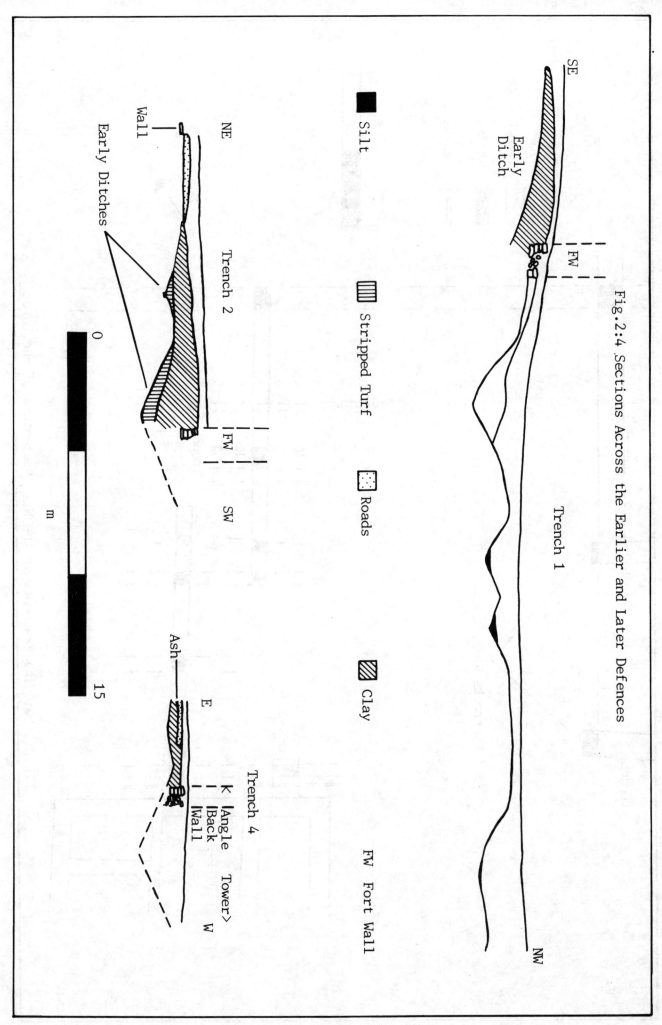

Fig.2:4 Sections Across the Earlier and Later Defences

Silt

Stripped Turf

Roads

Clay

FW Fort Wall

SE

Early
Ditch

FW

Trench 1

NW

NE

Wall

Early Ditches

Trench 2

FW

SW

0

m

15

Ash

E

Trench 4

K Angle Tower>
   Back
   Wall

W

attached. This distribution chamber might also have served as an inspection chamber and even as a deposition tank for sludge, though no suggestion of deposition from water was in evidence. How the water was further distributed within the fort is not known, since on emerging from the cover provided by the gateway ruins the conduit had been removed. The fate of the conduit where unprotected by the ruins of the defences is representative of the destruction which has everywhere befallen the later levels on the site.

The Pottery[44]

a) The Earlier Fort

Pieces 1–8 were all found below the structures of the later fort. Of these 1–4 were found in the earlier fort, as were 15 further unnumbered pieces.

1 Fragment from the rim and shoulder of a cooking pot. Late-first or early-second century. *Cf.* Birley and Birley (1938) No. 44. From below the clay spread sealing the early fort near the early barracks verandah.

2 Fragment from the rim of a cooking pot in smooth light grey fabric. Late-first or early-second century. *Cf.* Birley and Birley (1938) No. 42. From below the clay spread sealing the early fort below the later (granary) building south east of the *principia*.

3 Fragment from a mortarium of Bush-Fox's (1913) type 18, in yellowish white sandy fabric with white grit on the rim as well as inside the vessel. Late-first century. *Cf.* Richmond and Gillam (1951) No. 6. From below the clay spread sealing the early fort immediately north west of the later *principia*.

4 Several fragments from a mortarium of Bush-Fox's (1913) type 38, with heavy moulded spout, in very sandy light brown fabric with small black grit confined to the interior of the vessel; though the appropriate part of the rim survives there is no maker's stamp. Late-first to early-second century. *Cf.* Birley and Birley (1938) No. 56. From the same deposit as No. 1.

In addition to the four preceding pieces fragments from six south Gaulish samian dishes of Dragendorf's form 18, one with the stamp OF.RVFI, from the workshop of the first century potter Rufus, a fragment from a delicate south Gaulish cup of form 27, six wall fragments from as many rustic cooking pots, and a

reeded rim from a carinated bowl, were found at the same level; a wall fragment from a rough cast beaker was found in the filling at the butt end of one of the pair of early ditches immediately north west of the south west gate.

Fragments 5–8 were found either sealed by or incorporated in structures of the later fort, as described below.

5 Fragment from the rim and shoulder of a cooking pot in black fumed fabric with a lightly scored wavy line on the neck; vessels of this type first began to appear in small numbers on the northern frontier of Britain *circa* A.D. 125, just before the Stanegate forts were superseded (*Cf.* Birley and Birley (1938) No. 37; Gibson and Simpson (1909) No. 6; Simpson (1913) Throp No. 15). After this the type continued in common use, and there was no marked change in its style for several decades (*Cf.* Birley and Richmond (1938) Fig.8 No.8 from the deposit of an occupation beginning in A.D. 163). From the causeway across the early ditches in the angle formed by the later north west wall of the south west gate and the south west fort wall sealed by the later rampart.

6 Fragment from the rim and shoulder of a jar, with the rim ledged internally at the neck, in gritty, orange fabric, slightly reminiscent of Derbyshire ware. It is impossible to say exactly when this type first came into use; something not unlike it was still current in the later-second century (*Cf.* Richmond and Gillam (1950) No.8). From below the later intervallum road north of the later south west gate.

7 Large fragment from one side of the spout of a mortarium of Bush-Fox's (1913) type 46, with the stamp FECIT, retrograde, on the rim, in smooth light orange fabric with large sparse multicoloured grit. The word FECIT, retrograde, in its distinctive panel, is the counter stamp of the potter G. ATTIUS MARINUS. The two stamps were used on either side of the spout of a mortarium to form the phrase *G. Attius Marinus made (this)*. There is evidence that the potter worked at Radlett in Hertfordshire. The distribution of his stamps and counter stamps has been worked out and published by Prof. Eric Birley (Kenyon 1948, 215) and a further example may be added from High Cross, Leicestershire (pers. comm. Grahame Webster), making fourteen sites. Of these three are in Derbyshire and three in West Yorkshire. The type of rim made by G. Attius Marinus is closely matched by those of other potters of the south east Midlands whose wares have been found in successive layers ranging in date from A.D. 100 to A.D.125, at Corbridge in Northumberland; unstamped fragments of the same type have been found at Leicester in a level dated A.D. 110–120.

---

44 Since the pottery is not extant and the drawings are lost it has not been thought right to include editorial comment on the majority of this section or to update the bibliography. However, it may be noted that the majority of Gillam's dating conclusions have subsequently been confirmed.

Mortaria stamped by G. Attius Marinus have been found at Slack in the West Riding and at Melandra Castle, both forts of the period A.D. 80–140, and in two successive levels at Leicester dated A.D. 125–130 and A.D. 150–160; the examples from the later of these two levels are almost certainly pieces which had survived as rubbish, along with other early-second century vessels which were found with them. Although both earlier and later estimates have been made, it thus appears, on available evidence, that the potter's period of maximum production was from *circa* A.D. 110 to *circa* A.D. 130. The present fragment was from the heel of the later rampart above the filling of the earlier fort ditches near the west corner.

8 Fragment from a carinated bowl with a reeded rim, in smooth light orange fabric. Late-first to early-second century. *Cf.* Forster and Knowles (1911) No. 5. Found built into the south west wall of the headquarters, immediately north west of the shrine.

The group as a whole is internally consistent in date, and, save for one piece of slightly later date, belongs to the late-first and early-second centuries. One mortarium, No. 3, is of a type which did not outlast the first century, and the stamp OF.RVFI is at least as early. Nos.1,2,4 and 8, and most of the unnumbered fragments would be equally at home in a first or early-second century context. There can therefore be no doubt that the earlier fort was founded in the first century, not improbably when Julius Agricola was governor.

The date of the first occupation is approximately indicated. Leaving aside the orange coloured jar, about which there is an element of doubt, the latest datable piece is the black cooking pot No. 5. If this vessel was broken during the earlier occupation, then that occupation continued until *circa* A.D. 125; and the stamped mortarium, No.7, helps to bridge the gap between the earlier years of the century and this date. The cooking pot is the only vessel of its period in the earlier group, and only one other vessel that might conceivably be contemporary, No.36 below, was found anywhere on the site. Taken as a whole the group is remarkably similar in composition to that from the earlier occupation of the Stanegate fort at Chesterholm; in this, also, first and second century pieces are in the majority, and a single black cooking pot appears. It is thus by no means improbable that the first period of occupation at both sites was the same, and that the evacuation of both forts was a consequence of the decision to erect forts on the actual line of Hadrian's Wall.

It is, however, possible that the fragment No.5 came from a vessel broken while the later fort was under construction, and not during the occupation of the earlier fort. If the later fort immediately replaced the earlier, the dating of the earlier occupation is unaffected by this possibility. On the other hand, if, as is more likely, the later fort replaced the earlier only after an interval and the fragment came from a vessel broken then (as is not impossible, for vessels of the type remained current for several decades) the stamped mortarium, No.7, would become the latest piece certainly derived from the earlier occupation. This would allow a conclusion that the earlier occupation ended when Hadrian's frontier was first fortified in its Stanegate phase.

The available evidence does not allow a choice to be made between these alternatives, but the truth clearly lies between them, and the gap is narrow. It remains safe to conclude that the earlier occupation at Brough-on-Noe ended at the time of, and probably as a consequence of, the building of Hadrian's Wall, but the event cannot on present evidence be assigned to a particular stage of that fairly protracted operation.

b) The Later Fort

Some indication of the date of the later fort is given by the following pottery vessel:

9 The greater part of a samian dish of Curle's Newstead form 15. This type of vessel belongs exclusively to the second half of the second century, though a more delicate prototype appeared on the continent at a slightly earlier date. Found covered by silt at the bottom of the outermost ditch of the later fort.

Whether the cooking pot, No.5, discussed above, was broken during the earlier occupation or at the very beginning of the later, and whether the later occupation followed the earlier immediately or after an interval, the fact that a structure of the later fort sealed a cooking pot of the type that did not come into use in northern Britain before *circa* A.D. 125 is conclusive evidence that the later fort was not erected before A.D. 125; it may have been as early as this, or it may have been considerably later. The dish, No.9, of a type not in use before the middle of the second century and thereafter in fashion for some time, found its way into one of the earlier ditches of the later stone fort before silting was at all advanced. These two pieces of evidence, taken together, tend to suggest that the later fort was founded in the course of the second and third quarters of the second century; the occurrence of the dish tips the scales on the side of the third quarter. The pottery available does not allow of greater precision, but it tends to support the conclusion that the inscribed tablet of *circa* A.D. 155–159, noted above commemorated the original erection of the later fort.

c) The Phase 2 and 3 *Praetentura*

The date of the later stone buildings is indicated by the pottery which follows:

10 Three fragments from the rim and wall of a cooking pot in black fumed and burnished fabric. Early-fourth century. *Cf.* Richmond, Hodgson and St Joseph (1938) No.29.

11 Rim fragment from a large jar in smooth brick red fabric; while the profile with seating for a lid resembles that of Derbyshire ware the fabric is different; the piece is nevertheless probably contemporary with Derbyshire ware, and thus belongs to the closing years of the third century or to the earlier part of the fourth century.[45]

These two pieces were found together in the hole left by a post in one of the cobble packed foundation trenches of the building east of the headquarters.[46] The hole had been formed by setting the post upright and then packing cobbles tightly round it. The only moment when it stood empty was when the post had been withdrawn and the wooden structures to which it had belonged were in the process of being replaced by the stone buildings. Later, the hole would be sealed by the occupation layer of the stone buildings. The fragments therefore date the replacement, and indicate that it took place early in the fourth century.

d) The Duration of the Later Fort

The highly disturbed condition of the latest levels on the site meant that stratified material was not forthcoming. However, this did not prevent the occurrence in the plough soil of a scatter of unstratified fragments of pottery from these levels. Such pieces are of value in offering a general date for the later occupation and a group of them is now considered:

12 Fragment from the rim and shoulder of a small fine walled cup with rouletted pattern on the body, in white fabric with black coating. Though this type of Castor cup may have emerged before the end of the second century, it is more likely to be of third century date.

13 Rim fragment from a cooking pot in grey fumed and burnished fabric. Late-second century. *Cf.* Richmond and Gillam (1950) No.29.

14 Rim fragment of a cooking pot in black fumed and polished fabric. Mid-fourth century. *Cf.* Richmond, Hodgson and St Joseph (1938) No.69.

15 Fragment from the rim and shoulder of a jar in light orange fabric with a buff outer surface roughened by burning. This simple form is not closely datable.

16 Several fragments from the rim, shoulder and base of a jar, in thick coarse light grey fabric, bleached by fire at the base. The hollowed rim has something in common with the late-third century type represented by Simpson (1913) Milecastle 50 No. 117 and No. 118.

17–23 Rim fragments from seven separate jars or cooking pots in hard gritty fabric, "goose-flesh fabric" varying in colour from brick red to greenish grey. This is the so-called Derbyshire ware, datable to the closing years of the third century and to the fourth century. It is found more frequently on civil and military sites in what is now Derbyshire than any other contemporary type of vessel, and is found more frequently here than elsewhere; it is now known to have been manufactured at Hazelwood, near Duffield.[47]

24 Large fragment from a wide mouthed jar in thick smooth grey self coloured fabric; this simple type is not closely datable though generally similar vessels are found in third and fourth century contexts.

25 Large fragment from the rim of a mortarium in creamy fabric, with a small amount of brown grit surviving; rim, fabric and grit combine to make probable the attribution of this mortarium to a Midland potter of the middle or later half of the second century. *Cf.* Birley and Gillam (1948), *s.vv.* GRATINUS, LOCCIUS, SARRUS, AND SENNIUS.

26 Large fragment from the rim of a mortarium in red fabric with grey core and white slip; the grit is multicoloured and medium sized; though doubtless from another hand this mortarium resembles the products of a northern potter of the late-second century. *Cf.* Birley and Gillam (1948), *s.v.* BELLICUS.

27 Small fragment from the rim of a mortarium in a creamy white fabric, conveniently called pipe clay fabric; no grit survives. Mid-third century. *Cf.* Richmond, Gillam and Birley (1951) No. 18.

28 Fragment from the rim of a mortarium in pipe clay fabric; no grit survives; this is a slightly later development of the type represented by No.27. Late-third century. *Cf.* Richmond, Hodgson and St Joseph (1938) No.12.

29 Large fragment from a small hammer-head mortarium in pipe clay fabric with vertical stripes on the rim; no grit survives. Early-fourth century. *Cf.* Kenyon (1948) Fig. 18 No.23.

---

45 Derbyshire ware is now known to have been produced as early as c.140 and Gillam's following comments must rest only on No. 10.

46 I.E. the phase 2A barracks/stables in the south eastern half of the *praetentura*.

47 For dating see note 45. A number of kiln sites are now known, *Cf.* Kay (1962); Brassington and Webster (1988).

30 Small fragment from a mortarium similar in form and fabric to, and doubtless contemporary with, No.29; the surface has been flaked by fire.

31 Fragment from a large hammer-head mortarium with reeded rim, in brick red fabric, with medium sized dark brown grit. There seem to be no exact parallels, but the general form, which is reminiscent of the samian mortarium of form 45, is typical of the later-fourth century.

33 Many fragments making up the greater part of an imitation of a samian bowl of form 37, in soft smooth fabric of a delicate cream colour with a pinkish tinge; the zone of decoration on the prototype is represented by rouletting. *Cf.* May (1922), No. 171, dated by the excavator to the middle or later half of the second century. A comparison of the two vessels has shown them to be identical in fabric; they are doubtless both products of a kiln situated within reach of the two sites, which are themselves a mere sixteen miles apart.

34 Several fragments making up the greater part of a hemispherical bowl in smooth orange fabric. Late-second century. *Cf.* Richmond and Birley (1930) No.61.

35 Fragment of a hemispherical flanged bowl in imitation of the samian form 38, in white fabric with brown colour coating-Castor ware. Late-fourth century. *Cf.* Corder (1951) No. 30.

36 Fragment from a flat rimmed bowl in black fumed fabric, now in part of a lighter colour and roughened on the surface; rims of this type first came into use *circa* A.D. 125, but remained little altered for half a century. *Cf.* Simpson (1913) Turret 50b No.65.

37 Fragment from a straight sided flanged bowl in black fumed and burnished fabric, reddened by fire on the surface; the flange is very near the edge of the rim leaving quite a small bead. This is an early feature in the flanged bowl series. Third century. *Cf.* Birley and Richmond (1938) Fig.7 No.12.

38–40 Fragments from vessels similar in general form and in fabric to No.37, but with a higher bead and of slightly later date. Early-fourth century. *Cf.* Richmond, Gillam and Birley (1951) No.47.

41 Fragment from a straight sided flanged bowl with a short flange, in black fumed fabric; this is probably approximately contemporary with Nos.38–40.

42–43 Fragments from straight sided flanged bowls, each with a pronounced bead and thick flange, in light bluish grey fabric reminiscent of the products of the fourth century kilns of East Yorkshire. Mid- to late-fourth century. *Cf.* Kenyon (1948) Fig.19 No.29.

44 Small fragment from the rim of a straight sided flanged bowl in white fabric with warm brown coating-Castor ware. Late-fourth century. *Cf.* Corder (1951) No.35.

In addition to these pieces a fragment of a samian bowl of form 38, and four weathered fragments from as many bowls of form 37 were also found, though none with sufficient of the decoration surviving to make their attribution to individual potters possible or their illustration desirable.

The number of fragments assignable with fair certainty to the second half of the second century is relatively large. Fragments securely datable to the early years of the third century are rare, but, as the same phenomenon has been observed on other military sites, where there is independent evidence of early-third century occupation, it does not necessarily mean that Brough-on-Noe was unoccupied at this time. Fragments assignable to the later-third century are more common, and to the early-fourth century more common still. The fort was certainly occupied in the early-fourth century, probably after structural modification. The distinctive products of the latest and most active phase of the East Yorkshire kilns are absent but several approximately contemporary pieces of Midland origin appear, and are evidence that occupation continued at least until the second half of the fourth century; it is not improbable that the fort was occupied until the end of the Roman period.

d) The Economic Implications

The pottery from Brough-on-Noe is not without its interest from an economic point of view. The fort lies near the head of a valley which drains eventually into the Trent. It is therefore to be expected that its trade connections will have been mainly with the Midlands, and this, by and large, appears in fact to have been the case. The samian ware, naturally, was imported from Gaul, as were also, in all probability, the two earliest mortaria, but other vessels to which a place of origin can be confidently assigned come from Hertfordshire, Northamptonshire, Warwickshire and the south of Derbyshire, and it is highly probable that most of the pieces are of Midland origin. It has nevertheless been possible to quote exact parallels to many of the vessels from sites on the northern frontier. This is because, for the greater part of the Roman period, such sites obtained much of their pottery from the same Midland sources as forts in Wales and the south Pennines. Only after the upheaval caused by the Picts' War of A.D. 367 did the situation change. Then the frontier garrisons came to rely almost exclusively on East Yorkshire, while, as appears from the pottery here discussed, the garrison at Brough-on-Noe maintained its Midland connection.

Acknowledgements

In conclusion, thanks are offered to Mr. F. F. Nicholson, owner of the site, who kindly permitted its re-examination, and to Mr. Jesse Eyre who helped us with many local arrangements. Also to Mr. R. W. P. Cockerton, without whose initiative the work would not have been undertaken, and whose active interest was a stimulus and constant source of encouragement. Mr. William Lawson of Durham University helped manfully with the digging and earned, not for the first time, warmest gratitude.

Editor's Note

Whilst further detail and comment has been added to the text from the 1938 interim report and from the Richmond archive in the form of footnotes, one or two other matters require separate notes

a) The Extent of Excavation

The placing and extent of trenches in the north west corner of the fort, at the south west gate and north west end of the *principia* are not in doubt. However, the extent of the excavation in the rest of the *principia* is not clear. The archive plan suggests that the south east side wall and perhaps parts of the south corner and north east wall were revealed in addition to the areas described by Richmond in the text. Also the provenance of vessel No.2 in the pottery report indicates that some excavation occurred south east of the *principia*. How extensive the trenches in the *praetentura* were is uncertain but a fragment of, presumably, the intervallum road is marked on the archive plan a short way north east of the south east gate suggesting that trial trenching occurred south east of the main building fragments recovered.

b) The West Angle Tower

The west angle tower is not fully described in the present text. The interim report (Richmond 1938, 56) notes that the back wall was faced with three courses of hammer dressed masonry on top of 2 ft 9 in (0.8 m) of rubble, resting on the subsoil at the edge of the earlier ditches (their presence explaining the greater than usual depth of the foundations). Above the filled ditch behind the angle tower a thick ash deposit was found and overlying it was a deposit of ?road gravel (Figure 2:4). A plan in the site book adds the details that the back wall was 2 ft 8 in (0.8 m) thick and *c*. 9 ft 3 in (2.8 m) behind the main fort wall.

c) Finds

Richmond (1938, 60) notes that a silver *denarius* of Severus was recovered from the *principia*. The only other find of which a record exists is a small bronze mount or escutcheon in the form of a bust, known from a photograph in the Richmond archive labelled Brough. It cannot be certain that this find relates to Brough-on-Noe rather than another similarly named site. The bust is of a man with a round face and short, fairly crudely depicted hair finishing above the ears. He has disproportionately large, almost lozenge shaped eyes, a small, thin nose and wide mouth.

3. Excavations at Brough-on-Noe, 1958–9

J. E. Bartlett and M. J. Dearne

Introduction

Excavations at the Roman fort at Brough-on-Noe, Derbyshire (ancient *Navio*) by Garstang in 1903 and Richmond in 1938–9 identified the course of the defences of the later fort, established *c.* 154/8, on the north east, north west and south west sides (Garstang 1904; Richmond 1938; Richmond and Gillam this volume). However only two small fragments of the fort wall were known along the south east defences (Garstang 1904, plate 3) and moreover the defences of the earlier fort, examined by Richmond at the west corner had not been found elsewhere. Two seasons of work in 1958 and 1959 directed by one of the authors (J.E.B) for Sheffield City Museum in conjunction with a Sheffield University Department of Extramural Studies School based at Buxton aimed to establish the course and details of these earlier and later defences. A further aim was to examine an area south west of a building fragment next to the stone *principia* located by Garstang.

Interim reports on the work appeared at the time (*J. R. S.* 1959, 108; *J. R. S.* 1960, 216) but the publication of the present volume gave an opportunity to present a fuller account of the work. Thanks are due to the former owner of the site Mr. Knowles, and the then Ministry of Works for permission to excavate; to Mr. H. Foster, Sheffield City Engineer, for the loan of equipment; and to the late Messrs. R. W. P. Cockerton and J. P. Heathcote for help on many occasions.

The Excavations

Excavation in 1958 took the form of a long trench (trench A) bisecting the later fort defences at a slight angle on the south east side of the fort. The trench continued, with intermittent baulks, into the *raetentura* of the later fort, being in all some 175 ft (53.3 m) long and 4 ft (1.2 m) wide though it was widened slightly at the north west end to fully record a wall fragment (Figure 3:1). Two small box trenches to its north east were also cut to record further details of excavated features and cuttings were made to re-expose the *principia* cellar excavated by Garstang and the corner of the south west gate excavated by Richmond in order to use them as reference points. A further shorter trench across the defences was subsequently cut and a number of small trenches were eventually opened east of this in 1959 (Area B on Figure 3:1). Further trenches south west of the south

east part of trench A were cut to expose the line of a late wall (Area C on Figure 3:1).

Work in 1959 also included the opening of a trench (trench R), 45 ft (13.7 m) long and 4 ft (1.2 m) wide across the south angle tower of the later fort together with three smaller trenches (P, Q, and S) to confirm the position of the fort wall at the south angle and on the south west side.

Trench A was excavated to natural in the vicinity of the defences, though the three defensive ditches were not bottomed, and between the two baulks in the *raetentura*. However the north west end of trench A and other trenches were only cleared sufficiently to answer specific questions such as the line of the wall of the building in the *raetentura* and the nature of the late changes to the defences. The results of the excavation will be described in chronological order according to the phasing established by Jones, Thompson and Wild (1966).

The Phase 1 Fort (*c.* 80–120 A.D.)

Few traces of the first fort at Brough were recovered. However, excavation of trench R and areas adjacent to it revealed fragments of the defensive ditches also seen by Richmond in 1938/9. Both ditches were seen, though not excavated, and appeared likely to be turning a corner. Accurate measurement of their widths was problematic since the trench crossed them obliquely but they were probably much as Richmond found them to be. If they were indeed turning a corner, the south east side of the early fort may not have lain much more than 25 ft (7.6 m) south east of the line of the later fort wall. No trace of these ditches, or of the early rampart (which also eluded Richmond), was found in trench A but it is likely that the cutting of the later fort ditches would have obscured any trace of them. The only other features assignable to the first phase fort were a sleeper trench crossing trench A north east to south west, north west of the later fort wall and an occupation horizon below the later intervallum road, both presumably relating to barracks.

The Phase 2 and 3 Fort (*c.* 154/8–*c.* 350)

a) The Defences

The defences of the later fort were principally examined in trench A with certain further

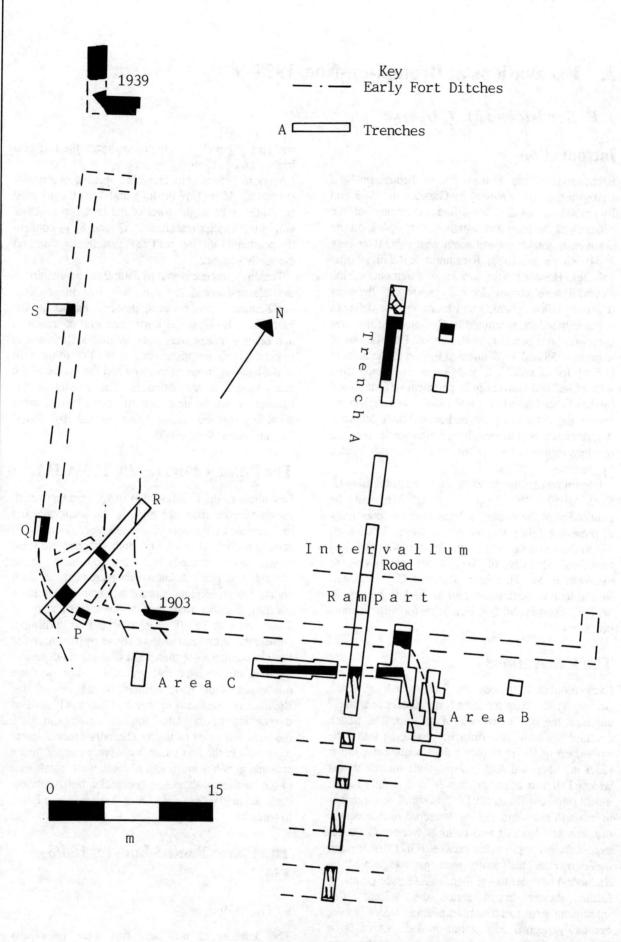

Key

— · — Early Fort Ditches

A ▭ Trenches

1939

S

N

Trench A

Intervallum
Road

Rampart

R

Q

1903

P

Area C

Area B

0   15

m

Fig.3:1 General Plan of Excavations

information coming from a trench in Area B. Three ditches were found, though none of them were bottomed. The outer ditch was 9 ft (2.7 m) wide, c.4 ft (1.2 m) deep and of V-shaped profile. It was separated from the middle ditch by a gap of about 10 ft (3 m), this ditch being 16.5 ft (5 m) wide, and of uncertain depth and profile. Another gap of c.10 ft (3 m) separated it from the inner ditch which was approximately 20 ft (6 m) wide (though the presence of a stone wall on its inner lip made ascertaining its exact width problematic). It was excavated to a depth of 7 ft (2.1 m) and was clearly considerably deeper. Its profile was probably V-shaped but it appeared to have a step on the inner face. The berm between the inner ditch and the fort wall was apparently just over 7 ft (2.1 m) wide though again defining the inner edge of the inner ditch was problematic (Figure 3:1).

The fort wall itself (which may have been a later insertion; below) had been entirely removed in trench A and was represented only by a ?robber trench some 4 ft (1.2 m) wide and a maximum of just over 1 ft (0.3 m) deep. Its fill of pebbly silt contained blocks of stone presumably derived from the demolished wall and further blocks from it or the later wall on the inner ditch lip were found in loose clay deposits above and to the north west of the ?robber trench. A second trench in Area B north east of trench A revealed the line of the fort wall surviving to a maximum of three courses at the north east end of the late entrance (below). It was found to be 5 ft (1.5 m) thick but poorly preserved.

The rampart was not clearly seen in the trench in Area B, it being too short but was sectioned in trench A. It survived to a maximum height of 3 ft (0.9 m) and was composed of compacted clay. At its rear it sealed a humic layer probably representing the pre-phase 1 ground surface, a phase 1 occupation horizon evidently having been removed from above it when the rampart was constructed (Figure 3:2). There was evidence that the front of the rampart had been constructed over a natural step in the ground, though the absence of the humic layer suggested that it had also been artificially deepened.

The insertion of the late entrance (below) had, at this point, removed the front 5½ ft (1.6 m) of the rampart, though rampart material had subsequently crept forward over deposits post-dating this late entrance. The original rampart would seem to have been 15–16 ft (4.6–4.9 m) wide at its base. Its rear face sloped at an angle of about 37°. This would suggest, if the stone wall was an original feature of the defences and allowing for a rampart walk some 6½ ft (2 m) wide, that the rampart stood to a height of some 16½ ft (5 m) which seems unlikely. Rather it seems more likely that the stone wall was a later insertion and that the original rampart was of the

more normal height of about 11½ ft (3.5 m) with both faces sloping.

The line of the front of the fort wall was also examined at three points at the south corner and along the south west side (Figure 3:1) by small box trenches. Trench R also revealed the main fort wall, still standing to eight courses, and the rear wall of the south angle turret. This rear wall only survived as rubble foundations.

b) The Internal Structures

Behind the rampart the phase 1 occupation horizon was sealed by a 9 in–1 ft (0.23–0.30 m) thick clay dump, as met with by other excavators, though below the intervallum road this was replaced by a thinner yellow gravel layer, perhaps being a make up for the intervallum road. This road was stated in the interim report (J. R. S. 1959, 108) to be 37 ft (11.3 m) wide. However, subsequent discoveries in 1969 (Jones and Wild 1970) suggest that the intervallum road was probably only in the region of 18 ft (5.4 m) wide and that the apparent continuation of the metalling north west of the first baulk in trench A within the defences (Figure 3:1) may relate to later changes in the interior of the fort (below). Some 7 ft (2.1 m) north west of the back of the rampart lay a small circular hearth represented by an area of burnt clay on the road, about 1 ft 6 in (0.45 m) in diameter with an inner circular area c. 8 in (0.20 m) in diameter being sunken by c. 3 in (0.07 m). Further traces of burning were found around it.

The principle feature encountered within the fort in trench A and in one small box trench to its north west was the corner and parts of two of the walls of the building partially revealed by Garstang. These stone walls, surviving in places to a height of nearly 3 ft (0.9 m) were constructed of roughly coursed masonry surviving to three courses. Excavations by Jones and Wild (1970) re-located the building fragment discovered by Garstang and revealed more of its plan, clearly identifying it as the phase 2B granary constructed on sleeper walls with external buttresses. Confirmation that the external walls were buttressed was provided in the present excavation by the discovery of three courses of the footings of a buttress between the building corner and a curved slab-covered water conduit presumably running towards the south west gate (Figure 3:3). The granary can now be seen to have formed a rectangle some 55 x 69 ft (16.7 x 21 m) though no internal features likely to relate to this phase were recorded.

No traces of activity in phase 2A, when at least the north east end of the site of the phase 2B granaries was occupied by a granary built on wooden posts (Jones and Wild 1970), were recovered. However the area excavated was not sufficiently large to draw any

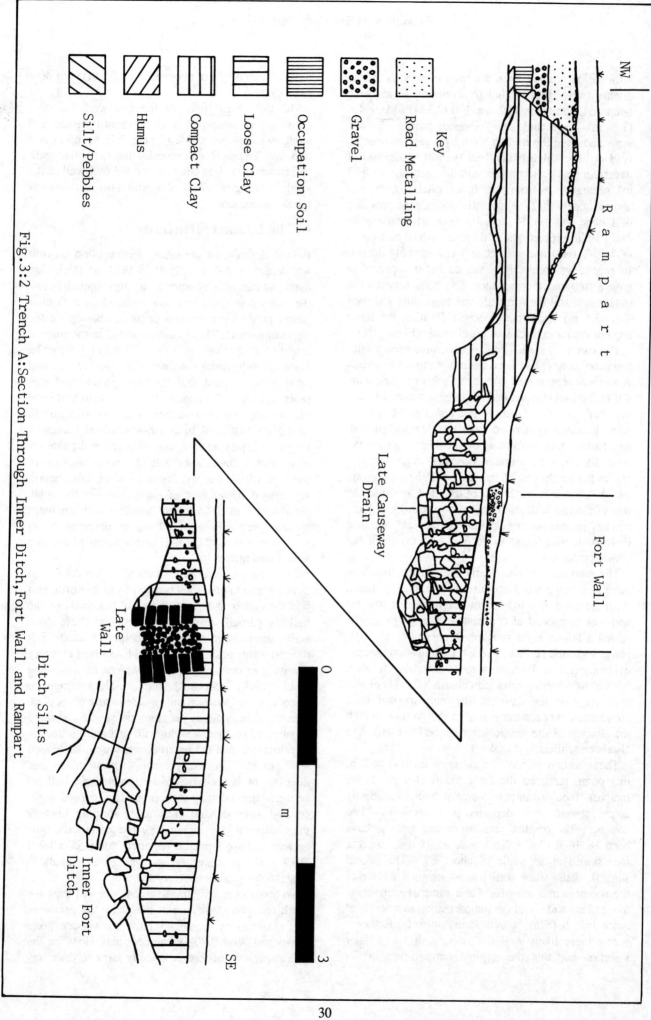

Key

Silt/Pebbles

Humus

Compact Clay

Loose Clay

Occupation Soil

Gravel

Road Metalling

Fig.3:2 Trench A:Section Through Inner Ditch,Fort Wall and Rampart

NW

R a m p a r t

Late Causeway
Drain

Fort Wall

Late
Wall

Ditch Silts

Inner Fort
Ditch

SE

0

m

3

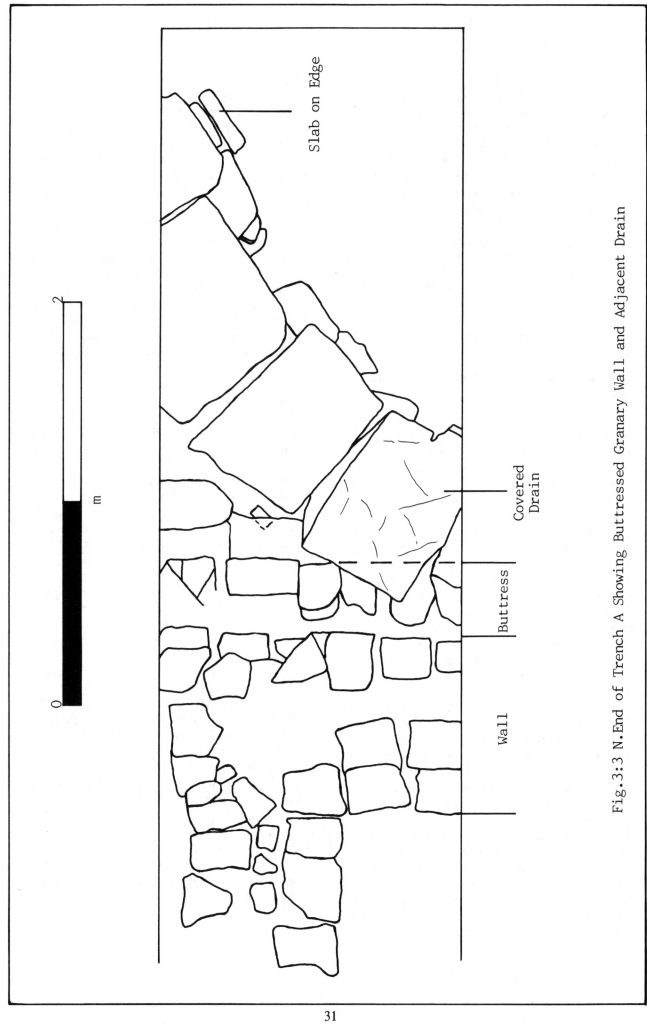

Fig.3:3 N.End of Trench A Showing Buttressed Granary Wall and Adjacent Drain

Slab on Edge

Covered Drain

Buttress

Wall

0 m 2

conclusions from this. Similarly no certain evidence was recorded in trench A for any building activity in phase 3 when the site of the earlier granaries appears to have been reused, probably for a *praetorium* (Jones and Wild 1970). However, even if the phase 3 *?praetorium* did reuse the whole of the earlier site of the granary the projected lines of its construction trenches would not necessarily have crossed trench A, given the position of the baulks, except at the extreme north east end. Some phase 3 activity is probably represented by the metalling which continued into the area of the earlier granaries, by traces of a hearth and perhaps by a boulder filled pit. The presence of a baulk means that it is not certain that the metalling was continuous with the intervallum road and the *Via Decumana*. This would be particularly likely in view of the presence of the probable late cavalry exit to the south east (below).

c) Late Changes to the Defences (Figure 3:4)

As already alluded to trench A revealed late changes to the defences, the nature of which were further clarified by work on trenches in areas B and C. By this time all of the fort ditches on the south east appear to have silted up or been filled in as was further demonstrated in 1969 (Jones and Wild 1970). The fort wall appears to have been removed for a distance of over 22 ft (6.7 m), one edge of the gap so created being observed in area B. The rampart was also cut back and probably revetted, traces of the stone revetting being noted immediately behind the line of the wall in area B. Given the position of the front of the cut back rampart in trench A it is clear that the intention was to create a way through the rampart obliquely to its line. Running approximately parallel to and 5 ft (1.5 m) in front of the former course of the fort wall another wall was discovered. This wall was traced south west from opposite the north east end of the gap in the fort wall for a distance of 45 ft (13.7 m). It was constructed over the inner lip of the former inner fort ditch and appeared to have been built in a construction trench packed on the north west side with compacted yellow clay, though traces of it on the south east side were less certain, only a gritty deposit containing charcoal and burnt clay possibly representing it. The wall itself was 2½ ft (0.7 m) thick and survived to a maximum of five courses. It was faced on both sides by dressed stone blocks with an offset two courses up on the south east face and had a rubble core. It appeared likely that the full extent of the wall had been recovered, no signs of return walls being detected and at least at the north east end its termination was fully faced.

Between this wall and the rampart revetment (or where it had been left *in situ* the fort wall) ran a causeway of pitched cobbles, uniformly 5 ft (1.5 m) wide with a central slab-covered drain. The drain was also seen in trench A, though here the causeway seemed to have been removed. This causeway presumably continued along the line of the oblique cut through the rampart. At the north east end of the wall over the inner ditch the causeway turned south east. The wall and causeway at this point appeared to be contemporaneous. The causeway with its central drain terminated some 26 ft (7.9 m) south east of the line of the fort wall near the outer edge of the former inner ditch. At this point removal of the drain cover slabs revealed that the drain channel was 6 inches (0.15 m) wide and constructed of large stone blocks. Along the north east side of the causeway as it ran south east the remains of another, much rougher wall were noted. The wall was 2 ft (0.6 m) thick and built of rough stonework surviving only to one or two courses and retaining a rubble core. The wall was built over the edge of the causeway and further evidence that it was later than the causeway was provided by the fact that one of the causeway drain cover slabs had been reused in it.

It is clear that these late changes to the defences, the date of which is indicated by the coin of Constantine found below the causeway where the rough wall overlay it to the north east, represent the insertion of a new entrance/exit. As Jones and Wild (1970, 105) have pointed out such an entrance/exit which incorporated two turns would have been particularly appropriate for the at least partly mounted unit which their work showed occupied the fort in phase 3. However, the details of these entrance/exit arrangements pose more of a problem. The wall over the inner edge of the inner fort ditch cannot as Jones and Wild (1970, 106) later suggested have been the main fort wall. However nor does it seem to have been part of any *vicanal* structure. No return walls were found and the presence of the offset on the south east face tends to argue that it was if anything the external face. Given that it and the causeway appeared contemporaneous it must be assumed that it was a defensive screen for the entrance. However, the rough stone wall to the north east of the causeway and the fact that Jones and Wild (1970) found a similar ?continuation of the causeway considerably north east of the present excavations but still lying over the former inner ditch may suggest some later changes to the arrangements, or the existence of two similar entrances/exits close together.

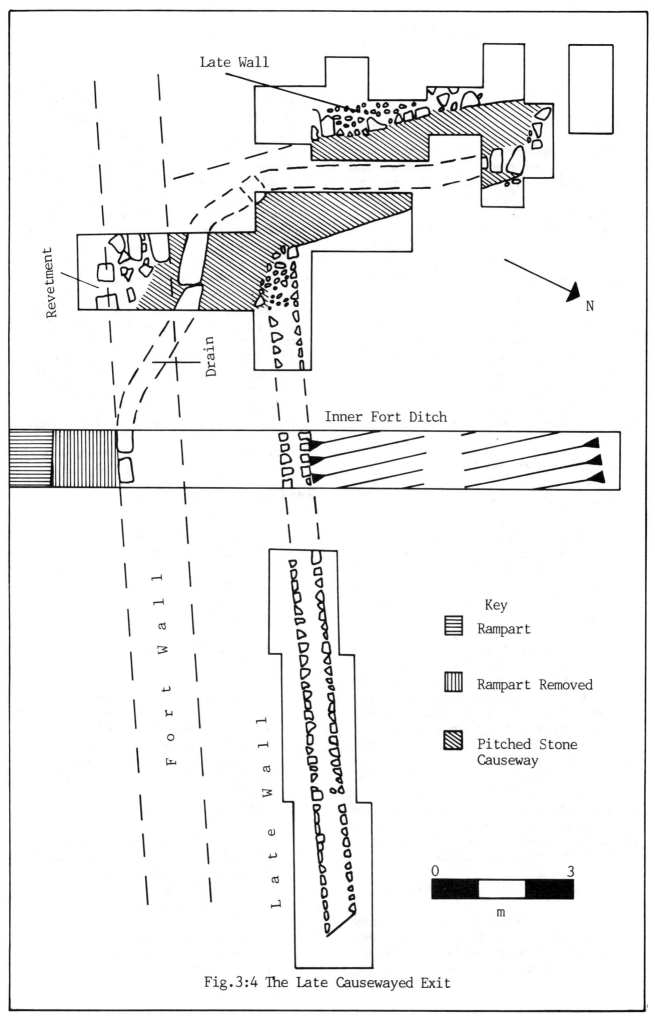

Late Wall

Revetment

Drain

Inner Fort Ditch

Fort Wall

Late Wall

Key

Rampart

Rampart Removed

Pitched Stone Causeway

0   3

m

N

Fig.3:4 The Late Causewayed Exit

The Finds

Samian

One hundred samian sherds were recovered, but the vast majority were small and abraded. A small number retained traces of moulded decoration but most of these were again abraded. The vast majority of pieces retaining any decoration or whose form could be ascertained were unstratified. The only pieces worthy of note were a 15/17 or 15/17R bowl and a very small decorated sherd from the phase 1 occupation layer; a probable 33 or 33a cup rim from the rampart material; and a form 30 bowl rim from the ?robber trench of the fort wall. A large part of a form 18 bowl mentioned in interim reports was probably derived from the phase 1 occupation but closer examination indicates that it was probably residual in a later context. Two partial stamps (OF P[and OF SA[) were recovered unstratified, though the form of the vessels carrying them could not be determined. The only other piece calling for comment was the rim of an unusual inkwell.

Coarse Wares and Mortaria

Some 432 Romano-British coarse ware sherds were recovered, together with 25 *amphora* sherds and 14 *mortaria* sherds. The vast majority were unstratified and of the stratified material few contexts produced sufficiently large groups of material to provide reliable dates since it was clear that much material was residual in nature. In terms of fabric the material included significant quantities of Derbyshire ware and BB1, but predominated in grey and orange wares of varying fineness, some with burnished finishes. A small amount of colour coated pottery, generally in a fine cream fabric with a red to brown wash, was also present, as well as two sherds of 'parchment ware' and a few sherds of 'Parisian ware' with incised decoration. The *amphora* sherds included eight large pieces probably from the body of the same vessel from the intervallum road surface, and nine sherds from the body of the rampart. The *mortaria*, with one exception, were all in white or cream fabrics, most of which were Mancetter/Hartshill products. The exception was a sherd in a very coarse pinky orange fabric with quartz and red tituration grits. Only three rim profiles were complete, all being hammerhead forms of the late-third to late-fourth centuries.

Only the following require more specific comment:

1 Twelve sherds representing a jar in a light grey fabric with large inclusions. Everted rim. Rusticated. (*Cf.* Wheeler 1985a Nos. 9–10; late-first/early-second century) From the rampart.

2 Seven sherds representing much of a bowl with a reeded rim and angled wall in a fine, hard buff to cream fabric with a quantity of red inclusions (*Cf.* Wheeler 1985a No. 15; late-first/early-second century). NB The material from the rampart included these pieces and other material which would be at home in a late-first/early-second century context, and BB1 was notably absent. However, there can be no doubt that the rampart was constructed on the re-establishment of the fort *c.*154/8. It seems likely that at this point the rampart was partly constructed from clay containing residual pottery, and most likely from material derived from the cutting of the later fort ditches. This suggests that these ditches were cut at least partly along the line of the ditches of the earlier fort.

3 Jar in a fine grey burnished fabric with barbotine decoration (*Cf.* Gillam 1957 No.70; 120–200). From the ?robber trench of the main fort wall.

4 Mortarium in a hard, cream coloured fabric with large red and black tituration grits. Hammerhead form with red painted swirls on the rim. Similar to Gillam 1957 No. 280; 270–350. From a possible robber trench on the line of the granary wall.

The Coins (*J.F. Drinkwater*)

1. Arg. *Denarius*
    obverse: Imperial bust (Nero), r.
    [IMP NERO CAESAR AVG P P]
    reverse: Legionary eagle, r., between two standards
    A.D. 67–8: Rome mint (*RIC* i [2nd ed., 1984], p. 154 no. 68 = *BMC* Empire, p. 214 no. 107).
    Unstratified in trench R.

2. Aes *Follis*
    obverse: Imperial bust (Constantine I), r., wearing laurel crown and cuirass
    IMP CONSTANTINVS PF AVG
    reverse: Sol (the sun god), standing l., wearing radiate crown, raising r. hand holding globe in l., with *chlamys* over l. shoulder
    SOLI INVICTO COMITI
    A.D. 312–318. It is difficult to be sure exactly where and when this coin was produced, but, if its mint-mark is read as TIF/PTR, it may be compared with *RIC* vi, p. 226 no. 866–Trier mint, AD 310–13. From below the causeway in area B.

3. ?Brass coin of indefinable denomination
    Obverse: Crowned or diademed bust of woman or young man, r.

Reverse: Illegible
Probably Greco-Roman but not a product of the late Empire. Perhaps first-century Roman, *perhaps* a Neronian *quadrans* of *c.*AD 63 (*cf.* R. A. G. Carson, *Coins of the Roman Empire*, 1990, p. 15).
Unstratified.

Other Finds

Except for a number of pieces of modern ironwork from the topsoil, and a small number of pieces of galena and lead splashes found unstratified only the following were recovered:

1   Mellon Bead (Diameter 2.5 cm; Length 1.6 cm). Half of a dark blue paste mellon bead. Unstratified.
2   Spindle whorl (Diam. 2.6 cm; Thickness 1 cm). Lead spindle whorl of flat form with central hole. Unstratified.
3   ?Bolt head (Length 14 cm). Very corroded probable iron bolt head with ?square sectioned shank. From the filling of the inner fort ditch.
4   Twisted rod (Length 17 cm). Circular sectioned iron rod twisted for most of its length and possibly originally ending in a corroded spatulate point. ?Roman. Unstratified.

4. Excavation and Geophysical Survey at Brough-on-Noe (*Navio*) 1980–3 and 1985

M.C. Bishop, M.J. Dearne, J.F. Drinkwater and J.A. Lloyd

Introduction

Until the 1980s no sustained archaeological research had taken place outside the fort at Brough-on-Noe, although antiquarian finds and one brief excavation had indicated the presence of a probable *vicus* (see volume introduction). It therefore seemed desirable in 1980, when the research programme whose results are described here was being drawn up, to devote resources to an investigation of what by inference from Brough's position as the only nearly continuously garrisoned site in the Roman Peak District may have been an important civil site. Attention was focused on the field south east of the fort known as the Halsteads by the location of antiquarian finds there and the likelihood that the road to Buxton (*Aquae Arnemetium*) ran from the south east fort gate across the field (e.g. Figure 1:1).

Although sloping quite steeply towards the Bradwell Brook the field includes flatter areas suitable for settlement; the slope may have facilitated drainage in the damp Peak District climate which would have been important given the predominantly clay subsoil.

The fieldwork aimed to obtain both a broad picture of the layout of the settlement through resistivity survey and some detailed indication of its character and development through excavation. Permission to carry out the project was kindly granted by the then DoE Ancient Monuments Division, the landowners, Blue Circle Cement PLC, and the tenant, Mr. Peter Eyre. Four two-week seasons of work were carried out in June/July of 1980–3, the final season being curtailed by the need to divert resources to the rescue work at Home Farm described below (Drage, this volume). Funding was supplied by the former Department of Ancient History and Classical Archaeology, University of Sheffield, for whose students the project served as a training programme. Considerable help in soil removal and in fencing the site was provided by the Hope works of Blue Circle Cement and Mr. P. Eyre kindly allowed the use of farm buildings for the temporary storage of finds and equipment. The site archives and finds have been deposited in Sheffield City Museum.

MJD directed a small resistivity survey in 1985 close to the south corner of the fort with the intention of assessing the extent of the *vicus*. Permission was again obtained from the land owners and the tenant and funding from the former Department of Ancient History and Classical Archaeology, for whose students the project again formed a training exercise.

The 1981–2 Resistivity Survey

The resistivity survey of 1981–2 carried out in the field known as the Halsteads (Figure 1:1) evolved in an attempt to understand something of the nature of the *vicus* following the results of a trial trench (later trench A below). The survey was undertaken on a one metre grid in three stages. Squares 1–3 (Figure 4:1) were surveyed in April 1981 using a Bradphys machine which, due to a malfunction, failed to complete square 3. This was re-surveyed in November 1981 along with an additional square (4) to the east of square 1. Subsequently square 4 was re-surveyed as square 5 in June 1982 and squares 6–10 were surveyed at the same time. The 1982 surveys were executed using a DIGS (Digital Impedance Ground Survey) machine custom designed and built by Dr. A.T. Barker of the Department of Medical Physics, University of Sheffield to whom the authors would like to record their warm thanks.

The 1981 survey was carried out after the trial trench (later trench A) had been backfilled but before it and trench B had been (re-)opened. Trench A appears as a high resistance feature on the survey (Figure 4:2 No. 1); this is due to the fact that it was lined with plastic sheeting prior to backfilling. Trench A demonstrated that the visible *agger* in the field did not represent the Roman Batham Gate (below) but at least in the excavated area, a later track. Its course is readily apparent on the survey as Figure 4:2 No. 2. It is possible that the indistinct feature 10 running parallel to and slightly west of 2 is in fact Batham Gate and the coincidence of feature 5 (below) with its turn to the s.s.w. strengthens this. From this point the south west stretch of feature 2 (the *agger*) probably overlies the course of the Batham Gate (see also Figures 8:5 and 8:6). Feature 3 on Figure 4:2 was shown by excavation in trench B to be a road (road B below). Its continuation in survey squares 7 and 8 shows that the road led from the south east gate of the fort down to the confluence of the Bradwell Brook and the River Noe, where the bath house was probably situated. High resistivity feature 4 (Figure 4:2) may be a branch from this road, heading for a crossing of the Bradwell Brook whence it will have led to that part of the *vicus* on the other side of the brook partly excavated in 1983–4 when a

BROUGH-ON-NOE RESISTIVITY SURVEY 1981–82

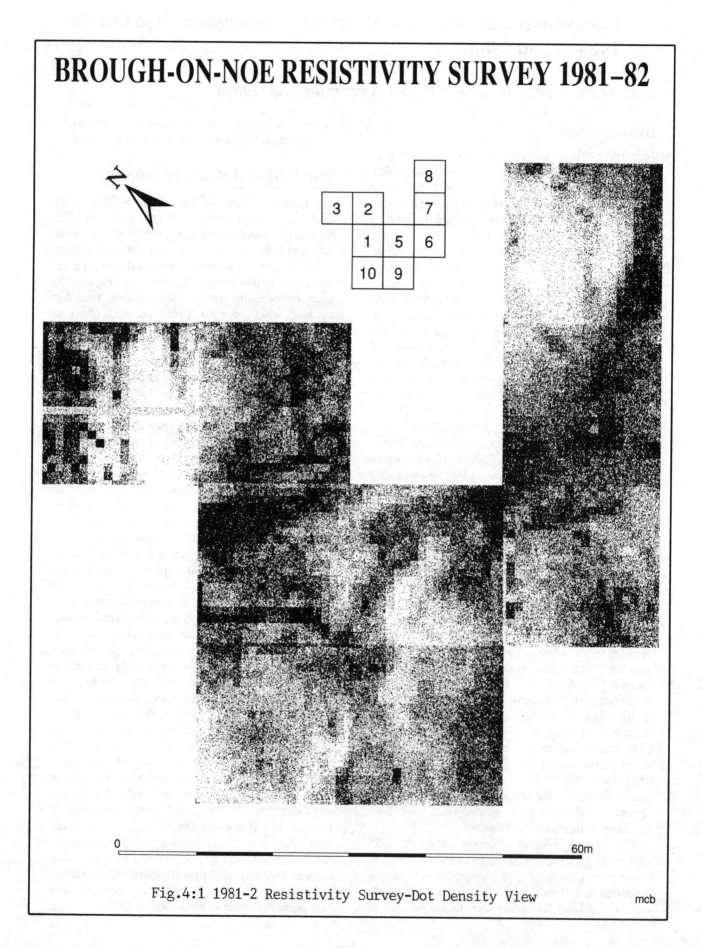

Fig.4:1 1981-2 Resistivity Survey-Dot Density View

mcb

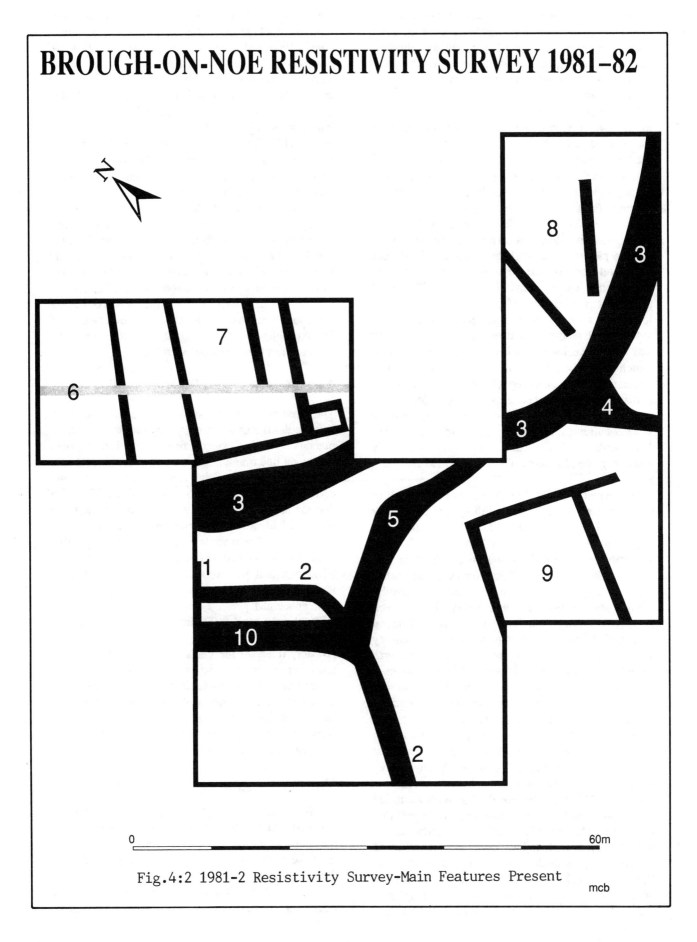

BROUGH-ON-NOE RESISTIVITY SURVEY 1981-82

N

8

3

7

6

3

5

4

3

1

2

9

10

2

0   60m

Fig.4:2 1981-2 Resistivity Survey-Main Features Present

mcb

39

road heading for ?Chesterfield was identified (Drage, this volume). Whether these roads are to be identified with each other is not certain but likely. Similarly feature 5 on Figure 4:2 is probably another road linking the baths and the eastern part of the *vicus* with Batham Gate.

Low resistance feature 6 may reflect the course of a modern water main trench, at least three of which run through the field, though it has not been possible to establish this categorically. Between feature 3 (road B below) and the bank of the River Noe to the east it is quite likely that a number of linear high resistance features (grouped as 7 on Figure 4:2) represent structures belonging to the *vicus*, possibly of the classic strip-building type. Their outlines on Figure 4:2 are plotted from heightened contrast dot density views and from contour views of the data which show them more clearly than Figure 4:1. The most prominent is a building 15m wide and at least 20m long with a small annexe 4m square on its eastern side. It is aligned so that it fronts feature 3 (road B) and lies immediately outside the area examined by trench B (below). Eight metres to the west of this structure another wall on the same alignment, is perhaps part of another strip-building. More linear features (8 and 9 on Fig 4:2) may also indicate *vicanal* buildings. At 9 there appears to be a structure 14m wide and at least 20m long, apparently respecting the alignment of feature 3 (road B) at this point.

The elements revealed by the survey need not all be contemporary, though the buildings represented by features 9 and especially 7 clearly respect the alignment of feature 3 (road B) and are likely to be contemporary with or later than its construction. The confirmation from trench B that feature 3 represents a road is important and must make the similar identification of features 4 and 5 very likely. Trench B also revealed cut and relatively ephemeral structural features not recognised by the resistivity survey. However, whilst the industrial structures including hearths immediately south of feature 3 (road B) were not clearly delineated by the survey, there is, undeniably, a medium resistance concentration in the same general area (Figure 4:1). A further implication of the resistivity technique on the site is that stone founded buildings are the most likely to show up and it seems that purely timber structures would be unlikely to be detected by the technique. This suggests that the buildings identified were stone founded at least and tends to suggest that they were constructed later rather than earlier in the site's history. Few stone founded let alone constructed buildings except bath houses are known in south Pennine *vici* and the few that are suggest that the use of stone even for foundations did not develop until well into the second century. Thus, at Melandra

where much of the *vicus* is known, only a single building had even stone footings for a timber construction and it belongs to the period *c*.120–140 (Webster 1971). In the Manchester *vicus* the use of stone footings does not seem to be attested before the later-second century (Walker 1986, 142), although there are antiquarian records of undated stone buildings in other parts of the *vicus* (e.g. Dearne 1986, 41f.). Thus the buildings identified by the resistivity survey probably belong to the second century at the earliest and relate to the *vicus* outside the fort re-established *c*.154/8.

The organisation of the site as revealed by the survey gives no indication of attempts to impose any systematic plan on it. Rather piecemeal development beside and between military roads (features 2, 3, and perhaps 4) and lesser road lines (e.g. probably feature 5) is suggested. None of the road courses betrays any sign of concern other than for the most convenient route to its destination and the only coincidences of building alignments appear to be determined by common frontages on adjacent roads.

The 1985 Resistivity Survey

The smaller resistivity survey carried out in 1985 again utilised a one metre grid system and the DIGS machine. It consisted of five 10 x 10m squares forming a line running south along (but offset from) a modern field boundary that runs south from the south corner of the later fort. To this was added a 10 x 45m dog leg at right angles to its northern end, and two additional squares running north and south from it (Figure 1:1). The work was carried out in June 1985 in tandem with a survey of the banks and beds of the River Noe and Bradwell Brook, whose results were largely negative as far as Roman features and finds were concerned.

The survey results (Figure 4:3) were also largely negative. Higher readings in squares B4, B5 and D1 probably relate to the course of Batham Gate or its successor track as one would expect from the indications of their courses in the earlier survey. One or two patches of higher readings to the north west of this might indicate the presence of walls but they form no coherent pattern and west of square B2 there is no trace of any feature.

The Excavations (*cf*. Figure 1:1)

The first trial trench opened in autumn 1980 was 8 x 2m and placed over a slight *agger* which was presumed to be the line of the Roman road leading from the south east gate of the fort. The position of the gate is now approximately marked by a modern field gate and stile. The remains of a small cambered track were revealed below the *agger* but finds of

BROUGH-ON-NOE RESISTIVITY SURVEY 1985

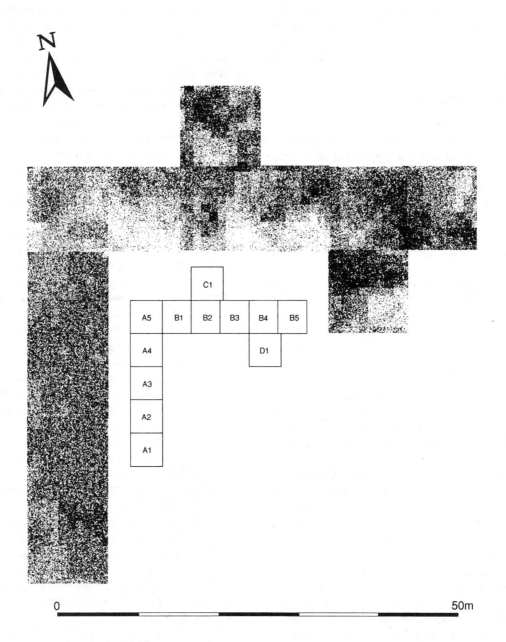

Fig.4:3 1985 Resistivity Survey-Dot Density View

mcb

Roman material (amphorae, coarse pottery, samian, glass and a lead object) below the track suggested that it sealed Roman levels. This trench was reopened in 1981 as trench A to investigate further this supposition, along with trench B, a 10m square to its north east separated from it by a 1m baulk. Trench B was placed partly over the area of high resistance readings detected in square 1 of the 1981 survey (above) and its aims were to establish the cause of these readings and to establish whether civilian settlement was present in the area. Topsoil was initially mechanically removed from the trenches but all features were excavated by hand. For the purposes of the following description and interpretation north is taken as site north, actually grid north east. The location of trenches A and B is shown in Figure 1:1.

Trench A (Figure 4:4)

Excluding the small cambered track noted above, the latest level encountered below a topsoil layer up to 25cm thick was an undulating spread of small stones and pebbles within an earth matrix (context 1), almost certainly an example of worm-sorted plough soil (the field had not been ploughed in living memory (*cf.* Limbrey 1975, 313)). The Romano–British features were sealed by up to 30cm of sandy silt loam below context 1. They were, from south to north:

i) Two surfaces, contexts 3 and 7, constructed of hard packed earth, pebbles and small flat pieces of Limestone (up to 15 x 10cm, but generally much smaller), but also including fragments of ironstone and amphora. The surfaces were separated by a thin layer of sandy silt loam (context 8) from which brooch 4.1 was recovered. Their edges were extremely ragged and had probably originally extended rather further to the north where the southern side of the cut feature 6 was much shallower and more elongated than the northern side.

ii) A cut feature and its fill of dark clay loam (context 6). To judge from its eastern part the feature may originally have been of flattened V-shape with a rounded base. Its fill contained a considerable amount of pottery including part of a Curle 11 samian dish.

iii) Cut into a compact yellow-brown clay loam (context 5), two features 11 and 2. Feature 11 was defined by a ring of small stones and contained a shallow fill of dark silty clay loam. From the fill came a lead weight (6.2) and a large lump of coal (10.1). A little to the north of 11 lay 2, an east–west rectangular slot with a stub-like northern return.

iv) Context 9 consisting of a large, deep, irregularly sided cut through the surface 5. Set into the

surface 5 (and possibly into the top few centimetres of the cut, although the stratigraphical relationship between the two was far from clear) was a stone feature (context 10) comprising a horizontally laid slab surrounded (and partly overlain) by upright stones on two sides.

v) All features were cut into the surface of 5. However when a section was placed through it at the south east corner of the trench there was no certain indication as to whether this was natural material or not.

The surfaces 3 and 7 are almost certainly successive metallings of a road (road 'A'), flanked by a V-shaped ditch (context 6). Sites such as Manchester provide parallels for the presence of roads of similar construction in *vici* (Jones and Grealey 1974). The road surfaces were probably cambered, although the amount of wear was too great to permit an accurate reconstruction of their profiles. It seems likely that this was the original military road linking the fort with the road line known as Batham Gate and heading for Buxton. The samian ware from both trenches A and B was uniformly of Flavian/Trajanic date, the earliest pieces belonging to the last fifteen years of the first century, and, since the first surface of the road (context 7) had apparently been lain directly on to the natural subsoil, the road is probably contemporary with the foundation of the first fort at Brough *c*.78/9. Its remetalling dates to the Trajanic period (98–117) or later: fragments of the same Curle 11 samian bowl came from between the metallings and from the ditch fill, and the brooch (4.1) from between the metallings is a predominantly second century type with Trajanic origins.

It is possible that the later road surface did not survive in use throughout Brough's occupation. The withdrawal of the garrison *c*.120 doubtless decreased the traffic along the road. However, with the re-garrisoning of the site *c*.154/8 and its continued occupation down to the mid-fourth century it is curious that there was no evidence for subsequent re-metallings. The samian ware from the road side ditch was Flavian/Trajanic, as was all the samian ware from the site; however, the coarse pottery evidence suggests that the ditch and road were still features of the site, even if the road was not strictly still in use as a major thoroughfare, long after the re-garrisoning of the fort. If road A had passed out of regular use some alternative approach of Batham Gate to the fort should be sought.

To its north, road A seems to have been flanked by a timber structure represented by slot 2, but its relationship to feature 10, interpreted as a post setting, is unclear. Feature 11 might have been another post setting, but the absence of packing stones may make it preferable to see this as a small pit (conceivably deliberately dug to conceal the lead

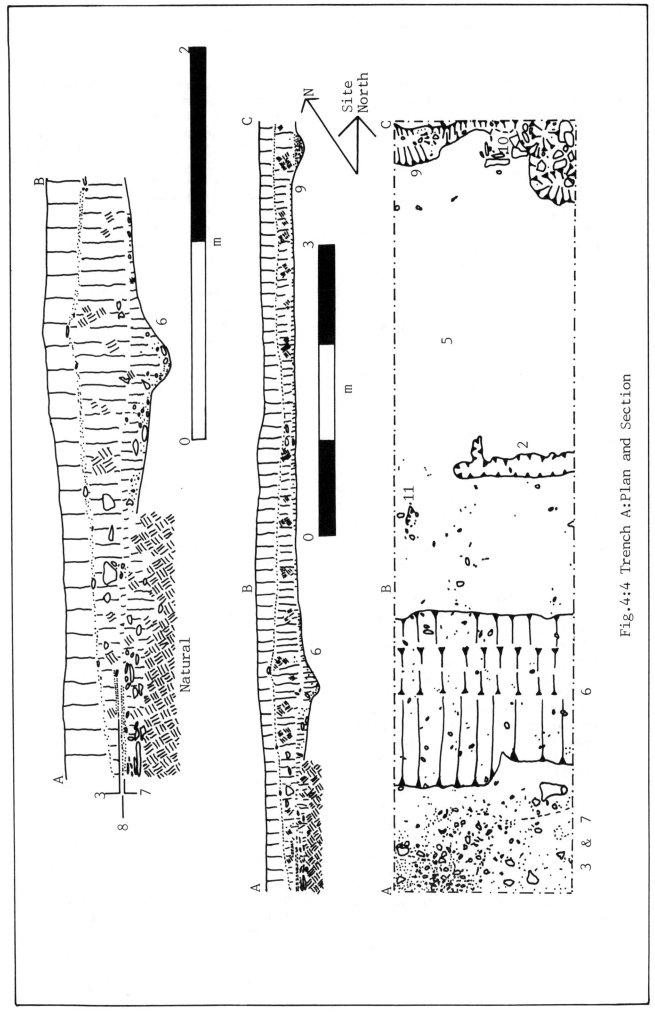

Natural

Site North

N

Fig. 4:4 Trench A: Plan and Section

43

weight). The cutting 9 may have been earlier than post setting 10, but its chronological relationship to features 2 and 11 was not clear. The possible timber building(s) will be discussed below together with the evidence from trench B.

Trench B (Figure 4:5)

Trench B revealed a similar horizon of small stones to that encountered in trench A at a maximum depth of 30cm below the modern ground level. Finds of post-medieval pottery and clay pipe fragments sealed below the surface give some indication of date. Only a few centimetres of soil separated this material from the uppermost Roman layers; indeed the tops of some of the larger blocks of feature 5 were incorporated within it. The main Roman features encountered were:

i) A mass of rubble and stone (feature 5/6) including some very large blocks (max. 80 x 45 x 25cm) which occupied much of the northern half of the trench, running at an angle across it west to east. Most of the stonework lay horizontally with a very few large blocks set vertically; the gaps between them were filled with a matrix that included smaller stones. In places there survived patches of a carefully finished compacted surface of small stones and pebbles (context 6). The surface of the feature was slightly cambered (Plate 1).
    Feature 5/6 was bounded to the south by an alignment of blocks (context 19), separated from it by a small gap, extending for just over 7m from the west section. There was no obvious indication (such as a robber trench) that the alignment had continued further to the east, although a possible foundation in the form of small compacted stones (context 23) ran up to the east baulk. The north side of feature 5/6 was not so clearly defined. In the north west of the trench it gave way to densely packed cobbling (context 54) which dipped sharply to the north. Bone, coarse pottery (including flagons) and an unusual sherd of Curle 15 plain samian were recovered from the fill (context 53).
    Feature 5/6 was c.4.6m wide and a section cut through it at right angles suggested that there was no more than one phase of construction, although there may have been repairs to the surface. The rubble core had been laid onto a thin matrix overlying a clay dump (see further below). A few scraps of occupation material, including fragments of samian and a piece of copper alloy, were present in this layer.

ii) An irregular but broadly rectangular spread of clay (c.1.45 x 1.20m) yellowish in colour at the edges but predominantly reddish. The surface of this feature (context 24) was pitted by numerous small in-filled holes and crossed by a linear east–west depression at its centre (Figure 4:6; Plate 2). The feature was subsequently investigated further, although the terms of the agreement with the DoE did not permit full examination. Two opposing quadrants were removed, allowing the recording of full east–west and north–south sections (Figure 4:7). These revealed a bowl-shaped depression filled with charcoal at the centre of what was clearly a hearth. The sides of the bowl were formed of clays burnt to various shades of red and magenta and of stones and it was surrounded by unaltered clays, typically yellow in colour above which in places survived traces of a maroon/red burnt cap.

iii) Similar remains, which were stratigraphically earlier than 24, and in a more fragmentary state. North east of 25 there was a considerable area of burnt red clay (context 12) along with a spread and patches of unburnt yellow material (context 22). Even more fragmentary were the remains (context 47) to the north west of 24 and beneath 24 itself were possible traces of another such feature (context 48; Figure 4:7). Context 47 may have been associated with a metalled surface in which there were three parallel 'ruts', as well as much charcoal (context 56). The silty clay deposit (context 13/15) surrounding and covering the burnt clay features to the south of 5/6 was rich in charcoal, patches of reddened clay, coarse pottery and fragments of iron including nails.

iv) A curved feature (context 16) next to the west side of 24 constructed of flat stones which had been discoloured by heat to a magenta in places.

v) A number of post holes or post pits (contexts 20–1; 31–2; and 34) some of which contained packing stones, e.g. context 32, which had been cut into a larger cut feature (context 59, below). The surviving packing stones had been set vertically as with context 10 in trench A.

vi) Partial removal of context 5/6 revealed two cut features, context 43 and 72 (respectively at the centre of the trench and below the northern edge of 5/6) which may possibly have been post-holes.

vii) In the south west corner of the trench and cut by later post hole 32 a pit (context 59), part of which lay under the west baulk. It was found to contain several fragments of pottery including decorated samian and much animal bone. It was evident upon full excavation that individual spade or

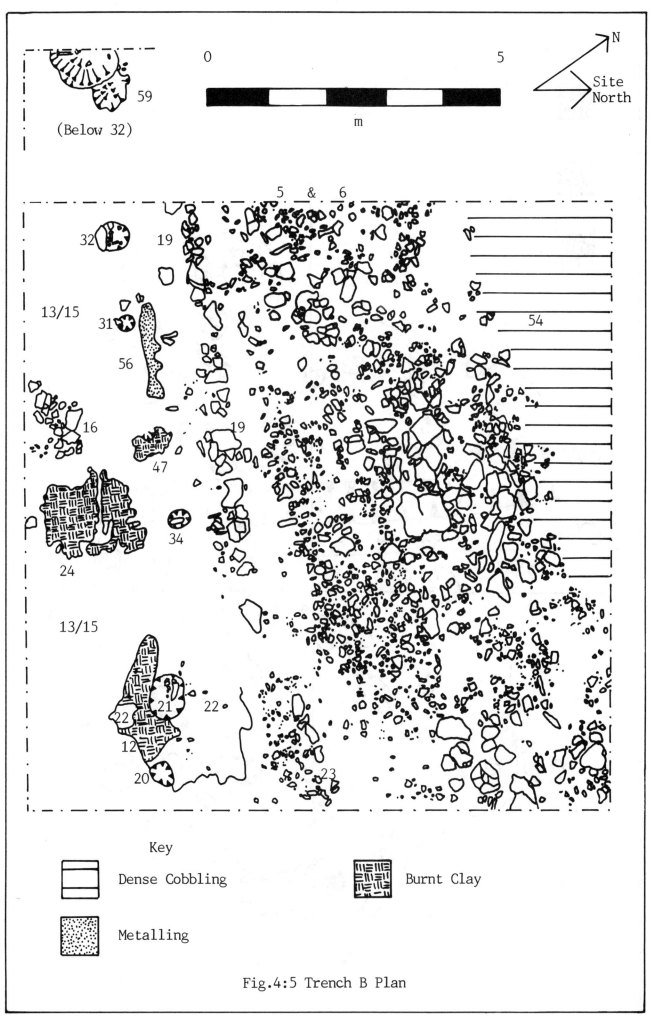

Key

Dense Cobbling   Burnt Clay

Metalling

Fig.4:5 Trench B Plan

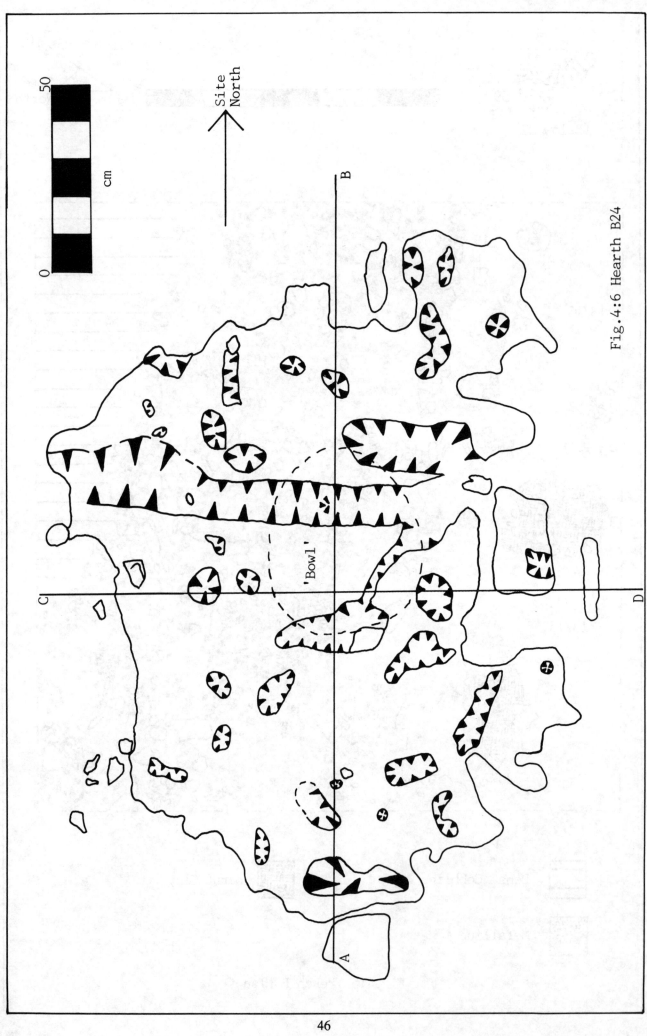

Fig.4:6 Hearth B24

50

cm

0

Site North

B

C

D

A

'Bowl'

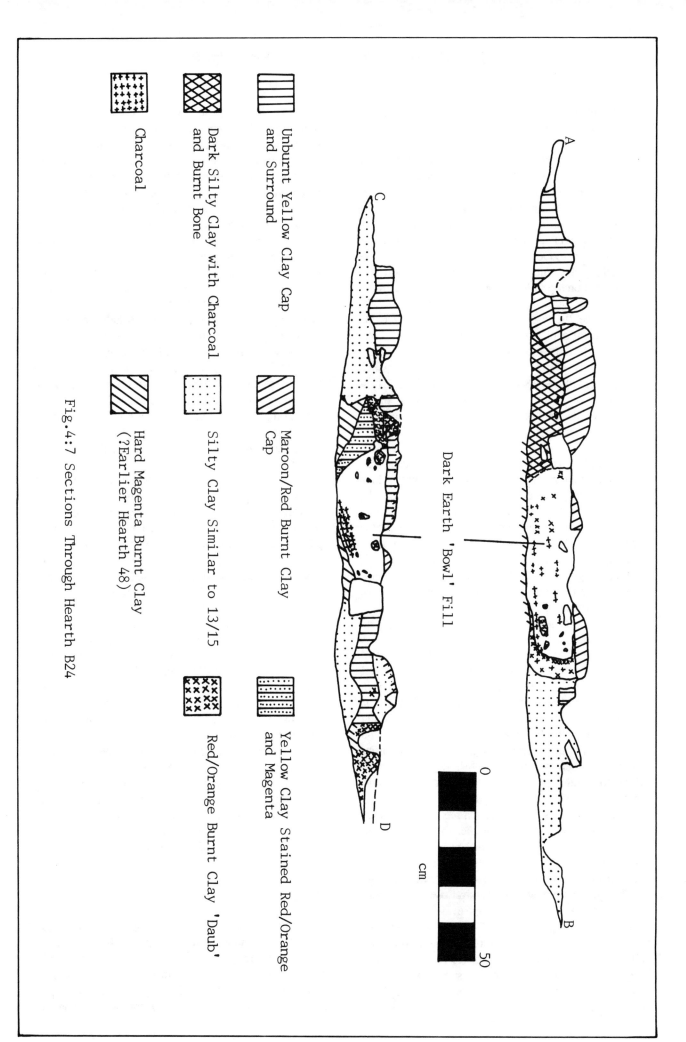

Unburnt Yellow Clay Cap and Surround

Maroon/Red Burnt Clay Cap

Yellow Clay Stained Red/Orange and Magenta

Dark Silty Clay with Charcoal and Burnt Bone

Silty Clay Similar to 13/15

Red/Orange Burnt Clay 'Daub'

Charcoal

Hard Magenta Burnt Clay (?Earlier Hearth 48)

Dark Earth 'Bowl' Fill

Fig.4:7 Sections Through Hearth B24

0

cm

50

shovel marks could be discerned, particularly around its eastern edge.

viii) A 4 x 1m sondage cut on the east side of the trench examined the deposits underlying the features described above, principally below 5/6. The natural was found to be overlain by some 60cm of yellow orange clay in which clear tip lines as well as charcoal smears and specks of pottery were identifiable. Above this was a layer of yellow clay and it was evident that a soil had formed on top of this, root holes descending into it from the soil. This soil was noted only in the sondage, the rest of the site not being excavated to sufficient depth to reveal it. Several slots were cut through the soil into the surface of the clay (contexts 36, 58, 69 and 71), one of which (context 58) was sectioned by the sondage. It was 0.2m wide and 0.3m deep and was traced westwards for about 2.2m in an area where 5/6 had been removed.

Feature 5/6 seems certain to have been a road (road 'B') leading from the south east fort gate (with which it is aligned) towards the south corner of the Halsteads field. It was evidently the stone construction of the road which was responsible for the high resistivity in this area, and the pattern of readings from the survey squares east of trench B strongly suggests that it took a slightly curving course towards the probable site of the military baths at the River Noe/Bradwell Brook confluence.

The nature of activity on the north side of the road was unclear. To its south however, between roads A and B, there is evidence for a minimum of two periods of settlement, in the last of which metal working was of particular importance. The most important evidence for the processing of metal is feature 24, which may be interpreted as a smithing hearth, in view of the evidence of the slag (below) and of its construction. Hearths of this kind are familiar from a number of Romano-British sites in northern England, notably Manchester. Bestwick and Cleland's research into the Manchester hearths (in Jones and Grealey 1974, 143–57) provides a model of how they may have functioned. Another example from Corbridge, Northumberland (Bishop and Dore 1989, 105ff and fig. 55) shows a central channel to have been a constructional feature of these hearths; the Corbridge example, which was never used, was stone-lined to form a flue. Additional evidence for metal working at Brough comes in the form of splashes of metal (4.5), offcuts of lead (6.5–6) and iron slag (10.2). The four intact lead objects (6.1–4) and the fragmentary iron objects are also suggestive of local metalworking, although they need not have been made at the excavated site.

Hearth 24 seems to have been placed within a workshop, the plan of which was only partly recoverable. This was sited in the angular space between roads A and B. The northern frontage of the property is probably represented by the line of large blocks (context 19), which could have served as a base for a wall constructed of timber and clay. The absence of blocks from the probable foundations of the feature further east may be explained by robbing (though no robber trench was noted); or an entrance might have existed here. To the south the only candidate for any formal property boundary is slot A2, which might indicate the position of a slight wall or perhaps a fence line built of perishable materials. By analogy (and by alignment) however this might belong with the slots located in trench B. Within these limits the presence of two almost certain post-holes or settings (contexts 21 and 32), together with A10, and possibly three more, contexts 20, 31 and 34, suggest that the building was at least partially roofed. The relationship between the post-setting 21 and the burnt clay spread 12 strongly suggests that the post was secondary.

The building with posts was the latest structure on the site. At least one earlier phase of activity is indicated by the various slots and by feature 59, whose nature and contents suggest a domestic rubbish pit. Traces of hearths in operation earlier than 24 may be represented by spreads of burnt clay and charcoal (contexts 12, 22, 47, 48). Associated with these levels was a patch of gravelled floor (context 56). It was necessary, however, to limit excavation of these features and we must be content with the knowledge that at least two phases of occupation were represented. There was no evidence beyond that already described for the construction techniques in use. Several scraps of tile and daub, a fragment of window glass and many iron nails were recovered, but none of them need necessarily have derived from buildings on the site.

The deposits revealed by the sondage below road B suggest that it was founded on a thin layer of yellow clay which may have been a deliberate makeup for it. Below this was a much thicker clay makeup dump. A soil horizon between them with traces of root holes and slots perhaps suggests some period of activity between the dumping of the clay and the construction of the road.

Dating

The principal dating evidence for the Roman levels is provided by samian pottery, supported by the coarse wares and the glass (discussed in greater detail below). A few sherds of later medieval, post-medieval and modern pottery, together with some clay pipe stem fragments, were recovered from the post-Roman levels. Although some of the coarse pottery belonged to the mid-second and early-third centuries A.D. and a little to later periods, the majority of the dateable finds and especially the samian ware form a coherent group of the late-first and early-second centuries.

The earliest samian sherds came from vessels manufactured in the period from the 80s to the end of the first century; the latest closely dateable piece is Trajanic. This evidence would seem to suggest that the development of this part of the *vicus* belongs firmly within the first period of military occupation at Brough, *c*.80–120. Within this period more precise dating is largely unobtainable. For what it is worth the pit (context 59), itself cut by the post-hole 32, produced sherds of Flavian date, and the fragments of samian recovered from the makeup of road B were also Flavian. This hints at, but does not prove, a pre-Trajanic date for both. The second metalling of road A seems to be an early-second century improvement as noted above. It does not necessarily follow, however, that the first metalling is of much earlier date.

The later material is exclusively coarse pottery from unsealed contexts or contexts sealed only by a general build up over the site. Notably it includes only one sherd of Derbyshire ware, which was abundant in later-second century contexts at Brough (e.g. Birss in Branigan and Dearne, this volume). It is probably to be associated with the well-attested activity within the fort from the mid-second to fourth centuries rather than with continued occupation of the excavated site. With the exception perhaps of the roads the site seems to have been an open area in which rubbish was accruing during the fort's later history.

Conclusion

The value of resistivity survey techniques in locating a number of features of the presumed *vicus* south east of the fort is indicated by the complementary excavation results which confirmed the identification of Figure 4:2 feature 3 as a road (road B). However the limitations of such a survey are demonstrated by its inability to locate smaller, poorly preserved or negative features such as the smithing hearth, slots and ditches. This is no cause for surprise, since, locally, the fills and constituent materials of such features are very similar in character and density to the 'background' soils, thus lessening the chance of significant variation being detected. A combination of resistivity and magnetometer investigation might be more successful in providing a fuller picture of the buried landscape (e.g. Clark 1990, 128ff).

However, the combination here of extensive resistivity survey with intensive but limited excavation, to provide a chronological framework and functional evidence as well as to confirm provisional survey interpretations, allows us to say a good deal about the *vicus* without the need for large scale excavation in a non-threatened area. It is now clear that two roads (roads A and B) left the south east fort gate. The former, or at least a later track on its line, turned south west before it had run far and was probably the road to Buxton (Batham Gate). How long it remained in use is not entirely clear but it was probably primary to the site layout. Road B sealed a makeup layer and some features and so was not, at least technically, primary, but it seems to have been built by *c*.120. Its destination was the Noe/Bradwell confluence, the probable site of the military baths, and the fact that probably stone (founded) buildings respect its alignment suggests that it was in use at least well into the second century. Two branch roads from it seem to have provided connections with the *vicus* area across the Bradwell Brook and with Road A.

Roofed timber buildings existed between roads A and B during the fort's first phase (*c*.80–120) and, although they are incompletely known, in the final phase they were associated with metalworking activity. This workshop with smithing hearths, associated slag and waste (suggesting that a variety of metals, iron, lead and perhaps copper alloy were being worked here) cannot categorically be said to be civilian. All the small finds from the excavation could fit into either a military or civilian context and the site, given the poorly known nature of this side of the early fort could have lain within an annexe; or indeed there might be good reason for the military to site any workshops outside the fort at a time when building in timber was the norm. This said, however, the location would have been a prime one for a civilian craftsman looking to serve the needs of the garrison as well as those of the *vicani*. The initial activity belongs to the Flavian/Trajanic period and, if indeed it was a civilian enterprise, it is rather tempting to believe that it closely followed the establishment of the garrison *c*.80 and was given up when the first fort was abandoned close to 120, with consequent loss of the military market. At the comparable Peak District site of Melandra the life of the *vicus* ended when the garrison left (Webster 1971) and *vicanal* dependence on the army's cash is a well worked theme.

The presencee of possible stone footings (context 19) for a presumably timber-framed wall fronting road B is of interest. As noted above the use of masonry for the footings of buildings in south Pennine *vici* is not otherwise attested before the later-second century. However, an alternative explanation for the feature is that it served as a kerb for road B, and only excavation on a larger scale is likely to resolve the issue. It would be unwise to place weight on this evidence when considering the date at which stone began to be used for *vicanal* building in the region.

Whether there was any reoccupation of the excavated site with the re-establishment of the fort 154/8 is not certain but it may well have remained unused, despite its prime location with only rubbish, from the fort and or *vicus*, accruing in the later-second and perhaps early-third centuries. It is unlikely that any abandonment was representative of the whole *vicus*. Its expanded extent in the later-second century has been demonstrated elsewhere (Branigan and Dearne, this volume; Drage, this volume) and the traces of buildings on the resistivity survey are likely, given the technique's sensitivity, to be those of stone (founded) structures most likely of the second century or later. If so they suggest a picture of an unplanned *vicus* south east of the later fort with ?strip buildings lining the roads in the north western and eastern parts of the modern Halsteads field and probably south east as far as the 1984 site.

Finally it may be noted that the excavated site showed some sign of modest wealth in the reasonably abundant quantities of glass, fine pottery and amphorae present. Why perfectly serviceable items such as the lamp and weights (6.1–3) were buried or left behind, most probably when the site was abandoned *c*.120 is not clear. Hurried abandonment is a possible explanation or alternatively such objects may have been easily replaceable.

The Finds

1.   Samian Pottery *Catherine Johns*

The total assemblage is a small one (86 catalogue entries for plain ware and 30 for decorated sherds) and most sherds are very fragmentary and in very poor condition. This means that the identifiable sample is very small indeed; nevertheless, it is possible to make some general statements about the date and source of the group as a whole.

The date of manufacture of most of the sherds can be placed within the last fifteen years or so of the first century and perhaps the first few years of the second. Most of the material is of South Gaulish origin; the few sherds of Central Gaulish ware from Les-Martres-de-Veyre would appear to pre-date the major influx of imports from that region which took place in Trajanic times. There is no example of first century Lezoux samian, though it must be said that the chances of survival of this ware in the soil of Brough would seem to be slight.

Plain ware

The general impression is of a typically Flavian South Gaulish group, with the expected forms — Dr.27 and Dr.18 and 18/31. It should be stressed, however, that

of 86 entries, no fewer than 45 — over 50% — have had to be described as `indeterminate' because of their small size and worn condition. One example of form Hofheim (Ritterling) 12 was noted, and there was one exceptional form for the period, a fragment of Curle 15 in what appears to be a standard Flavian South Gaulish fabric (Context B53). This form is normally a later-second century type manufactured in Central (and East) Gaul.

There is a small proportion of Central Gaulish sherds, including a couple of probable Dr.27 fragments, one sherd from a cup of Dr.33 (Trench A unstratified), and a Dr.18 sherd in typical Les-Martres ware (Context B2). However, a disproportionate number of entries for Central Gaulish ware is accounted for by the survival of several sherds from the same bowl of form Curle 11. Sherds from this vessel are from contexts A1, A5, A6 and A8 and possibly also contexts B13 and 32. Given the condition of the material, it is only the distinctive form of this vessel which makes it possible to establish that all the sherds are from the same bowl, and the general implications for quantitative analyses of small samples should not be ignored.

Decorated ware

Of the 30 sherds from decorated vessels, 24 are from South Gaulish bowls of form Dr.37, one from a Central Gaulish 37, and five from South Gaulish 29s. All are likely to have been made between the early 80s and the beginning of the second century. No example of Dr.30 was found, but in such a small sample, this is to be expected.

The sherds definitely from Dr.29 bowls are from contexts A4 and B13 (including 1.1 below); sherds from A6 are probably from this form.

The one sherd from Central Gaulish decorated ware (1.4 below) is the work of an early and distinctive potter, the Potter of the Rosette. It is of Trajanic date, but may well be early in that period.

The four sherds illustrated, and described below, have been selected partly as representative of the whole group (one of the earliest sherds, two typical Flavian 37s, and the one Central Gaulish piece), and partly because their condition is just adequate to allow them to be drawn.

Illustrated sherds (Figure 4:8)

1.1 Dr.29, South Gaulish

Part of the lower frieze; below a very narrow central moulding is a middle zone of short upright leaves or lozenge-shaped gadroons, divided by a wavy line from a zone of reversed S-motifs. The condition of the sherd, which is very worn and has lost most of its slip, makes close comparisons difficult, but similar zones of vertical leaves are used on vessels stamped by Passenus and by

Modestus (Knorr 1952, Taf.43, E, F; 48, C). Note also several related sherds in Knorr 1912, especially those with the same S-frieze: Taf.VI, 10, Taf.I, 13, Taf.II, 1 and 6.

The sherd belongs to a late phase in the manufacture of South Gaulish 29s.

Flavian.

Context B13.

1.2 Dr.37, South Gaulish

Two non-joining sherds. The panelled decoration includes a triple-leaf basal wreath, a panel with a leaf-cross incorporating the same leaf, and a longer lower sub-panel containing a leaf-scroll with a small fan-shaped leaf. The basal wreath was widely used by the later Flavian potters; *cf.* Knorr 1919, Textbild 12, top, 2nd right, listed for Iucundus, Mercato, Niger, Secundus and Vitalis. The small leaf in the wreath was used by Mercato; Knorr 1919, Taf.57, 25. The scheme of decoration is slightly unusual, and as far as can be judged from the present state of the sherd, the moulding and finish was originally of good quality.

Flavian.

Context B59.

1.3 Dr.37, South Gaulish

A fairly large sherd with panelled decoration, the surface very abraded (all the slip is lost on the interior). In the first surviving panel is a warrior with sword and shield, O.185A or O.992: there is a size difference, but it is not certain which is represented here. A divided panel follows, the upper containing a biga to the left, O.1161, attributed by Oswald to the potter Cornutus; the lower panel has a group comprising a small cupid, O.406, and a small dancing satyr, O.646: this latter type is also recorded for Cornutus (Knorr 1919, Taf.25, 1). The next panel is occupied by an incomplete standing figure to the right, which looks as though it ought to be a flute-playing satyr (*cf.* O.614-616), but has not been identified. A leaf-cross motif incorporates the common `leek' (grass-tuft) used by the majority of later Flavian potters, while below the smaller panels only is a triple-leaf basal wreath which is rather slighter and smaller than the very common Flavian type seen on (1.2) above. The warrior, O.185A/992, occurs in a similar general style on Knorr Rottenburg (1910), Taf.1.

Flavian.

Context A1.

1.4 Dr.37, Central Gaulish

A small sherd, slightly burnt so that the slip, where it survives, is blackened, while the fabric retains most of its original orange-red colour. The decoration consists of crowded panels and numerous decorative details; the edge of a South-Gaulish-type leaf-tip and diagonal wavy line panel

can be seen. Decorative details of a `crown' (Bacchic clapper), Rogers U.64, used as a border junction, the bow and quiver U.216 across a wavy line, and a small, tightly-curved ram's-horn wreath used as a horizontal panel border; this is G.380, characteristic of the Potter of the Rosette. The details and the general style are typical of his work, *cf. CGP*, Pls.20–23 for his panelled designs.

Trajanic.

Context B2.

2. Coarsewares M. J. Dearne based on identifications and an archive report by Simon Tomson

The coarsewares recovered from the 1980–3 excavations were without exception poorly preserved . Much of the pottery was identifiable only by fabric, the sherds mainly being small. Given this, the low percentage of the material from sealed and uncontaminated contexts as opposed to the amount from the lower levels of the topsoil, and the better preserved collections from more secure contexts published in the present · volume, only a brief summary of the coarseware is presented here.

Amphorae (Vessel forms follow Dressel (1899) and Hawkes and Hull (1947))

Sherds of the large Dressel 20/Camulodunum 187 occurred throughout the vertical sequence and could theoretically all be from one 32–37Kg, 80 litre vessel (Riley 1979). However, this is unlikely given differences in fabric. The form was used to transport olive oil from the Guadalquivir valley in southern Spain to the western provinces in the first and second centuries (Peacock 1971); the lack of neck and oval shape (*cf.* Webster 1976, No.35) suggested by the Brough sherds indicate a post-Flavian date for the majority of these vessels (Tchernia 1967). Two plano-convex disc lids with pinched lugs were noted in a similar fabric. They differ from Dressel 20 stoppers examined (by ST) in Cordoba Museum, where hollow stepped ceramic bungs from slightly earlier vessels are displayed.

One sherd was positively identified as from a southern Spanish Dressel 38/Camulodunum 186c fish sauce amphora of the first and second centuries (Peacock 1971). Sherds from several Dressel 30/Camulodunum 188 amphorae were also identified, together with two lids. The form was used for wine transport from Mediterranean Gaul in the first to third centuries (Peacock 1978). Two further lids, though no body sherds, also seemed to belong to Dressel 2–4/Camulodunum 182, 183 amphorae in Peacock's (1971) fabric 1. Fabric 1 probably originated from the Falerian region around Pompeii and the form dates to the first and early second centuries (Peacock 1971).

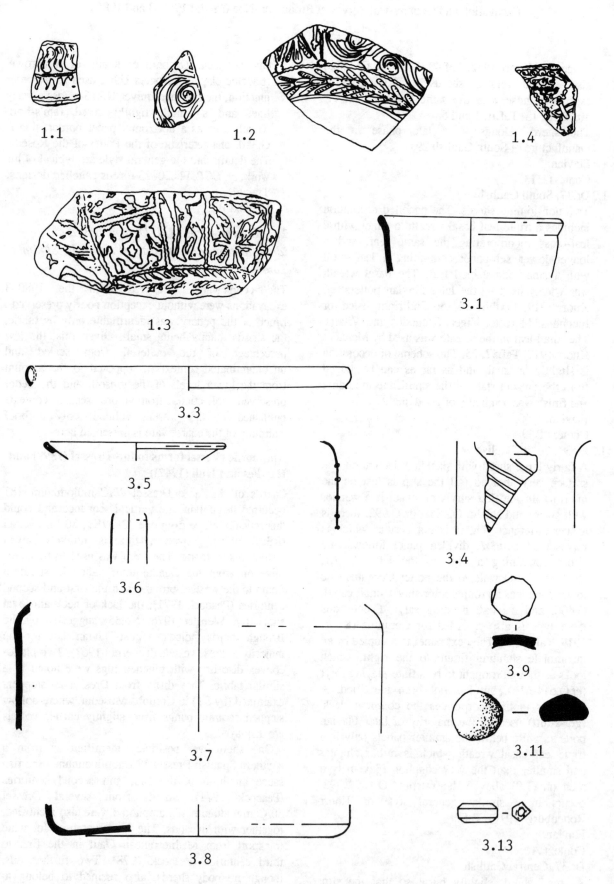

Fig.4:8 Samian and Glass (1:2 Except 3.9-3.13 at 1:1)

The presence of wine, fish and olive oil containers in Flavian/Trajanic auxiliary army contexts is not uncommon (Peacock 1971; Parker 1973). That the original contents of the amphorae rather than just re-used vessels were reaching the site may be indicated by the lid/stopper fragments (*cf.* Greene 1984, 410ff for an association of coins, amphorae and lids implying re-sale of the contents inside a military base).

Mortaria

Only seven mortarium sherds were found and no stamps were present. Three were in a Verulamium region fabric of 70–120 A.D.and one each in a Mancetter/Hartshill fabric of 80–110 and a Lincoln fabric of 100–130. The other two, both from the general build up B13, were in a Mancetter/Hartshill fabric of 110–60 and a Lincoln fabric of 140–80.

Other Coarsewares

The majority of coarseware fabrics were grey and orange wares, with some mica-dusted, creamware, North Gaulish, Lower Rhineland, Colchester and Verulamium products. BB1 and BB2 were also present but only one Derbyshire ware sherd was recorded. In terms of forms jars predominated (104 vessels), mainly Flavian/Trajanic rusticated or plain types but with some Black Burnished forms in later levels. Twenty four bowls were noted, again mainly Flavian/Trajanic flanged types but there were also some simple Black Burnished types and a hemispherical colander or strainer. A shallow Trajanic mica-dusted bowl of London type 36 (Marsh 1978) was also found. Only twelve beakers occurred, mostly in North Gaulish I and II and Lower Rhineland I fabrics with a few British fineware examples. The earlier were imports of colour-coated, rusticated cornice rimmed types (Anderson 1980; 1984) whilst the later domestic products were colour-coated folded or indented forms (Gillam 72, 74). Fifty four flagons also occurred, all reconstructable vessels being Flavian/Trajanic, usually with multiple ring necks. Most were in creamwares or in white slipped wares imitating them.

The majority of the dated vessels were mid-Flavian to Hadrianic and no vessels earlier than *c*.75/80 A.D. were identified. Some sherds from contexts either unsealed or sealed only by B13/15, a general build up south of road B, were identified as post-120 in date and it is likely that rubbish from the fort or *vicus* areas continued to accumulate in the excavated area during the later-second and probably third centuries. However, there was no sealed material from occupation features necessarily dating later than *c*.120, though later sherds suggest that both roads A and B and the roadside ditch A6 were still open if not

in use. None of this later material need not be dated before *c*.154/8 A.D., when the fort was re-established.

However, eleven sherds representing four vessels were tentatively identified as belonging to forms current between *c*.120 A.D. and *c*.154/8 A.D. (A6 and B56: Gillam 116 of 125–50 A.D.; B56: Gillam 220 of 125–60 A.D; B38: Gillam 219 of 120–50 A.D. (the last two in BB1)). All of these could have been lost immediately after a reoccupation 154/8 and/or lost within a few years of 120 A.D. (the fort's evacuation date is known only approximately). Indeed it is possible that some were items of 'old stock' at the time of re-garrisoning. If these sherds belong, on the other hand, to the period of the garrison's absence they need not indicate more than casual activity.

Evidence for activity (most likely rubbish disposal from the fort) in the later-third and fourth centuries is sparse. However, a small number of sherds were identified as of this period including a flanged bowl of Gillam type 229 and a carinated vessel of Gillam type 178. The latter came from the fill of the ditch beside road A.

The assemblage as a whole is fairly typical of vessel forms used in food and liquid transport and storage, cooking and serving. A few grey jars retained traces of sooting, heat discolouration and spalling due to thermal fracture and one BB1 Gillam 220 bowl was sooted on the inside.

3.   The Glass *Jennifer Price*

The excavations produced 86 items of Roman glass, of which 80 came from vessels, 5 from objects and 1 from a cast window pane. Most of the pieces were blue green, though 7 were colourless, 4 were yellow brown, 1 was purple, 1 light green and 1 (the bead 3.13) dark green.

Thirty nine of the vessel fragments came from tablewares and ordinary domestic vessels and 41 from containers. None of the first category was of great luxury and only a very limited range of vessels was represented, including a minimum of two drinking cups or bowls, two large cylindrical bowls, one light green ribbed bowl, jar or jug, one purple vessel, probably a jug (Isings 1957, forms 44, 52, 55 and 67c), and one jar, all of which were in use during the last quarter of the first and first half of the second century.

All but one of the pieces of containers came from square and cylindrical bottles, both of which were in common use during the late-first and early-second century (Isings 1957, forms 50 and 51), and the last piece was from a small unguent bottle.

It is noteworthy that most of the fragments found are very small, and represent only a tiny part of the complete vessels. This may be fortuitous, though an alternative suggestion could be that the larger pieces of broken glass were collected for re-melting, either at

Brough or elsewhere. Broken glass is completely re-usable and was certainly collected for this purpose in the late-first century in Rome, and a growing body of evidence, especially from military sites such as Inchtuthil, indicates that this practice also occurred in Britain when suitable conditions prevailed (Price 1985, 304).

The affinities and dating of the fragments catalogued are discussed in greater detail below.

Catalogue (Figure 4:8)

Cast Vessels

3.1 Two joined fragments, rim of bowl or cup. Colourless. Dull, some pitting, few small bubbles. Everted rim, edge ground with three flat facets on top and outside edge, part of convex curved body. Wheel polishing marks visible on all surfaces.
Present ht. 31mm; rim d. (approx.) 100mm; t. 3mm.
Unstratified.

Blown Vessels

3.2 Small body fragment, bowl or cup. Colourless. Dull, some usage scratches; few small bubbles. Part of straight side. Two close set horizontal wheel cut lines.
Dimensions 14 x 9mm; t. 1.5mm.
Unstratified. (Not illustrated.)

3.3 Rim fragment, bowl. Pale yellow brown. Few usage scratches; few small bubbles. Part of tubular rim, edge bent out and down.
Present ht. 11mm; rim d. (approx.) 180mm; t. 1mm.
B38

3.4 Five joined fragments, body of cylindrical bowl. Blue green. Slightly dull; small bubbles. Part of everted rim (edge missing) and vertical side with six diagonal ribs.
Present ht. 48mm; d. at top of body (approx.) 150mm; t. 1–1.5mm.
B13

3.5 Six fragments, five joined, rim of jar. Blue green. Slightly dull, small bubbles. Part of everted rim with uneven tubular edge (partly rolled out and down and partly rolled in and then out and down to form a double fold), concave curled neck tapering inwards.
Present ht. 13mm; rim d. 100mm; t. 1mm.
A1 and A5

3.6 Body fragment, tubular unguent bottle (?). Blue green. Slightly dull; few small bubbles. Part of narrow vertical side with constriction.
Present ht. 28mm; body d. 20mm; t. 1mm.
B38

3.7 Three joined fragments, body of cylindrical bottle. Blue green. Dull, many vertical usage scratches; bubbly. Part of curved shoulder and vertical side.
Present ht. 66mm; body d. (approx.) 200mm; t. 3mm.
B15

3.8 Two joined fragments, base of cylindrical bottle. Blue green. Dull, ring of wear on base edge, bubbly. Part of lower body curving into slightly concave base.
Present ht. 16mm; body d. (approx.) 140mm; t. 3mm.
A6

Objects

3.9 Roundel, from body of cylindrical bottle. Blue green. Dull; bubbly. Roughly circular piece of vertical side, edges carefully grossed for re-use.
D. 12mm; t. 2.5mm.
B56

3.10 Intact plano-convex counter. Opaque white. Ring of wear on under side; bubbly. Small object, oval in plan.
Ht. 7mm; dimensions 16.5 x 15mm.
Unstratified.

3.11 Intact plano-convex counter. Blue green and opaque `black' in streaks. Dull. Wear on most of underside; bubbly.
Ht. 7mm; d. 13mm.
B59.

3.12 Intact plano-convex counter. Opaque `black'. Wear on underside.
Ht. 6.5mm; d. 11.5mm.
Unstratified.

3.13 Complete bead, pentagonal, wide perforation. Dark green. Dull.
L. 11mm; max. w. 5mm; perforation 2mm.
B74

The fragment of colourless cast bowl (3.1), is an unusual vessel form. A wide range of cast colourless plates and bowls are known in late-first and early-second century contexts in Britain and throughout the Roman world. The best known of these is the shallow bowl with a wide over-hanging rim, which is sometimes decorated with egg and dart cutting, as may be seen on fragments from Fishbourne (Harden and Price 1971, nos. 26 and 33), Cramond (Maxwell 1974, nos. 6 and 7) and elsewhere, but other bowl and plate forms also occur. The Brough-on-Noe piece has a small everted rim which has some features in common with a fragment from Chilgrove (Down 1979, fig. 57, 8), though that has a more horizontal rim and appears to be a rather shallower vessel.

Although the exact form of 3.2 cannot be established from the surviving fragment, the quality of the glass and the nature of the cutting suggest that it comes from a late-first or second century drinking

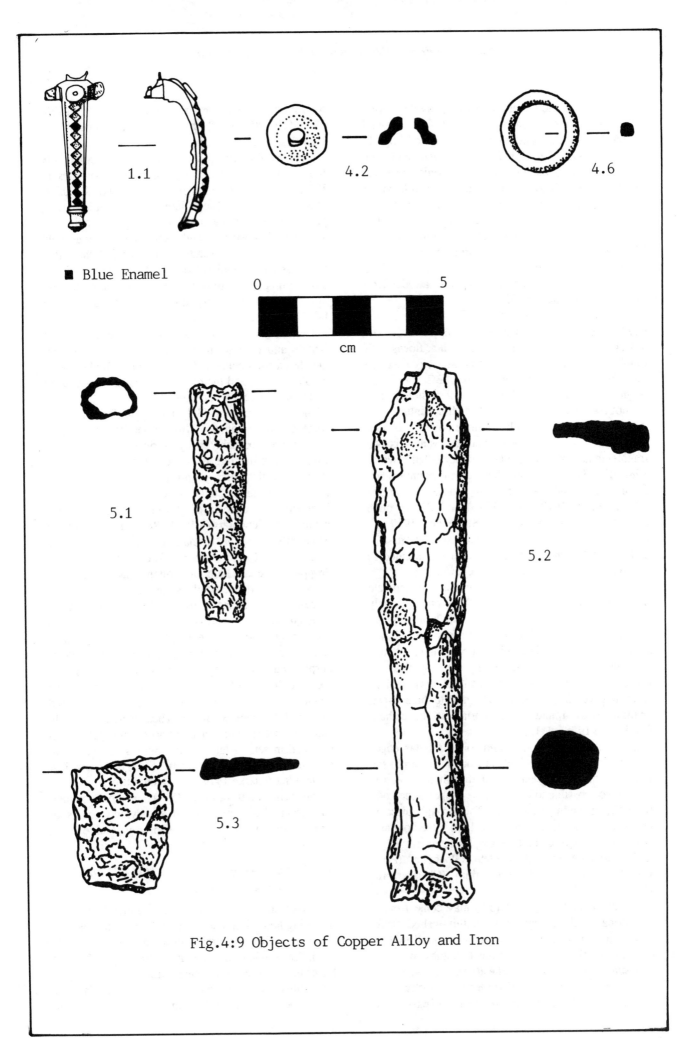

Blue Enamel

1.1

4.2

4.6

0   5
cm

5.1

5.2

5.3

Fig.4:9 Objects of Copper Alloy and Iron

cup. Colourless blown tablewares with cut decoration occurred in the western provinces from around AD65–70 onwards, and eventually replaced brightly coloured vessels. The drinking vessels were made in a variety of shapes, including truncated conical beakers, and cylindrical, biconical and hemispherical bowls or cups. In Britain, many of the vessels with cutting like the Brough piece have been found in second century contexts, as at Verulamium (Charlesworth 1972, fig. 77, nos. 41–4, 46; Charlesworth 1984, fig. 63, 45–51), but some are known from the last years of the first century as in the amphitheatre at Caerleon (Wheeler and Wheeler 1928, pl. xxxiv, 2).

The fragment of tubular rim (3.3) comes from a bowl, though whether this was a deep or a shallow vessel it is not now possible to determine. Bowls with tubular rims were in use in Rome and elsewhere in Italy by the end of the first-century BC, and some occur in Britain in the Claudian period, though they are not common finds until the later-first century.

Many of the large tubular rimmed bowls in Britain have been found in Flavian contexts: yellow brown fragments are known from Cirencester (Charlesworth 1981, fig. 34, 84–5), and blue green examples are frequently found, as at Red House, Corbridge (Charlesworth 1979, fig. 20.3–5) and Richborough (Bushe Fox 1932, pl. xv, 63; Bushe Fox 1949, pl. lxviii 369 and 372). Others come from late-first or early-second century contexts, and they continued in use until at least the mid-second century.

The colour of the Brough fragment may indicate that this was a first century bowl, as most strongly coloured vessels tend to disappear after the Flavian period, but yellow brown jugs, jars and bowls sometimes occur in Hadrianic and Antonine contexts.

Some tubular rimmed bowls have vertical or diagonal ribbing on the body, and 3.4 may well be from one of these vessels; a complete blue green example was found in a burial at Faversham (Brailsford 1958, pl. 12, 6).

Jars with funnel mouths and rolled tubular edges (3.5) are quite common finds in Roman Britain in the late-first and second century AD, though, as here, it is usually not possible to establish the shape of the body from the surviving fragments. The Brough piece is unusual because the rim edge has been folded out and down, whereas most other examples have rim edges folded inwards, as at East Gate, Gloucester (Price 1983, fig. 98.9), and Verulamium (Charlesworth 1972, fig. 76, 30).

The small body fragment (3.6) may come from a cylindrical neck, perhaps from a thin-walled flask, though it is more likely to be part of a small tubular unguent bottle. Tubular unguent bottles were in widespread use throughout the Roman world in the first century (Isings 1957, Form 8); they mostly occur in Britain in Claudian and Neronian contexts, as at Kingsholm, Gloucester (Price and Cool 1985, fig. 19, 39 and fig. 20, 69–82), though a few are known from later-first century sites.

Cylindrical bottles (3.7 and 3.8) are very commonly found on Flavian and early-second century sites in Britain as elsewhere in the Roman world (Isings 1957, Form 51). They, like square bottles, were produced as containers for a variety of liquid and semi-liquid substances and were standard household vessels. The vertical scratch marks on 3.7 show that this vessel has regularly been lifted in and out of a close fitting case, probably made in wickerwork, and both bottles were clearly in use for some time before breakage.

Two forms of cylindrical bottle are known in Britain and both seem to be represented at Brough. One has a squat wide body, as at York (Harden 1962, pl. 66, HG 53), and the other a tall narrow body, as at Inchtuthil (Price 1985, fig. 94, 11).

The small roundel (3.9) has been fashioned for some secondary purpose from a broken piece of a thick vessel, probably a cylindrical bottle. The re-working of broken glass is a common occurrence on Romano-British sites of all periods. The size and form of this piece suggests that it may have been intended as a counter or gaming piece. The three plano-convex counters (3.10–3.12) are a type of object commonly found on Romano-British sites from the first to the fourth century. They were made by dropping a small blob of molten glass onto a flat surface and were used both as counters and as gaming pieces. These objects were usually opaque white or dark green, blue or brown, appearing black, though translucent blue green examples are also common, and other translucent and opaque colours, such as purple, yellow and turquoise are sometimes found. In the late-third and fourth centuries, some of the counters were decorated with coloured spots marvered flush with the convex surface. These were presumably gaming pieces and have very occasionally been recorded in sets in late Roman burials in Britain, at Lullingstone (JRS xlix, 1969, p.132–3) and Lankhills, Winchester (Clarke 1979, 251–4 and pl.Ib).

The pentagonal bead (3.13) is a type common throughout the Roman world and which occurs in Britain from the first to fourth centuries (Guido 1978, fig. 37, 8).

4. Copper Alloy D.F. Mackreth (4:1) and M.J. Dearne (4:2–4:6) (Figure 4:9)

4.1 Headstud Brooch. The pin is hinged, the axis bar being housed in a semi-circular projection behind the wings. There are traces of a cast-on loop on the head. Each wing has a curved front face bearing traces of two recessed lozenges with infilling triangles for enamel; some red survives in one of the triangles. The stud has a red enamel annulus on it.

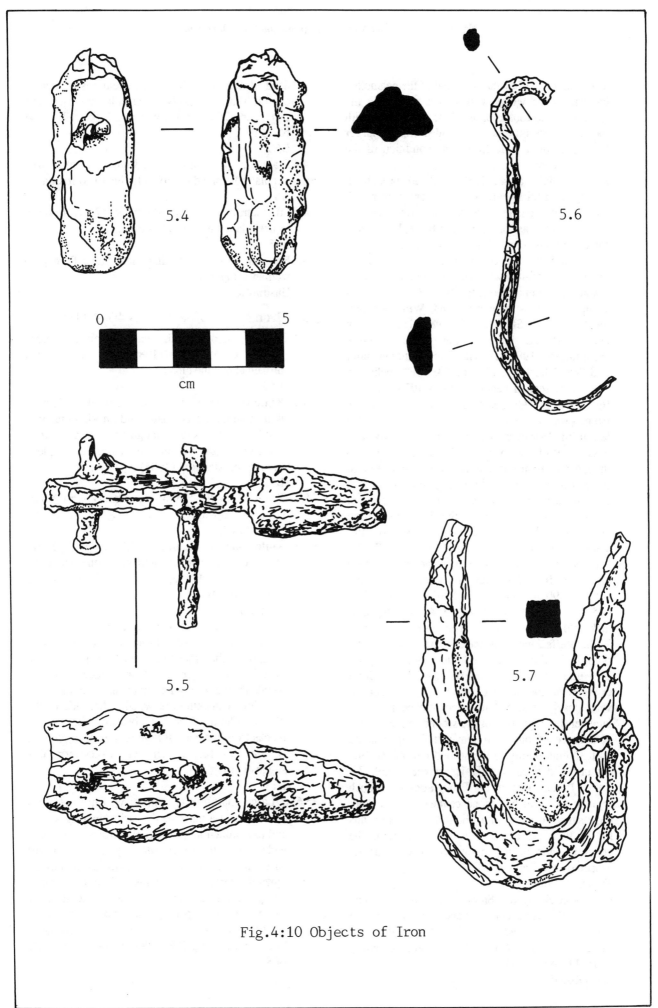

0   5
cm

5.4

5.6

5.5

5.7

Fig.4:10 Objects of Iron

The front of the bow has a repeat of the enamelled pattern on the wings with a trace of blue in the lozenges. The foot-knob is of the usual form with the triple cross-mouldings divided from a larger basal pair by a wide flute. The condition of the brooch is poor.

At first sight a standard Headstud brooch, it belongs to a fairly narrow general group in which the central lozenges down the bow may be reserved; the cast-on loop may be replaced by a freely moving one mounted in the ends of the wings; and the cells on the wings may be flanked by buried bead-rows. The commonest added feature is an unpierced crest above the stud. In this group dating is exiguous; Old Winteringham, third century (Stead 1976, 198, fig. 99, 12); Derby, second half of the second century (Brassington 1980, 18, fig. 8a); Nettleton, after 270 (Wedlake 1982, 128, fig. 53, 60); Chichester, after early-second century (Down 1978, 279–80, fig. 10.26, 11). On this evidence, the date range is from, probably, the early-second century to the late-third. However, it may be that the type had passed out of use in the earlier-third rather than the later: there are not enough dated specimens for the *floruit* to be properly established. Turning to the standard form with wings having a series of steps running back from the bow, two from Newstead belong to the period 80–early-third century? (Curle 1911, 323 pl. lxxxvi, 19, 20; Hartley 1972, 54). There is some ambivalence about one from Camelon which should be either before *c*.90 or after *c*.140 (Christison 1901, 405–6, p. A.5; Hartley 1972, 13, 42–4). The same lack of definition emerges from an example from Wall, Staffs., which is merely earlier than some point in the third century (Gould 1964, 43, fig. 18, 2). Perhaps the best indication that the main form of the Headstud, to which the present Headstud is very closely related, had come into being at the latest at the beginning of the second century is the occurrence of one in a grave at Cologne along with samian dating to the second half of the first century and a coin of Trajan (Exner 1939, 73, Taf.6, 1.I.1). In short, the Brough-on-Noe brooch is most likely to be second century and may not have survived in use into the third. It would thus tie in with its antecedents and also with the general tenor of the dating of bow brooches, especially the Trumpet type.
Trench A, context 8.

4.2 Boss or caulking (ht. 8mm; d. 16mm; d. of hole 5mm) with raised centre pierced by a circular hole and recessed on the base. *Cf.* Allason-Jones and Miket 1984, 333 No. 8.97 (in lead); Crummy 1983, 117 No. 3.168.
Unstratified.

4.3 Stud (d. 20mm; t. 4mm) with remains of slender central shaft, probably of circular cross-section. Damaged. *Cf.* Allason-Jones and Miket 1984, 248 No. 3.977.
B5/27

4.4 Fragment (l. 23mm; w. 23mm; t. 3mm) with circular hole on edge probably due to corrosion.
A5

4.5 Fragment or splash (l. 20mm; w. 17mm; t. 4mm) of irregular shape. Highly pitted.
B46

4.6 Ring (d. 21mm) with flattened sides. Perhaps a woman's finger ring.
Unstratified.

5. Iron M.J. Dearne (Figures 4:9–4:11)

5.1 ?Ferrule (l. 60mm; d. (max.) 15mm), probably similar to Manning (1985) 140 No. 60 but broken above the closing.
B53

5.2 Knife (l. 141mm; w. 26mm; t. (max.) 17.5mm) with a single edged blade and an ?integral iron handle of sub-rectangular cross-section, somewhat narrower in the centre. Incomplete. Perhaps of Manning (1985) type 1A.
B15

5.3 Knife blade (l. 35mm; w. 22mm) with single edge. Incomplete.
Unstratified.

5.4 Knife tang (l. 60mm; w. 25mm; t. 17.5mm) attached on one side to half of a bone handle by two iron rivets. Perhaps from a knife of Manning (1985) type 1B.
Unstratified.

5.5 Oval plate (w. 35mm; t. 4mm; d. of projection (max.) 17mm) broken at one end and thickening abruptly at the other to a conical projection. The plate is pierced by two nails and retains traces of wood. The surviving length of the nails indicates an original thickness of wood either side of the plate of 30mm+. Possibly a bearing with wooden blocks from the central hole of a grinding wheel. (I am grateful to Dr. G. Coles for this suggestion.)
B13

5.6 ??Large chainlink (l. 90mm; w. (max.) 15mm) consisting of a narrow, flat strip tapering at one end to a broken loop of circular cross-section and widening at the other into a gentle downward curve and then tapering again to a broken upward curving extension. Although other interpretations are possible (e.g. some form of harness fitting) perhaps a broken and bent chainlink or possibly a small, contorted latch lifter (*cf.* Manning 1985, 88 e.g. nos. 04 and 09).
B68

5.7 Staple (l. 80mm) with a stone embedded between the prongs. *Cf.* Crummy (1979) 120 No. 4071.
B5

5.8 Staple (l. 99mm) similar to 5.7.
Unstratified.

5.9 Staple (l. 60mm; w. 13mm) of `joiner's dog' form. *Cf.* Crummy (1979) 120 No. 4072; Manning (1985) 131 No. R52.
B15

5.10 Staple (l. 34mm) similar to 5.7 but smaller.
Unstratified.

5.11 Part of bradawl or awl (l. 46mm; w. (max.) 12.5mm; d. of tang (max.) 5mm) of rectangular cross-section set in a wood or bone handle, originally of ?circular cross-section. Incomplete. The loss of the tip and the uncertain form of the handle fixing make differentiation between a leather working awl and a woodworking bradawl impossible (*cf.* Manning 1985, 28), but a bradawl such as Manning (1985) 28 No. B78 is perhaps more likely.
B15

5.12 Hook (l. 51mm; w. (max.) 30mm). Tip of a large hook.
B13

5.13 Stud or fixing (l. of bar 13mm; 1 of shaft 5mm; d. of head 15mm) with rounded head attached by a round shaft to a bar of square cross-section (now detached).
B2

In addition 77 unidentifiable iron fragments were recovered.

Nails and Pins

5.14 Nail (l. 61mm) with rounded head and rectangular shank of Manning type 1B (Manning 1985, 134).
Unstratified.

5.15 Pin (l. 60mm)
Unstratified.

5.16 Pin (l. 36mm)
Unstratified.

In all 169 nails were recovered (though some of the unidentified iron objects could be nails). Sixty nine round-headed nails were present and eight square-headed, though not all the nails retained their heads and many were too corroded to classify. It was rarely possible to classify the nail shanks due to corrosion. Most of the examples probably belong to Manning type 1B (Manning 1985, 134).

6. Lead *M.J. Dearne* (Figures 4:11–4:12)

6.1 Lamp or lamp-holder (l. 135mm; w. (max.) 60mm; ht. 25mm; weight 575.7 grams) made from a single sheet of lead, crimped at the front of the lamp. A handle made from a lead strip (w. 32mm) folded back on itself is attached to the back. It is decorated with four 20mm long lead strips attached to the sides, two halfway along each side of the main chamber and two at the point where it narrows.
B13

Several lamps or lamp-holders made from lead are known from Roman Britain, but with little apparent stylistic uniformity. The decorative strips may imitate the strengthening bars on some bronze lamps such as Walters (1914, 19 No. 117).

Mr. D. Bailey suggests that they would adequately serve as lamps, rather than lamp-holders, if a wick was lain in them projecting beyond the front lip. In either event they would clearly be more stable than a clay lamp. The presence of several examples in the south Pennines and north and south Wales may suggest that lead was cheap enough in these mining areas to replace clay for lamp production.

Similar open lamps are known from London (Milne, 1986, plate 7b) in clay; and from Melandra Castle (Conway 1906, Appendix 99ff) in lead but without decoration or crimping. Other lead lamps/lamp-holders are known from PenLlystyn (Hogg 1968, 183 nos. L1 and L2); Caerleon (Nash-Williams 1932, 91 nos. 5 and 6); Slack (Dodd and Woodward 1922, fig. 4; Richmond 1925, 63); Colchester (two unpublished examples in the British Museum); Chester (Thompson 1976, fig. 29 No. 54); Ravenglass (Potter 1979, fig. 28 No. 80) and Gellygaer (Ward 1903, 86, citing others from Wilderspool and in York Museum).

6.2 Weight (d. (max.) 49mm; d (min.) 30mm; ht. 25mm; weight 311.3 grams). Biconical. The underside is slightly concave; the top has a roughly rectangular punch mark in the centre.
A11

6.3 Weight (d. 31mm; ht. 16mm; w. 127 grams). Cylindrical with a flat base and top, slightly recessed around the middle. The top has five circular punch marks arranged as on a die.
Unstratified.

The weights are a one *libra* (6.2) and a five *uncia*, conceivably from the same set. Roman weights seem to have varied slightly from set to set but 6.3 seems to be in proportion to 6.2. The marks are the standard ones for a *libra* and a five *uncia*, although a number of other markings are known (*cf.* for example May 1922, 77; and May 1903, 115ff). May 1922, No. 6 and May 1903, No. 19 are close parallels for 6.2.

6.4 Strip (l. 65mm; w. 17mm) with flat base and convex top. There are two holes (d. 5mm), one in each end. Probably part of a repair clamp.
Unstratified.

6.5 Bar (l. 38mm; d. 10mm) of circular cross-section, ? cut obliquely at either end and slightly bowed. Possibly an off-cut from lead working.
B74

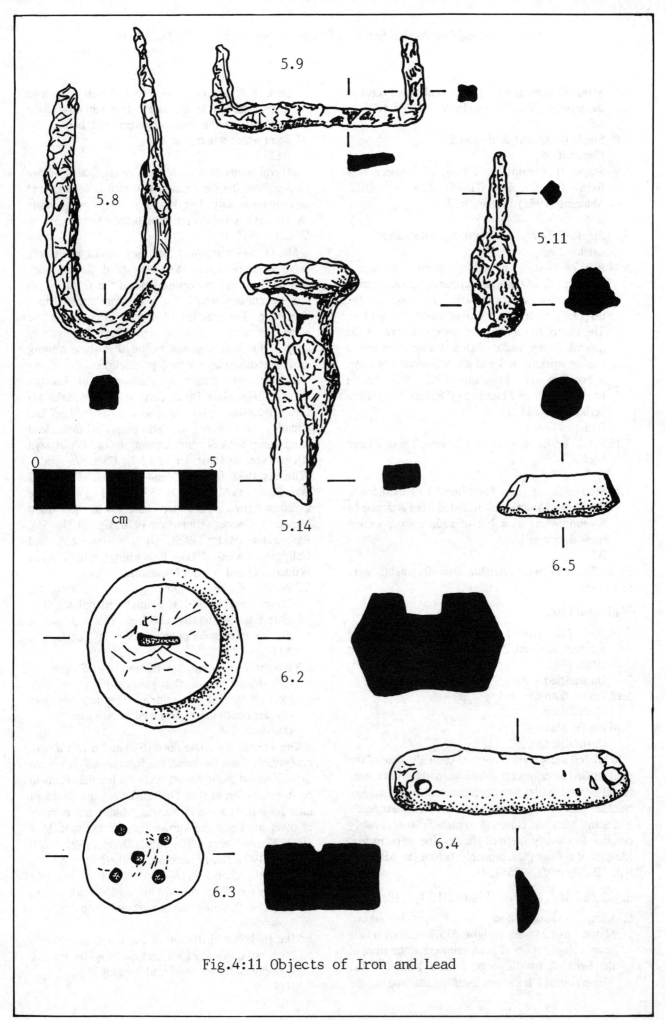

Fig.4:11 Objects of Iron and Lead

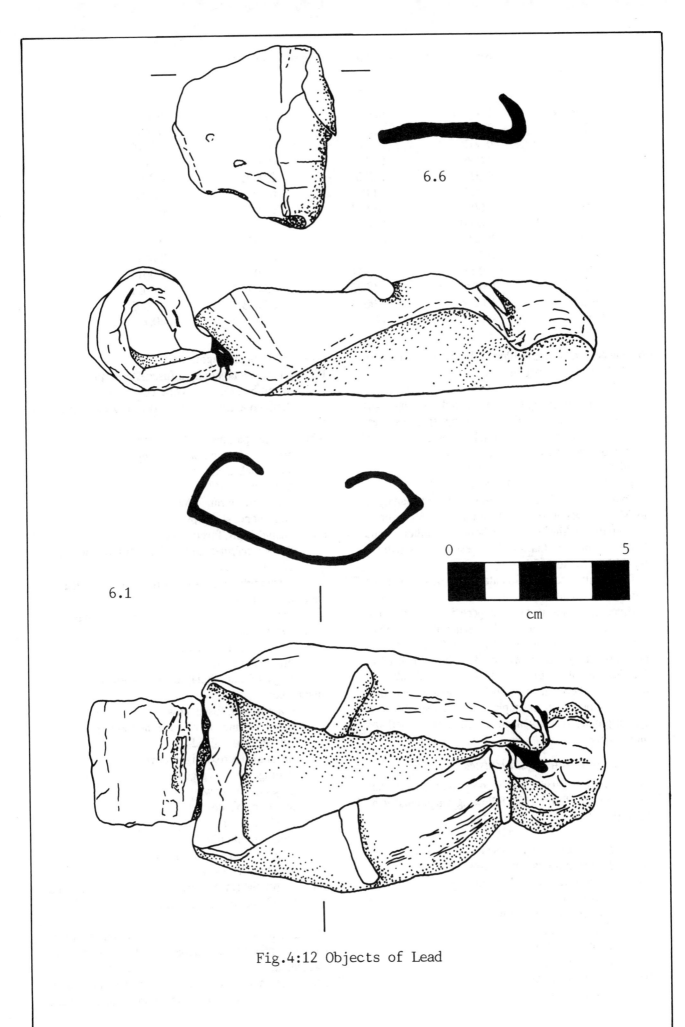

6.6

6.1

0   5

cm

Fig.4:12 Objects of Lead

Object No.	6.4	6.1	6.2	6.3
%Cu	0.032	0.019	0.03	0.007
%Mn	0.003	0.0002	0.0004	0.0002
%Ni	0.006	0.004	0.007	0.004
%Co	0.005	0.0004	0.0005	0.0005
%Fe	0.0082	0.0075	0.007	0.0057
%Ag	0.0061	0.0031	0.0057	0.0058
%Zn	0.0061	0.0014	0.003	0.0013
%Al	0.088	0.07	0.069	0.081
%Sn	0.019	0.006	0.29	0.099
%Bi	0.0009	0.0014	0.0012	0.0014
%Sb	0.0049	0.0025	0.0097	0.0051
%Cd	0.0006	0.0004	0.0003	0.0003
%As	<0.1	<0.1	<0.1	<0.1

6.6 Sheet (w. (max.) 40mm; l. (max.) 50mm; t. 1–3mm) folded over on itself.
B53

In addition four small pieces of lead showing signs of having been worked or of being splashes were recovered. Thirteen pieces of galena and two pieces of galena or lead slag were also recovered.
Lead splashes/frags., : B2, A5, B6/18.
Galena/slag: B2, B18, B24, B5, B52, B61.

Four of the lead objects were submitted for analysis to Mr. M. Dobby of the Department of Metallurgy, University of Sheffield (to whom the author would like to record his thanks), The results are shown in the table at the top of the page.

The results seem to indicate that 6.4, 6.2 and 6.3 have been made from lead that has not been desilvered, which is to be expected for Derbyshire lead which has a variable but generally low silver content in the range 0.005% – 0.01% and was probably rarely if ever desilvered by the Romans. No. 6.1 lies in the silver content range (0.002% – 0.005%) where it is hard to assess whether desilverisation has taken place or whether the lead was originally very low in silver. The latter is perhaps more likely.

7. Animal Bones *Paul Halstead*

Bone generally survived very poorly and most of that recovered was burnt. The following fragments were identifiable.

A5 radius, distal, right, fused, burnt, ?cow
A9 ?3rd mandibular molar, cow
B2 phalanx 1, proximal, fused, cow
incisor tooth, pig
mandibular molar, cow
molar tooth, cow
tooth frag., ?cow
molar tooth, cow
B13 1st/2nd maxillary molar, pig
limb-bone frags., cow-sized

B15 ?calcaneum, right, pig
B23 lateral metapodial, unfused, burnt, pig
mandibular molar, worn, cow
limb bone frags., burnt, cow- and sheep/pig-size
B24 metacarpal, distal, fused, cow
tibia, shaft frag., burnt, sheep/goat
tail vertebra, ?cow-size
B27 jaw frag.
B32 ulna, left, burnt, ?cow
limb-bone, sheep/pig-size
B53 scapula, left, fused, cow
metacarpal/metatarsal, distal, fused, cow
rib, sheep-sized
mandibular 3rd molar, left, at `mature' wear stage (i.e. adult), cow
mandibular 1st/2nd molar, left, wear suggests *c.* 1–2½ years, sheep/goat
femur, proximal, cow
3rd phalanx, cow
frags. of mandibular molars, worn and unworn, cow
scapula, left, fused, cow
mandible, incl. female canine tooth, pig
vertebra, cow-sized
metatarsal, prox., right, cow
?astragalus, sheep/goat
scapula, left, cow
femur, prox., cow
pelvis, right, fused, pig
incisor tooth, pig
B56 phalanx 1, prox., fused, cow
vertebra, ?cow-sized
B74 limb-bone frags., burnt and unburnt, cow-sized
B76 limb-bone, frags., v. burnt, cow-sized

The assemblage is mostly cow, but pig and sheep or goat are present. A range of body parts are represented. The poor preservation perhaps biases against the smaller animals, though the latter often tend to be burnt more than large animals and in these

Context	%Fe$_2$O$_3$	%SiO$_2$	%Al$_2$O$_3$	%CaO	%MgO	%TiO$_2$	Total
A5	11.1	41.5	30.2	10.9	0.9	–	94.6
B1	22.8	40.6	26.6	1.7	0.9	–	92.6
B2	36.7	30.3	4.8	0.5	0.2	–	72.5
B13	3.1	40.0	3.1	6.1	0.2	–	52.5
B5	9.6	67.6	11.4	0.6	0.5	–	89.2
B15	38.8	33.2	8.2	1.3	0.3	–	81.8
B41	17.9	41.5	16.8	4.0	3.0	3.88	87.02
B18	9.0	28.8	20.2	8.0	4.6	4.02	74.62

soil conditions that would perhaps have been an advantage. The small size and poor preservation of the group preclude further analysis.

8. Stone, Clay and Plaster *M.J. Dearne*

8.1 Pumice (l. 75mm; w. 50mm; h. 50mm) block, flat on one side.
A11

8.2 Tile frag. (l. 123mm; w. 56mm) marked with an X. Probably hatching rather than graffiti.
Unstratified.

8.3 Tile frag. (l. 91mm; w. 74mm) marked with two Xs. Probably hatching rather than graffiti.
Unstratified.

8.4 Wall plaster. Twenty two small fragments of ?ochre painted plaster.
Unstratified in two groups.

In addition 56 fragments of tile/brick, mainly small and eroded, were noted probably including imbrices, tegulae, box tiles and bricks. A number of daub fragments were also noted but all were friable and abraded with no wattle impressions.

9. Flint *Donald Henson*

9.1 Primary flake with abraded river pebble cortex. Internally flawed.
B18

9.2 Thinning flake, possibly from axe preparation.
B27

9.3 Thinning flake with stained pebble cortex on platform and edge. Distal and damaged.
B32

9.4 Blade, hinge fractured with no signs of use.
B42

9.5 Blade, medial fragment, heavily hinge fractured and with primary cortex on one edge. Proximal end snapped, ?to remove the hinge.
B53

No certain conclusions can be reached on just five items about the prehistoric context of the finds. What can be said is that the five artifacts represent three types of knapping activity.

Primary reduction of pebbles is indicated by 9.1, the raw material being river gravel flint. Nos. 9.2 and 9.3 represent core tool manufacture - the thinning down and shaping before final finishing off. Blade manufacturing is represented by 9.4 and 9.5.

Typologically, nothing can be said as to the contemporaneity of any of the artifacts. As far as raw material is concerned most of the artifacts seem to be in flint from the tills of the Cheshire Plain area and the western edge of the Peak. The exception to this is 9.3 which resembles much more closely the flint from the tills of the Trent Valley and eastern England. From the position of the site this pattern of material procurement is much as one would expect.

10. Coal and Slag *M.J. Dearne*

10.1 A fragment of coal from Trench A (context 11) was submitted for analysis to the Yorkshire Regional Laboratory of the N.C.B.. A.H.V. Smith reports that it is a low rank bituminous coal from the upper middle coal measures of Smith and Butterworth (1967), zones IX and X. Such coal outcrops immediately west of Castleford.

10.2 A number of pieces of slag from iron working were recovered, though most were single small lumps and very few were securely stratified. Eight representative samples were submitted to Mr. M. Dobby of the Department of Metallurgy, University of Sheffield for analysis. The results are shown in the table at the top of the page.

Tap slag, which ought to contain *c.*70% iron oxides and *c.*10–20% silica (Tylecoate 1986, 176), does not seem to be present and most examples are probably either smithing slags or hammer scale. The sample from B13 of which 47.5% is unaccounted for is thought to contain a significant proportion of coal.

Other contexts which produced slag are B5, B14, B42 and B54.

5. Brough-on-Noe, Derbyshire: Excavations in the *Vicus* 1983–4

Christopher Drage

with contributions by D.A. Allen; P.M. Barford; B. Dickinson; M. Harman; R.S. Leary; D. Mackreth; L. Moffet; G. Morgan; C.R. Salisbury; D.F. Williams

Introduction

Over a number of years chance finds have been made in the properties fronting the B 6049 at Brough-on-Noe. In 1972 a rescue excavation in advance of road widening located possible traces of timber structures and artefacts of the later 2nd and 3rd centuries; only a small amount of earlier 2nd and 4th century material was recovered (Lane, 1973). From the mid-1970s a large, modern farmyard developed to the east of the main road. Broadly level, west–east platforms, for buildings and areas of hard-standing, were constructed across the north–south slope of the land; in places the southern side of the farmyard was bounded by a more or less vertical, quarried-face, 1–4m high, of shale and clay. In the course of this work archaeological strata, up to 4m deep, including extensive spreads of burnt material, were observed by C. Hart (Derbyshire County Council Sites and Monuments Record 2612). In 1979 in the course of

further levelling a large, inscribed altar (Plate 5) was located and dug out by hand; a second, small, uninscribed altar was recovered from dumped spoil. To the east of this, no finds have been recoverd and no archaeological strata have been located.

Excavations in the *Vicus* 1983–4 (Figure 5:1)

In 1983 in the course of the excavation of a level platform to create an area of hard-standing on the southern side of the farmyard archaeological levels were observed and an opportunity was allowed for their examination. A team from Sheffield University, then excavating in the Halsteads close to the south east gate of the fort, was diverted to carry out a salvage excavation. The salvage excavations, directed by D. Kennedy and supervised by P. Freeman, M.J. Dearne, G. Wilson and others, cleared some 1,500 sq.

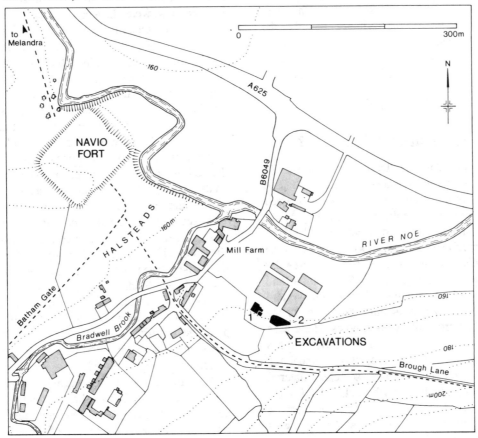

Figure 5:1 Location of the 1983 (1) and 1984 (2) Excavations in Relation to the Fort (The Postulated Course of the Roman Roads Follows Wroe (1982))

metres of ground, revealing structural features, stone surfaces, a stone-lined drain, hearths, and post-holes, together with extensive spreads of burnt material and clay. There was sufficient time to plan the archaeological levels, to excavate selected features and to recover some evidence of date.

In 1984 it was proposed to extend the area of hard standing to the east, removing an area of south-facing slope to create a levelled platform. The western side of the proposed area comprised a vertical face, up to 2m high, in which strata and features containing Roman pottery were evident, sealed below a layer of clay over 1m thick. The northern side of the proposed area contained a modern pit [ABL], from which the large altar had been removed. Funds were provided by the Historic Buildings and Monuments Commission for England, English Heritage, and the site excavated by the former Trent Valley Archaeological Research Committee, now the Trent & Peak Archaeological Trust, from April to July 1984. Additional labour was provided by Derbyshire County Council's Archaeological Team, funded by the Manpower Services Commission, and supervised by J. Barnett.

The finds and the primary records, plans, context sheets and photographs, of the 1983 excavation were passed to T&PAT, for analysis and publication; this part of the post-excavation programme was funded by the Peak Park Joint Planning Board. The finds and excavation archive will be deposited at Sheffield City Museum and Art Gallery, Weston Park, Sheffield. The archive comprises, the primary records, the plans, context sheets and photographs from the 1983 and 1984 excavations, and the processed records generated by the post-excavation analysis conducted in 1985–7. The present report is essentially a digest of the evidence contained in the archive.

The 1983 Excavation (Figure 5:2)

An area 16m by 12m was cleared and planned; 20 contexts were partially excavated and recorded. The eastern and southern sides of the area contained expanses of stone slabs, rubble and small pebbles; possible structures included a discrete spread [005] of large irregular rubble forming a surface 3x2m, to the south a less discrete spread [015] of large, irregular rubble and an irregular spread [014] of rubble and large stone slabs, incorporating a drain on the western and southern sides. At the south west corner of the excavation was a group of five post-holes. There were extensive spreads of clean yellow clay, perhaps redeposited natural, layers of sandy clay, charcoal and burnt material, and some areas of scorched material or *in situ* burning. Possible hearths included a discrete area of burning [012] and an area of burning overlying the three large stone slabs at the north west side of [014]. No ditches or gullies were located.

Artefacts included, an iron spearhead, staples, a collar, broken knives (83–93 in Figure 5:14), nails, and unidentifiable objects, a lead spindle whorl (94 in Figure 5:14), two copper alloy brooches (80–81 in Figure 5:13), one complete and two fragmentary quern stones, two ballista bolts, and a stone mould for casting ingots (97–102 in Figure 5:15). The pottery was broadly comparable to that recovered from phases 4–13 of the 1984 excavation, with a date-range from the late-second to mid-third century. The period of occupation, the range of artefacts, and the type of contexts located in the 1983 excavation are broadly similar to the 1984 excavation. In 1984 it was established that the 1983 excavation lay immediately north of a principal road [ACB] through the *vicus*.

The 1984 Excavation

Excavation methods and site conditions

Prior to excavation the site comprised a triangular area of sloping land 1–2.5m above the general level of the farm yard. The northern and western limits of the site were defined by quarried faces in which archaeological strata were evident, sealed below a layer , over 1m deep, of clay hill-wash . To establish the depth of topsoil at the southern limit of excavation a trench 1m wide was excavated by hand to the base of the topsoil, which was then removed by machine. No features were located and no artefacts were recovered by cleaning the surface of the hill-wash. North–south trenches were then excavated by hand across the area to establish the depth of hill-wash, overlying the archaeological strata. The hill-wash was then removed by machine, in two arbitrary spits, to within 0.1m of the archaeological strata. The remainder of the excavation was carried out by hand. Features and layers were excavated in plan. The site was examined by open area excavation, but was sub-divided by three control baulks (Figure 5:5); the baulks facilitated access and their section was drawn. In the later stages of the excavation a 2m wide strip was excavated as a separate cutting, immediately east of section line 2, in advance of the remainder of the site, to elucidate an area of slumping. Particularly in the earlier stages of the excavation all artefacts were assigned an individual code and their distribution was plotted. Considerable time was devoted to the removal of the lowest layers of hill-wash; although this produced negative evidence of occupation, this rare opportunity to examine the undisturbed upper levels of a site was fully exploited.

The natural was a yellow-grey clay, interspersed with bands of grey-brown shale; in places there were outcrops of shale. The parent materials, shale and clay, are reflected in the excavated strata, which were commonly clays or a mixture of clay and coarse,

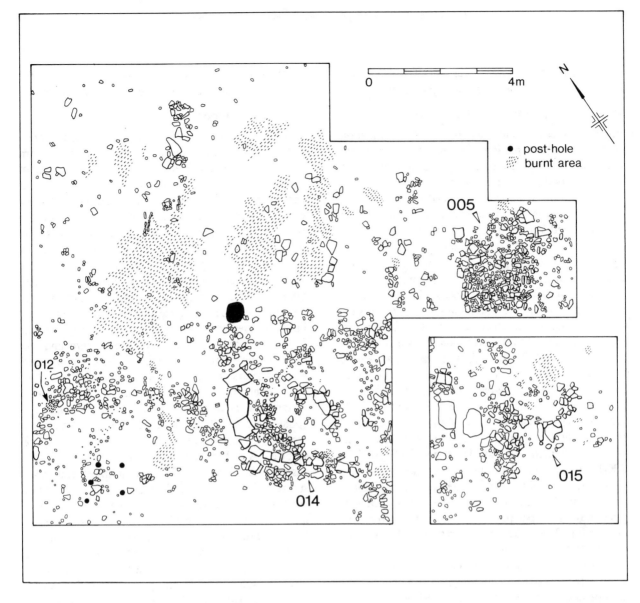

Figure 5:2 Plan of the 1983 Excavations

sandy, material. On excavation strata were commonly grey, oxidising on exposure to a grey-brown colour. In places areas of scorching or burnt material had survived only where they were overlain by a stone, or a layer of rubble; percolation of ground water had leached many layers to a uniform grey-brown. The acidity of the strata, ph values of 4.5–6.0 were measured, accounts for the small quantity of animal bone recovered, the paucity of bronze objects and the poor condition of the iron work.

The site was excavated from April to July 1984, a period of relative drought with drying winds. To conserve soil moisture the site was covered with polythene sheeting and periodically hosed down. Although the site was not subject to widespread cracking till July, dry soil conditions, on occasions, hindered the process of excavation and made interpretation difficult.

The site comprised an upper and lower terrace, which were, for the most part, stratigraphically isolated. The lower terrace was subdivided by a ditch

system, which was recut on several occasions; it was possible to correlate the stratigraphic sequence across the lower terrace. Many postholes contained open voids, where the post had rotted *in situ*; at the base of one void [BEZ], 1.15m long and 0.15m wide, a post stub was recovered. Several post-voids were partially filled by a plastic grey clay, sediments deposited by the passage of ground water. The post-voids encouraged local subsidence and in places collapsed during the course of excavation. In these circumstances it may be doubted that the correct stratigraphic relationship of these features was always recovered.

The stratigraphical sequence and phasing

For the purpose of interpretation the sequence of archaeological strata has been divided into 15 phases; the phases, essentially a grouping of stratigraphically related contexts, are of significance only in respect of the 1984 excavation, and should not be confused with historical periods. Phases 1–11 are of Roman date; phases 12–15 span the intervening period up to 1984.

Phases 1–4 (Figure 5:3; Plates 3–4)

The first phase of occupation comprised the formation of two west–east platforms or terraces, across the north–south slope of the land; at the eastern end of the excavation an area of ground, which had been subject to little disturbance, retained its natural 30% slope. The lower or northern terrace extended 21m west–east and 9m north–south; the eastern end of the terrace was defined by a north–south ditch [BEM]. At the western end the lower terrace was only a little below the surface of the upper terrace, but the eastern end lay 1.5m below. The clay/shale slope separating the terraces was not revetted. Only the northern side of the upper or southern terrace lay within the excavated area. With the exception of a single, stone-packed pit [BAF], the upper terrace was solely occupied by a road [ACB], in excess of 4m wide, extending some 18m through the area of excavation and rising from the west to the east with an 8% gradient. Two enclosures were formed on the lower terrace. The western enclosure, approximately 9m wide, was defined by a wide 'U'-shaped ditch [AGS & AHJ], up to 1.8m wide and 0.60m deep, running east–west, parallel to the upper terrace road; the ditch turned north, down the slope, and became progressively deeper (up to 1m) towards the limit of excavation. Beside the upper terrace road [ACB] the ditches terminated in butt ends to form an entrance 2.4m wide. The eastern enclosure was defined on the south side by a slope to the upper terrace and, at the eastern side, by a north–south ditch [BEM]; the ditch 0.5m wide and up to 0.5m deep, became shallower and terminated in an irregular butt-end at the southern, uphill, end. Within the enclosures no features were located which were contemporary with the first phase of occupation and a clean grey clay fill [BDI] accummulated in the ditch [AGS].

In Phase 2 a layer [BDA & BDH], up to 0.25m, thick of yellow clay, re-deposited natural clay, sporadic rubble, burnt clay and charcoal was deposited at the northern side of the lower terrace, in part filling the enclosure ditch [AGS].

In Phase 3, on the lower terrace, the ditches [AGS & AHJ] of the western enclosure were recut and subsequently silted up with a relatively clean fill of grey sandy clay and fragments of shale. In the western enclosure a large straight sided pit [BCB], 0.80m deep was excavated and back filled with a mixture of burnt and unburnt clay and charcoal.

In Phase 4 (not illustrated) on the lower terrace 2 pits [AGT & AGU], containing slag and charcoal, were cut into the fill of the silted ditch [AGS]. At the northern side of the lower terrace spreads of clay and sandy clay were deposited. The raising of the lower

north side may have been preparatory for the construction of structures in the succeeding phase 5.

Phases 5–6 (Figure 5:3)

In Phase 5 three structures (1–3) were constructed, two in the western enclosure and one in the eastern enclosure. Structure 3 comprised a discrete area of densely packed pebbles; to the east lay a spread of rubble, two large post-holes and a shallow pit [BEK] containing stones and burnt clay. The ditch of the western enclosure was recut on at least two occassions in phase 5. The recut enclosure ditch, up to 0.6m wide and 0.5m deep, was smaller than its predecessor [AGS], but was associated with a series of post-holes, perhaps a fence-line; later recutting has destroyed the western continuation of the phase 5 enclosure ditch, but post-holes to the south of structure 2 suggest that a boundary between the western enclosure and the upper terrace was maintained. Structure 1 comprised a single course of large flat stones, bedded in yellow clay, extending in an arc. Structure 2, a discrete rectangular area of Gritstone rubble, overlain by cobbles and gravel, lay at the western end of the lower terrace. A quantity of slag was embedded in the floor surface. A robber-trench extended along the the eastern side of structure 2. At the southern end was a sub-rectangular pit [AEF] filled with clean yellow clay; the southern side of the pit was cut away by a later recutting of the enclosure ditch. Beside the pit lay a kiln [AEM] comprising two rounded depressions, filled with grey brown sandy clay. The northern depression contained a lining of baked red clay. At some period during phases 1–5 a vague linear depression, probably a wheel rut, had worn into the upper terrace road [ACB]; the road surface was patched and edged in places with larger Gritstones.

In Phase 6 (not illustrated) a pile of Gritstone rubble (3m by 1.5m and 0.75m high), was deposited over the western enclosure ditches immediately south west of structure 1; this may be debris left behind after the robbing of structures 1 and 2. Subsequently a layer [ACN] of grey-brown sandy clay , 0.2–0.5m deep, with occassional pebbles and much charcoal was deposited over the lower terrace.

In Phase 7 (not illustrated), in the eastern enclosure, Structure 4, a discrete spread of pebbles, was constructed; the structure overlay layer [ACN] and occupied the same site as structure 3. At the eastern end the boundary ditch [BEM], an irregular broad scoop up to 1.5m wide and 0.5m deep, was recut. The western enclosure ditch was also recut, but within the enclosure there was little demonstrable activity beyond the deposition of a further layer [BCO] of yellow-brown sandy clay and charcoal.

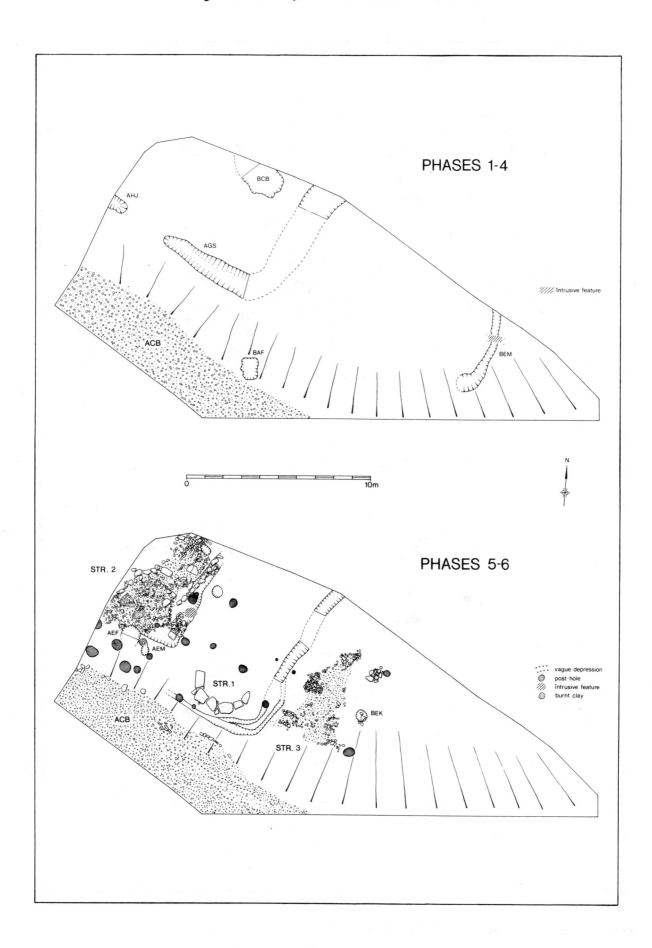

Figure 5:3 Plan of the 1984 Excavations (Phases 1-4 and 5-6)

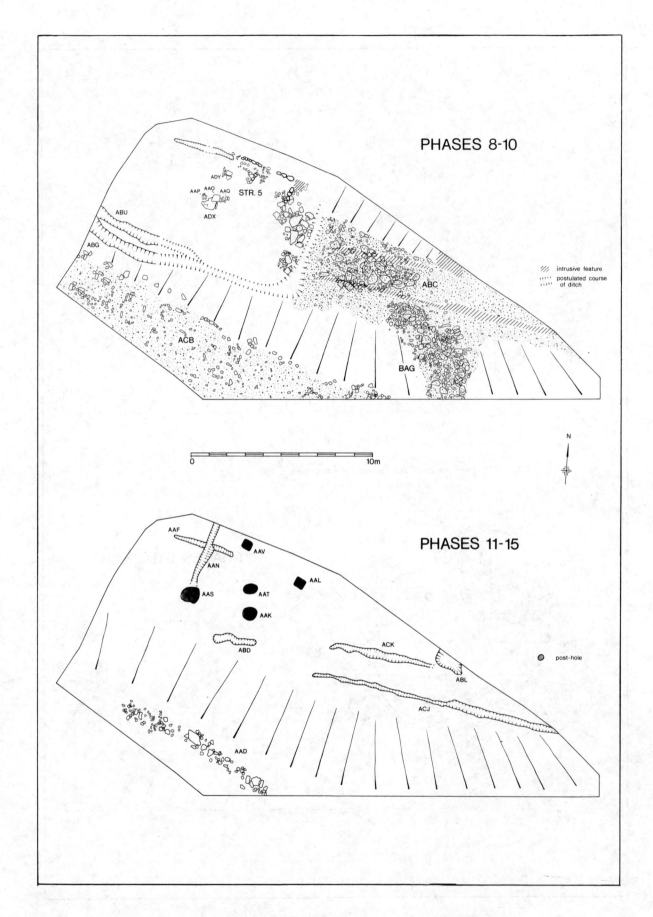

Figure 5:4 Plan of the 1984 Excavations (Phases 8-10 and 11-15)

Phases 8–10 (Figure 5:4)

In Phase 8 a road [BAG], 2.5–3.4m wide, constructed of large Limestone slabs and occassional shale rubble, with gravel metalling up to 0.1m thick, was constructed across the eastern enclosure, rising up the side of the slope to the upper terrace. The presumed junction of road [BAG] with the upper terrace road [ACB] lay outside of the area of excavation. The road terminated immediately east of the western terrace. Linear spreads of rubble defined the north and east walls of structure 5; a paved area, perhaps a continuation of [BAG], lay on the eastern side. To the west of structure 5 were two hearths [ADX & ADY]. The western enclosure ditch, 0.6m wide and 0.4m deep, was recut [ABU].

In Phase 9 a layer of brown sandy clay [ABE] up to 0.1m deep (not illustrated) with dense inclusions of fine black charcoal, and occassional fragments of scorched clay was deposited over the western enclosure and ditch [ABU]; the layer [ABE] encroached upon the southern edge of the paved area at the eastern side of structure 5, but the walls were not coverered (unless stone robbing has removed the evidence) and structure 5 may have remained standing. Slight traces of the layer [ABE] encroached on to the upper terrace road, but not the eastern enclosure.

In Phase 10 the ditch, 0.5m wide and 0.35m deep, of the western enclosure of the lower terrace was recut [ABG]; a clear plan and profile was recovered at the south east end, but the continuation to the east, cutting layer [ABE] was evident in plan only and the ditch appeared to be a vague, scooped depression in the top of earlier, subsided fills. Within the western enclosure structure 5 perhaps remained in use and a hearth, comprising a paved area [AAO] and two stone-packed post-holes [AAP & AAQ] was constructed, overlying the phase 8 hearth [ADX]. In the eastern enclosure, road [BAG] was resurfaced and a west–east extension [ABC], 4.5m wide and 0.1m thick, was constructed of water-worn pebbles.

Phases 11–15 (Figure 5:4)

In Phase 11 thin, clean lenses of yellow-brown sandy clay, with occasional flecks of charcoal, up to 0.06m deep, formed, in places, throughout the site. Although not stratigraphically linked the lenses appear contemporary and are interpreted as hill-wash.

In Phase 12 the deposition of hill-wash continued, interspersed with thin spreads of pebbles; the latter perhaps represent the erosion of road metalling. On the upper terrace a dry-stone, field-boundary, wall [AAD], represented by a linear scatter of irregular Gritstone rubble, 0.5m wide was constructed. It extended 9m west–east on the northern edge of the terrace; to the south, retained by the wall, a deep layer

of hill-wash accumulated. In Phase 13 the wall [AAD] collapsed or was demolished, the rubble lying down hill to the north, and was replaced by a new boundary system. On the lower terrace at the eastern side, two west–east ditches [ACK & ACJ], 1.6m apart, 0.12m deep and with a sharp 'V' profile, were dug. On the western side of the lower terrace, short and irregular lengths of west–east ditches [ABD & AAF] and a north–south ditch [AAN] represent the continuation of this system. Large, stone-packed post-holes [AAS, AAT & AAK] are interpreted as gate posts. The new system of boundaries aligns with and underlies field ditches and hedges which have only recently been removed. The boundaries, perhaps mark the introduction of a changed agricultural regime. In the succeeding phase 14 a deep layer of hill-wash up to 0.7m forming over the site may indicate ploughing on the higher slopes. In phase 15 a thin stone free topsoil 0.17m deep developed over the site, cut through by modern gate posts [AAV & AAL], and a pit [ABL], dug to remove the large altar in 1979.

Dating

Pottery (below) provides the dating evidence for the occupation of the site. Phases 1–3, which contained relatively little material, may be dated to the early/mid-second century. Phases 5–10 contain pottery of the later-second to mid-third century; cross joins between the phases are indicative of a history of redeposition and disturbance over the site. Pottery of similar date was recovered from phases 11–13, but the contextual evidence suggests that phase 13 is relatively recent, perhaps post-medieval, with the introduction of ditches and hedges as field boundaries. Third/fourth century pottery and medieval sherds were recovered from phases 14–15; this material is residual. The small quantities of third/fourth century and medieval pottery from the site confirm the contextual evidence; there was no occupation on site and the excavated area was part of a field system.

The terraces and ditch system

Superficially the construction of terraces implies a high degree of planning, organisation and resources sufficient to command considerable labour; such investment seems unnecessary, compared with the level of subsequent occupation. The construction of the upper terrace was structurally essential to carry the road [ACB] to the east, ascending a north-facing slope; road building is likely to have been supervised by engineers and funded by the imperial treasury. By contrast the development of the lower terrace is essentially a pragmatic and localised response to the topography, the levelling of a small area to create yards and building platforms, on sloping ground close to the road. There is insufficient dating evidence to show that the upper terrace and road was constructed significantly before the lower terrace; it is suggested that the lower terrace and enclosures were formed after the upper terrace, respecting an important route through the *vicus*. There is no evidence that their construction is strictly contemporary or was the result of a unified plan. The difficulty and labour required to construct the lower terrace on sloping ground does not necessarily imply that space within the *vicus* was limited; land adjacent to and accessible from an important route through the *vicus* was limited and throughout the occupation, work was undertaken to ensure continued access to the upper terrace road (below).

In phase 1 the western enclosure was formed by the construction of a wide 'U'-shaped ditch [AGS & AHJ], 1.10m wide and 0.60m deep, running east–west, parallel to the upper terrace road; the ditch turned north, down the slope, and became progressively deeper (up to 1m) towards the limit of excavation. The ditches terminated in butt ends to form an entrance 2.4m wide. The eastern enclosure was defined on the south side by a slope, up to 1.5m high, to the upper terrace; at the eastern side was a north–south ditch, which became shallower and terminated in an irregular butt-end at the southern, uphill, end. Within the enclosures, there was little evidence of occupation during phases 1–3; a relatively clean grey clay accumulated in the ditches.

Defences have been recognised at a number of *vici*, including Melandra (Webster, 1971) and Ribchester (Olivier, 1982). There was no trace of an internal bank or rampart associated with the ditches on the lower terrace. The ditches have the appearance of field boundaries. At Little Chester, Derby large ditches, 1.5–2m wide and up to 0.85m deep, were an early feature of the *vicus*, covered by later buildings

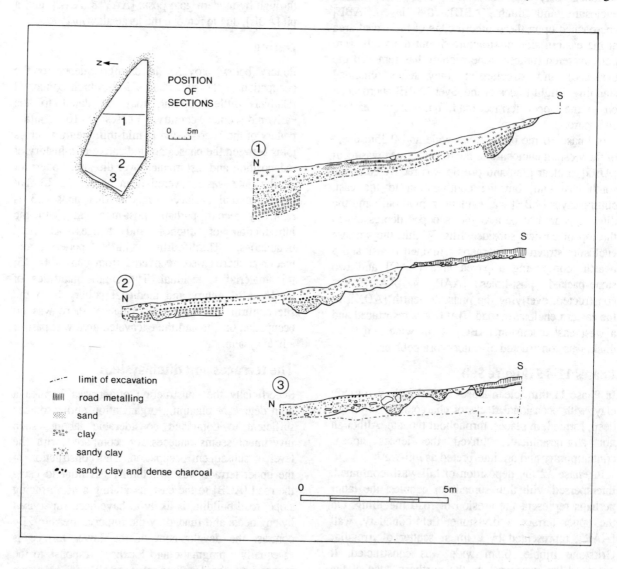

POSITION
OF
SECTIONS

0   5m

limit of excavation
road metalling
sand
clay
sandy clay
sandy clay and dense charcoal

0   5m

Figure 5:5 Sections Across the 1984 Excavations

(Dool 1985a, 158). Aerial photography suggests that certain *vici*, including Newton Kyme and Old Carlisle (Jones, G. D B, 1984, 80–85) have extensive ditched fields and enclosures, perhaps allotments, gardens or yards associated with houses. It seems probable that the phase 1–3 ditches on the lower enclosure, on the periphery of the *vicus* at Brough-on-Noe had a similar function and should be interpreted as agricultural enclosures.

The ditches around the western enclosure were maintained and recut through out the occupation of the site. No post-hole structures were located but a significant number of post-holes were associated with the western enclosure ditches in phases 5–10. One post-hole void, 1.15m long, extended vertically through the recut ditches at the northern limit of excavation, suggesting that the post was standing throughout phases 5–10. It would appear that the western enclosure was defined by a ditch and a post and rail or hurdle fence, or possibly a hedge with occasional reinforcing posts.

The road system (Figures 5:1, 5:3, 5:4; Plates 3–4)

Three roads were located; a road [ACB] on the upper terrace, a road [ABC] on the lower terrace and a road [BAG] linking the two terraces. One feature, a stone-filled pit was associated with the upper terrace road.

The road upon the upper terrace was not fully excavated, its southern edge lying outside the limit of excavtion. The road [ACB], 0.4m thick and over 4m wide, was constructed in phase 1. A foundation of large Gritstone and Limestone rubble, including some weathered blocks, was laid in a matrix of clay and shale upon an uneven, stripped clay surface. The road surface was composed of small water worn pebbles and shaley-clay. Between phases 1–6 there was some resurfacing, with water worn pebbles; an irregular linear depression, a traffic rut, wore in to the surface and an irregular kerb of Gritstone rubble blocks was constructed on the north edge. An extensive resurfacing of the road, using thin irregular slabs of Limestone (up to 0.3m by 0.2m and 0.05m thick) and large waterworn pebbles and cobbles is attributed to phases 8–10; this resurfacing extended over pit [BAF]. The road extended 18m, rising in a gradual 8% slope to the east. The road formerly continued at least 40m to the west; a thin line of gravel and stone was observed in the bank forming the south side of the farmyard. The only other feature on the upper terrace was a subrectangular pit [BAF], with straight sides and a flat base 1.2 x 0.9m and 0.37m deep, filled with large angular Limestone and Gritstone rubble set in grey clay. There was no evidence of a post-setting. The function of this feature is uncertain. The feature formed a carefully constructed foundation or base, to support a road-side feature, such as a monument, or some other mundane purpose. The feature may be contemporary with the first phase of road construction and was covered by later, phase 8–10, metalling.

Road [BAG], constructed in phase 8 comprised a layer of large Limestone slabs and shale rubble (the largest 1.4m by 0.4m and 0.30m thick) overlain by a metalling of water-worn pebbles (0.05–0.1m), 3.4m wide. The road extended from the eastern edge of the western enclosure, and turned south ascending to the upper terrace in a curve to reduce the gradient. The slope accounts for the massive foundations. Road [BAG] presumably joined the upper terrace road, but the junction lay outside of the excavated area.

Road [ABC], constructed in phase 10, comprised a single layer, 4.5m wide and 0.1m thick, of water-worn pebbles and cobbles (0.05–0.20m) set in yellow-brown sandy clay. Road [ABC] overlay the south eastern end of the link road [BAG] and extended across the eastern enclosure to the limit of excavation. No continuation of the road was observed in the bank forming the south side of the farmyard and the destination of the road is unknown.

The upper terrace road [ACB], on account of its extent (58m), the several phases of construction and its wear, may be interpreted as an important route through the *vicus* and a prominent feature of its plan. The road is parallel with, and 50m to the north of, the postulated course of a road to Chesterfield (Figure 5:1); it is possible that the upper terrace road [ACB] is the actual road and the postulated course along a modern lane is a diversion. To the east of Brough-on-Noe sections of terrace and holloways on the postulated road to Chesterfield were examined in 1969. A road 3.2m wide on a levelled platform or terrace 7.2m wide was located; there was no certain evidence of Roman date (Richardson, 1969). The other roads [ABC & BAG] are later and less carefully constructed; [BAG] is a short, link road and road [ABC] was perhaps not extensive. Within the *vicus*, road [ACB] gave direct access to the western enclosure through a gap in the ditches (Phases 1–3). Road [BAG] restored access from the upper terrace to the western enclosure, serving structure 5. Road [ABC] also served the western enclosure.

The structures

Structure 1 (Figures 5:3, 5:6)Structure 1 comprised an arc of large slabs of Limestone 0.05–08m thick, set in yellow clay; the upper surfaces of the stones were smooth and flat, but without any sign of having been worked. The slab at the north west had been dressed into an irregular trapezoid; there were traces of chisel marks

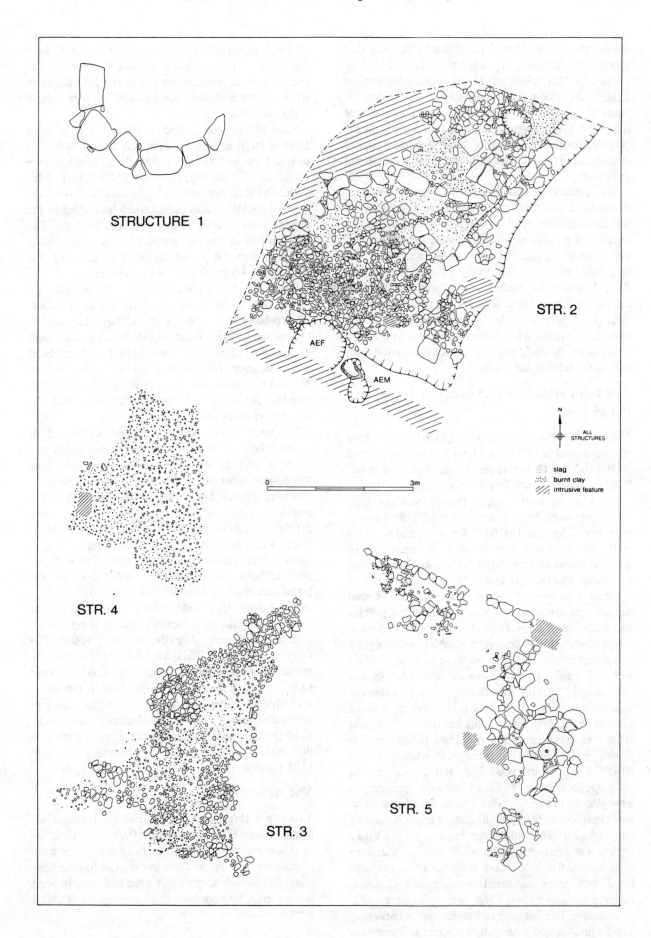

Figure 5:6 Structures 1–5

on the edges; the base was flat. The bases of the other five slabs were deeply eroded by weathering and they appear to have lain exposed for a considerable period of time. The stones were carefully placed and, on account of their smoothness, appear to have formed a surface. There is insufficient evidence to warrant comparison with such apsidal-ended structures as the late-first early-second century, timber structure excavated in the north west sector of the fort at Littlechester, Derby, tentatively interpreted as a shrine, but in an area concerned with animal husbandry (Wheeler, 1985a, 43–4) and the Corbridge *schola*. Irregular, curved lines of slabs can be seen in the floor of structure 2 and in context 014 (Figure 5:2), where they may define a drain. In the absence of other evidence it is possible that the slabs forming structure 1 were formerly part of a more extensive spread of stones, perhaps forming an area of hard standing or the floor of a building.

Structure 2. (Figures 5:3, 5:6)

Structure 2 (Phase 5) consisted of sub rectangular area (5.75m by 4.5m) of hard-packed, random-sized Limestone and Gritstone rubble, overlain by patches of water-worn pebbles and cobbles. Contemporary with the floor was a stone packed post hole [AFX]; the post-pit was sealed by gravel, but the post-pipe projected through the floor. At the north end was a small depression [AFN] or pit, filled with gravel. On the east side of Structure 2 was an irregular robber trench, 0.75–0.9m wide and up to 0.18m deep, and a stone packed post-hole [AID]. To the south of Structure 2, was a subrectangular pit [AEF], which cut the floor, but was in use at the same time as the building, and a kiln [AEM]. Thirteen kgs. of slag from the floor and the kiln [AEM] indicate that metalworking was carried out within or close by structure 2.

The robber trench indicates that there was a wall on the east side. The structure appears to have been open at the southern end; there was no evidence of a wall, but the shallow scoop at the south east corner suggests that some stone or metalling has been removed. It is probable that post hole [AID] marks the south eastern end of the structure; the remaining floor to the south being an exposed area of hard standing. The form of the east wall is uncertain; a low stone wall to support the superstructure is probable.

Structure 3 (Figures 5:3, 5:6)

Structure 3 comprised an irregular spread (5.6m by 4m by 0.1m thick) of densely packed water-worn pebble and cobbles, and irregular Gritstone rubble; the west side of the structure was destroyed. A discrete area of larger stones, including a broken quern stone is suggestive of a hearth, but no trace of burning was located. To the east of Structure 3 were two post holes and an area of burnt clay, possibly an oven. Structure 3 may be no more than a discrete area of gravel and rubble, a hard standing, but it is probable that it formed the floor of a building, whose superstructure was carried on sill beams.

Structure 4 (Figure 5:6)

Structure 4 comprised an irregular spread (2.5m by 3.5m by 0.05m thick) of densely packed water-worn pebble. Structure 4 overlay Structure 3, but was separated from it by a layer of yellow brown silt (0.25m thick); it may be a rebuild of Structure 3. Structure 4, like Structure 3 may be no more than a hard standing, but it is possible that it formed the floor of a building, whose superstructure was carried on sill beams.

Structure 5 (Figures 5:4, 5:6)

Structure 5, comprises two walls, indicated by lines of thin, irregular, Limestone rubble, extending at right angles; only a single course of walling survived and the intersection of the walls has been destroyed by a modern intrusion. To the east is a surface, paved with large irregular slabs of Limestone and a single quernstone. South of the north wall, a linear scatter of rubble suggests a further wall, sub-dividing the structure. The walls possibly supported sill beams. Structure 5 was constructed in phase 8 and probably remained standing through to phase 10.

Discussion

In view of the tenuous structural evidence no detailed discussion of the buildings can be sustained. It seems that the buildings were dismantled and their materials taken away for re-use, as soon as they were redundant. It should be noted that although there were many stone-packed post-holes on the site, there were no post-hole structures and a single construction method, with sill beams directly on earth or on low stone walls, was used for structures 2–5. Sill beam construction, with either beam-slots or low stone footings, was also used exclusively in the *vicus* at Melandra (Webster, 1971, 60–65). The purpose of the buildings, whether industrial or domestic, is unknown.

Metalworking (Figure 5:7)

The evidence for the working of metals in the areas excavated in 1983–4 comprises, a mould stone, six hearths and a small quantity of iron slag. One small piece of galena was recovered in the 1983 excavations and 24 small pieces in 1984; the latter are all from recent phases (13–14) of the site. A few fragments of iron slag and a mould stone for a small ingot (102 in Figure 5:15) were recovered in 1983, but the composition of the metal cast in it cannot be determined.

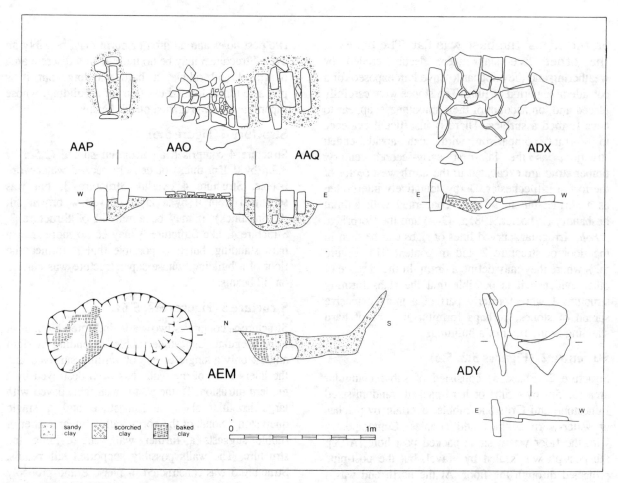

Figure 5:7 Metal Working Features

29kgs. of iron slag was recovered in the 1984 excavation; 13kgs. from floor of structure 2 (phase 5), and significant quantities from the phase 6 levelling layers and the western enclosure ditch, phase 10. Analysis of the slag (below) suggests that there is no evidence for iron smelting on site, but blooms were brought to the site, perhaps already partially forged; several partially-forged billets of iron bloom were recovered including one from the floor of structure 2. The blooms were probably then reforged on site either into finished objects or into bar stock for later redistribution. A probable source for blooms and fuel lies some 15–20km to the east in the Coal Measures, where there are deposits of clay-ironstones (Edwardes and Trotter, 1954, 4).

Pits AGT & AGU (Phase 4 not illustrated)

Two subrectangular, straight-sided, flat-bottomed pits ,0. 5–6m wide and 0. 25m deep, were cut into the infilled ditches of the western enclosure; in each case the fill was grey-brown, sandy clay, with quantities of ash and charcoal. Pit AGT cut AGU. There was no trace of any scorching. From pit [AGU] 0.6 kg of iron slag was recovered.

The pits resemble a mid-second century or later bowl hearth (VI F46) at Little Chester, Derby, (Dool , 1985a, 169).

Kiln [AEM] (Phase 8) (Figures 5:4, 5:7)

The feature, which resembled a pottery kiln, consisted of two flat-bottomed, intersecting pits, 0.4 x 1m and up to 0.5m deep. Only the lower part of the feature survived, the top was cut away by the western enclosure ditches. The northern pit, the oven, contained an area of baked clay, interpreted as a fragmented lining. At the junction of the stokehole and oven the fragmented lining appeared to form a fire arch; the arch, which had been formed over and incorporated a mortarium rim, overlay a large stone, probably a blocking. With the exception of the baked clay, there was little trace of heat and the fill, a sandy clay, contained only a little charcoal and 1.65 kg. of iron slag. The feature resembles a possible furnace for crucible melting of non-ferrous metals (VI F96) at Little Chester, Derby, (Dool 1985a, 170). However no evidence of crucibles or working of non-ferrous metals, other than the mould stone, was found.

Hearth [ADX] (Phase 8) (Figures 5:4, 5:7)

The hearth comprised one vertical stone and one horizontal slab. The cracked, horizontal, Sandstone slab (0.72m long x 0.63m wide by 0.05m thick) appears to have been laid in a slight hollow or depression, where scorching was noticeable. The vertical stone (O.35m long x 0.10m wide by 0.05m thick) was set in the ground to a depth of 0.20m, projecting 0.10m above the surface of the adjacent slab.

Hearth [ADY] (Phase 8) (Figures 5:4, 5:7)

The hearth comprised one vertical stone and one, or possibly two, horizontal slabs. The cracked, horizontal, Sandstone slab (0.51m long x 0.41m wide by 0.06m thick) appears to have been lain in a slight hollow or depression.. The vertical stone (O.55m long x 0.05m wide by 0.06m thick) was set in the ground to a depth of 0.38m, projecting 0.11m above the surface of the adjacent slab.

Hearth [AAO] (Phase 10) (Figures 5:4, 5:7)

The hearth consisted of an area of paving between two post-holes [AAP & AAQ]. The paving, comprised a single, fragmented slab of Sandstone (length 0.48m, width 0.60m, thickness 0.03m), laid in yellow sandy-clay; immediately to the east was a vertical stone. To the west was a stone packed post-hole [AAP]; the packing-stones, roughly-shaped, rectangular, Gritstone rubble, were placed around a rectangular post, (0.17 wide x 0.10m deep), set in an irregular scoop (0.45m deep and 0.24m wide) packed with brown clay; the packing stones appear to have been driven into position to stabilise the post. To the east was a stone packed post-hole [AAQ]; it was very similar to [AAP] but the scoop was sub-rectangular

The common features of the three hearths were a horizontal stone with an adjacent vertical stone slab; ADX and ADY are contemporary structures. AAO overlay ADX. At Little Chester, Derby, a large, burnt slab of Sandstone (VI F76) was interpreted as a smithing hearth, although there was no directly associated slag (Dool 1985a, 174–5). The three hearths could be for secondary smithing, the forging of implements from purified blooms or repair work.

The Finds

1. Romano–British Coarse Pottery (Figures 5:8–5:10) Ruth Leary

Some 1,781 sherds from a minimum of 55 vessels were recovered in 1983 and 4,181 sherds from a minimum of 437 vessel in 1984. The pottery was examined by context and a fully quantified archive is available at Sheffield City Museum comprising a catalogue recording fabric, sherd count, form, part, rim diameter, rim percentage, decoration and other conditions; fabric and form type descriptions; illustrations of form types and tables quantifying the forms and fabrics by phase using sherd counts and rim percentages. The mortaria archive was compiled with the help of K.H. Hartley. The fabrics present on

the site are described below. The range of forms represented is illustrated regardless of context and phase, because of the lack of typological change throughout the stratigraphic sequence, and the assemblage is treated as one ceramic group. A small number of sherds indicated some slight typological progression through time and this is commented upon below.

Fabrics

A sample of sherds was examined under a x20 binocular microscope to identify the fabric groups and thereafter identification was carried out using a hand-held lens except in doubtful cases.

All the sherds were wheel-thrown except those in fabric BB1 and some examples of DW/CTA2.

GRA:	Grey, often with darker core and lighter margins. Hard with sparse, fine, angular quartz, black/grey oxides and mica. Similar to a fabric produced at Derby Race-course (Brassington, 1971 and 1980).
GRB:	Grey. Hard, sandy fabric with moderate quantities of medium, subangular quartz and black/brown iron oxides, usually well-sorted.
GRC:	Grey. Hard rough fabric with moderate quantities of well-sorted, coarse, angular quartz and sparse black iron oxides.
OAA:	As GRA but orange. Quantified with GRA.
OAB:	As GRB but orange. Quantified with GRB.
OAC:	Orange. Rough, slightly soft fabric with abundant coarse, subangular quartz and red/brown iron oxides. Made in rebated-rim and cupped-rim jars. Similar to Brassington's pre-Derbyshire ware (1971, 59). Quantified with DBY.
OBA:	As GRA but buff/cream. Quantified with GRA.
OBB:	As GRB but buff/cream. Quantified with GRB.
OBC:	As OAC but buff/cream. Quantified with DBY.
OBD:	Buff/brown. Hard, rough fabric with moderate quantities of very coarse, angular, ill-sorted quartz and brown/red iron oxides. Only two unstratified sherds. Quantified with NSP.
DBY:	Derbyshire ware as Kay, 1962.

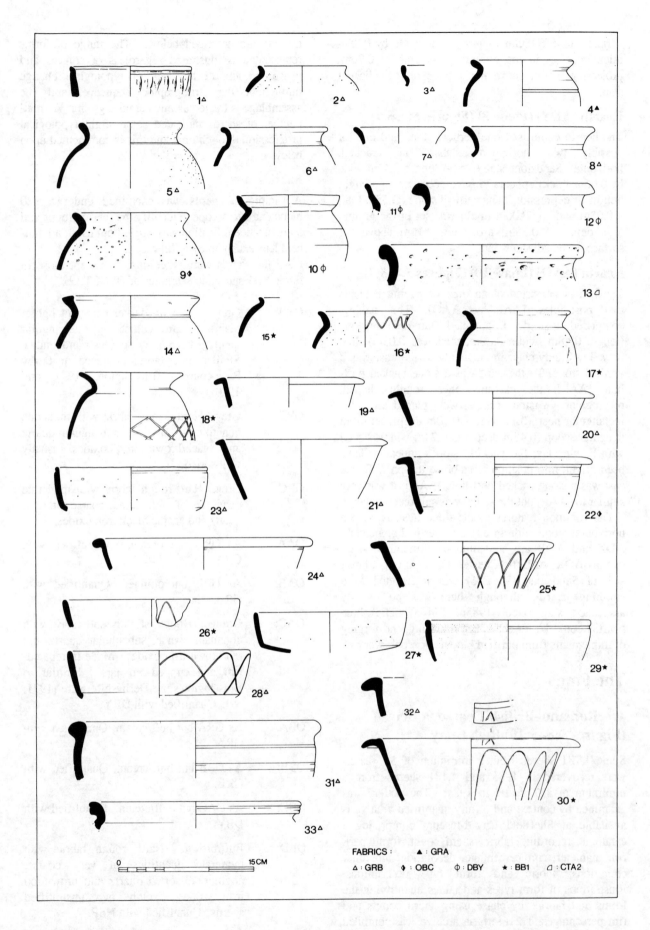

Figure 5:8 Coarse Pottery

FABRICS :   ▲ : GRA

△ : GRB   ◊ : OBC   Φ : DBY   ★ : BB1   ⊿ : CTA2

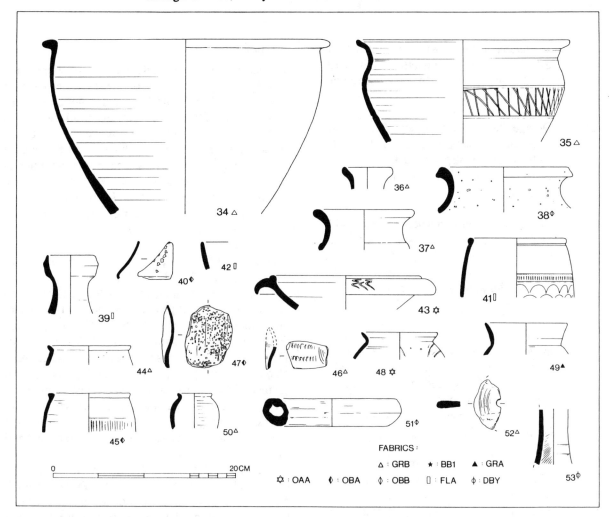

Figure 5:9 Coarse Pottery

NSP: General group of sandy wares not closely defined.

BB1:   Black Burnished ware category 1, as Farrar, 1973.

FLA/PMT: White or Cream fabric. Fairly hard, smooth or slightly powdery with moderate, fine, subangular, well-sorted quartz and sparse, fine, rounded brown/red iron oxides. FLA is a flagon fabric and is sometimes self-slipped. PMT is similar to FLA but painted.

FLB: Orange with cream slip. Flagon ware. fairly soft and sandy with moderate quantities of well-sorted, subangular, medium-sized quartz and red/brown iron oxides.

BSB: Brown. Hard, sandy fabric with moderate quantities of ill-sorted, medium-sized, rounded quartz and sparse brown iron oxides.

CTA2/DW: Brown or dark grey. Fairly soft, soapy fabric with laminar fracture and abundant coarse, ill-sorted, platey vesicles, sparse, fine, subangular quartz and fine brown/red iron oxides. Dales ware (Loughlin, 1977) or South Midlands shelly ware (Young, 1980, 27).

C: colour-coated ware: OB: orange with black/brown colour coat.
                          CWB: white with black/brown colour coat.
                          CWO: white with orange colour coat.

All the colour-coated ware was similar to Nene Valley ware in fabric and form except two rough-coated sherds comparable to North Gaulish colour-coated ware.

M: Mortaria fabrics.

M1: White/cream fabric with red/brown/black trituration grits and quartz. All these sherds were identified as Mancetter-Hartshill products.

M2: Orange fairly hard, sandy fabric with abundant medium-sized, subangular, well-sorted quartz and sparse black iron oxides. Brown trituration grits 2–5 mm. North, ? local source.

M3: Cream/buff soft, powdery fabric with moderate quantities of well-sorted fine, rounded quartz and clay pellets/?grog and sparse, fine black/brown iron oxides. Quartz trituration grits 2–3 mm. Probably an import.

M4: Orange/buff fairly hard, sandy fabric with moderate quantities of well-sorted, medium-sized, angular quartz, sparse, medium-sized, rounded white inclusions and sparse iron oxides. Orange slip all over. Quartz trituration grits 1–2 mm. Possibly Little Chester.

M5: Cream with grey core. Soft, powdery fabric with moderate quantities of well-sorted, fine, subangular quartz and ill-sorted, medium-sized, orange-grey grog and sparse brown iron oxides. Black and white trituration grits. Possibly Little Chester.

M6: Orange, soft, powdery fabric with abundant, well-sorted, medium-sized, subangular quartz and rare, medium-sized, rounded white inclusions. Cream slip. Many quartz and red/brown trituration grits 1–2 mm. Northern source.

M7: Cream/orange, soft, powdery fabric with moderate quantities of well-sorted, fine, rounded clay pellets, fairly sparse, medium-sized, rounded quartz and sparse, medium-sized, brown iron oxides. Central France group 1 (Hartley, 1977).

M8: Cream with pinkish surfaces. Hard, smooth fabric with moderate quantities of well-sorted, medium-sized, angular quartz and sparse, fine red clay pellets and black iron oxides. Trituration grits not present. Perhaps fairly local.

Chronology

The material from the 1983 excavations was similar to that from phases 4–13 of the 1984 sequence in fabric (tables 1 & 2) and form and is not commented upon further although details are available in the archive. The pottery was divided into groups according to the site phases initially but the bulk of the fabric and form types occurred intermittently throughout the sequence and little typological progression could be detected. Derbyshire ware jars (nos. 9–12) and grey ware everted-rim jars (nos. 5–8) were present from phase 3. Similarly ovoid jars (nos. 36–8) were present in phases 3–9 and 14, flat rim dishes (nos. 19–25) in phases 3–8, 11 and 14, plain-rim dishes (nos. 26–28) in phases 4–9, grooved-rim dishes (nos. 23–29) in phases 4–6, 9 and 11 and deep bowls (nos. 31–5) in phases 4–8 and 10–11. Few of these forms are closely datable. Derbyshire ware dated from the Antonine period (Wheeler, 1985a, 116) and everted-rim jars superseded the earlier, more globular form (nos. 2 and 4) during the second century. The flat-rim dishes were most common in the second century but the plain- and grooved-rim dishes were long-lived types. The deep bowls were common from the later-second century (Buckland and Magilton, 1986, 110).

A few more closely datable forms were present and their incidence refines the dating. Phase 1 and 2 yielded little pottery. Sherds of an indented beaker (as no. 46) and a BB1 vessel from phase 1 gave a *terminus post quem* of 120 AD and a Mancetter-Hartshill mortarium dated to 140–200 AD was the latest sherd from phase 2. Pit BCB, phase 3, contained a mortarium dating to 130–180 AD (no. 56) and a mid-second century BB1 dish came from the ditch (AGS). Thus on the available evidence the first three phases are best dated to the early/mid-second century.

A small number of diagnostic forms appeared in the stratigraphic sequence in chronological order. For example, early/mid-second century BB1 jars (nos. 16–7, *cf.* Gillam, 1976, nos. 3–4) occurred in the earlier phases and the mid-third century type (no. 18, *cf.* Gillam, 1976, no. 8) did not appear until phase 7. Similarly third/fourth century Dales ware and South Midlands shelly ware jars (no. 13) did not occur until phase 6 and, apart from a beaker from phase 4 (Howe *et al.*, 1980, no. 45, probably third century), there was no third century colour-coated ware before phase 7. However, the beaker and a mortarium (no. 62) dated to 160–220 AD from the phase 4 layers reverses this sequence. In addition, the mortaria (nos. 60, 61, 59 and 58, *cf.* at Brough-by-Bainbridge, Hartley, 1960, fig. 7, nos. 41–3) from phases 5–13 place all these phases within the late-second/mid-third century with only a few mid-second century types (no. 57). The cross-joins between phases 5 to 11, 8 to 12 and 2 to 6 suggests a history of disturbances and redisposition of deposits on the site. Phases 14 and 15 contained similar pottery to the preceding phases with the addition of a small number of third/fourth century sherds (mortaria nos. 63 and 64) and some Medieval sherds. These were not closed groups so are not discussed further.

Some diagnostic first or early-second century types were found such as the mortarium from phase 5 (no. 54), a French import dating to 50–85 AD (Hartley, 1977, Group 1), and some vessels similar to the products of the Derby Racecourse kilns (nos. 1, 2, 4, 36, 40–4, *cf.* Brassington, 1971, nos. 183, 169, 160, 145, 1, 25 and 37–112 respectively and mortaria no. 55 *cf.* Wheeler 1985a, fig. 48). Of these, only the bowls, represented by body sherds only, were restricted to phases 3–5 the remainder being scattered throughout the sequence.

It is, therefore, concluded that the pottery from phases 4–13 can be regarded as a single assemblage sealed by hill-wash and dated by the coarse pottery, mortaria and samian to the late-second/mid-third century. The pottery from phases 1–3 along with the earlier-second century sherds scattered throughout the later contexts suggest some activity in the early/mid-second century.

Viewed as a single assemblage the pottery types from phases 4–11 compared well with late-second/third century groups from Derby Little

Chester (Wheeler 1985a, 101–3), Manchester (Jones and Grealey, 1974, 102–4) and the kilns at Rossington Bridge, outside Doncaster (Samuels, 1983, 535–600). The everted-rim jars were common at Rossington Bridge (Samuels 1983, fig. 119 nos. 25–40, fig. 120 nos 6–21) and present at Manchester (Jones and Grealey, 1974, fig. 36 nos. 80, 89 and 101, fig. 37 no. 134) but not at Little Chester where Derbyshire ware jars predominated. The rebated-rim jars (nos. 3 and 14) can be parallelled at Little Chester (Brassington, 1971, nos. 204–226) and Torksey, Lincs. (Oswald, 1937, Plate II, 12b and 13b) respectively. The small number of BB1 vessels at Brough-on-Noe was parallelled at Little Chester but contrasted with Manchester (Jones and Grealey, 1974, 93) and the earlier assemblage at Melandra (Webster, 1971, 107). The dish forms (nos. 19–30) were similar at Brough-on-Noe, Little Chester and Manchester although those at Derby and Manchester were nearly all in BB1 while those at Brough-on-Noe were in both BB1 and GRB. The deep bowls were parallelled at Rossington Bridge (Samuels, 1983, fig 124) but were scarce at Little Chester and Manchester, replaced by Derby Racecourse and Severn valley wares respectively. All the assemblages included comparable fine ware bowls and colour-coated beakers (nos. 44–49) in small quantities. Thus the differences between the assemblages are probably a result of different supply arrangements rather than date and equivalent vessel forms can be suggested where precise parallels are absent.

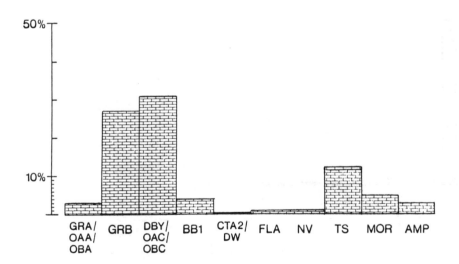

Table1   1983 – Relative percentages of pottery fabrics by sherd count.

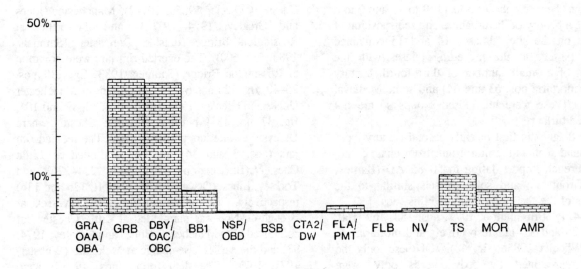

Table 2   1984 – Relative percentages of pottery fabrics by sherd count.

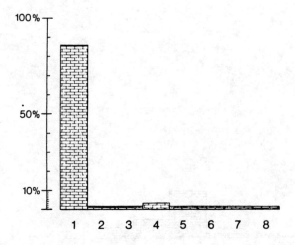

Table 3   1983–84 –Relative percentages of mortaria fabrics by sherd count.

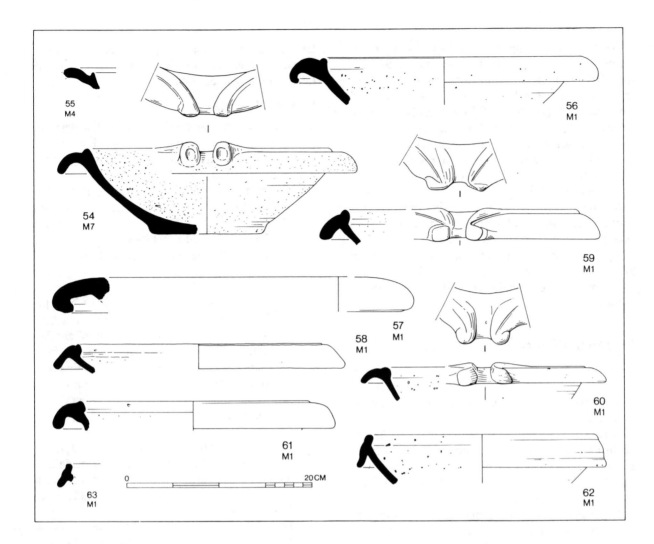

Figure 5:10 Coarse Pottery

Date Range Approx.	Mancetter-Hartshill	North/Local	Little Chester	Import
50–85				1
100–130/40	2		2	
100/110–170	2			
130/40–170/80	9			
140/50–190/200	16			
2nd century		2		
Antonine		1		
160–220	7			
170–240	3			
180–250	2			
200–260	1			
250–350	2			
Indeterminate		2		1

Table 4.   Summary of mortaria from the 1983 and 1984 excavations by kiln source and date using minimum vessel count.

The site was drawing *c*.40% of its pottery from the Derby Racecourse and Derbyshire ware kilns, 6% from BB1 kilns in Dorset or Rossington Bridge, 4% from Mancetter-Hartshill, Warwicks. and 10% from the Continent (samian and North Gaulish colour-coated, Tables 1–3). A further 35% comprised grey wares comparable to the Rossington Bridge pottery, although possibly made at kilns nearer to Brough-on-Noe working in the same tradition. Small quantities of flagon (no. 39), Dales and Nene Valley ware were also present along with mortaria from Derby Racecourse, unspecified northern kilns and France. One spindle-whorl, made from a pot sherd, the ring of a triple vase and a miniature jar (nos. 50–2) were found. One object, a funnel in Derbyshire ware (no. 53), has not been parallelled and its function is unknown.

2. Samian (Figure 5:11) *B. Dickinson*

Severe chemical and mechanical erosion has made much of the samian in this assemblage useless for dating purposes. A full itemised catalogue is held in the archive.

There is, however, a small quantity of South Gaulish ware from La Graufesenque, most of it late-first or early-second century, but, apparently, very little Trajanic material from Les Martres-de-Veyre or Hadrianic Lezoux ware.

The datable pieces are preponderantly Antonine ware typical of Lezoux. An appreciable proportion of them are later than *c*. 160 AD The small amount of

East Gaulish ware, apparently all from Rheinzabern, is either contemporary with the later Antonine Lezoux vessels, or early-third century.

Decorated Samian

(69) Form 37, central Gaulish. A similar detached chevron festoon occurs on a bowl in one of Pugnus ii's late styles from Baylham Mill, Suffolk. *c*. 150–180 AD. ACN.

(70) Fragments of Form 37, Central Gaulish. The ovolo (Rogers B52) and ring terminals joining the borders suggest Divixtus i. The sequence of the panels is not clear, but they include:
1. Mars (D94), as on a stamped Divixtus bowl from Worcester.
2. A small double festoon containing a mask (D.696). There is also a bear to left, with the fore-quarters only impressed. The medallion and mask, which recur at the top of another panel, are on a stamped bowl from Cirencester. Another sherd has a Venus at an altar (D.184) at the bottom, as on a bowl in Divixtus style from Carrawburgh. *c*. 150–80 AD.

(71) Form 37, Central Gaulish, in the style of Do(v)eccus i. One panel contains a medallion with a beaded outer border (Rogers E8), over a row of fan-shaped motifs (Rogers G259). *c*. 165–200 AD.

(72) Form 37, Central Gaulish. The ovolo (Rogers B103) and large double medallion containing a

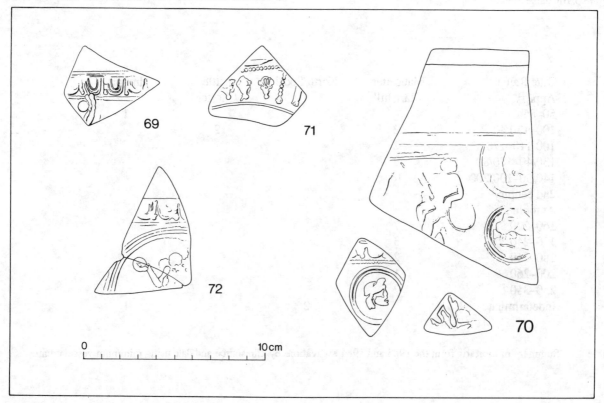

Figure 5:11   Decorated Samian

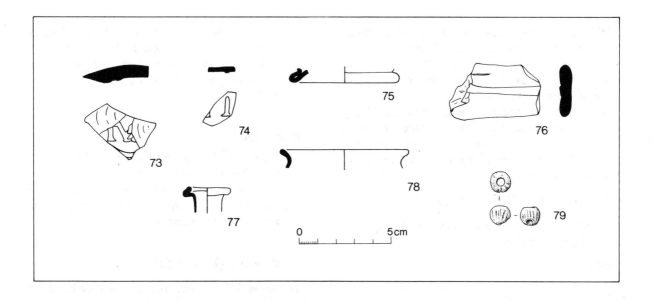

Figure 5:12 Glass

3. Amphorae *D.F. Williams*

29 sherds (2,514 grams) from Dressel 20 amphorae were recovered from the 1983 excavations and 42 (3,593 grams) from the 1984 excavations including four handle sherds. this is the most common amphora type imported into Roman Britain and was made in the southern Spanish province of Baetica, along the banks of the river Guadalquivir and its tributaries between Seville and Cordoba, and carried olive oil (Ponsich 1974;1979). This type of amphora has a wide date range, from the Augustan prototype (Oberaden 83) with a fairly upright rim, a short spike and a less squat bulbous body than the later form, to the developed well-known globular form which, with some typological variation, was in use at least up to the late-third century A.D. (Zevi 1967) and possibly into the fourth century (Manacorda 1977).

4. Glass (Figure 5:12) *D.A.Allen*

A total of 89 vessel fragments, seven window fragments and one bead was found. Of the vessel fragments, 78 were natural blue-green in colour and eleven were colourless, the latter including six bags of extremely tiny shattered pieces, too numerous to count individually and therefore included as one each. Their possible significance is discussed below.

By far the commonest vessel type represented is the blue-green bottle which occurred in a wide variety of shapes as containers for an equally wide range of liquids. Fifty-one fragments were found, and where body shapes were determinable, all were prismatic — some definitely square and one definitely hexagonal. The latter shape went out of use from the second quarter of the second century, but the squares continued from the second half of the first century to at least the end of the second and possibly into the third century. Two base fragments (73–4) are of interest in that they appear to include parts of letters of the alphabet in their markings. This is not an uncommon feature (Charlesworth 1966), and they can sometimes be interpreted as abbreviated names or places, thought to refer to the manufacture of the vessel rather than the contents. Insufficient remains of these fragments to permit identification.

Other blue-green vessel fragments include a base-ring (75), 11 pieces from the body of a globular jug or flask, a ribbed handle fragment (76) and a flask or jug rim (77). None was sufficiently diagnostic to allow certain identification, but the latter two may well represent a group of long-necked jugs common in later-first and earlier-second century contexts. They have been much discussed elsewhere (e.g. Price 1977,155–8).

The colourless glass included one beaker rim (78) which again cannot be identified with certainty, but probably belongs between the late-Flavian period and the earlier-third century. The six bags of shattered fragments all very much resembled what often remains of a type of facet-cut beaker common in Flavian and Trajanic contexts in Britain, particularly on military sites (*cf.* a complete example from Barnwell, Cambs., Harden et al 1968, 79, no. 101). For some reason this specific group often weathers and shatters in this way. However no conclusive evidence of facet-cutting was found on any of the minute fragments found at Brough-on-Noe, so the identification remains tentative.

Victory (D474) are all on a stamped bowl of Advocisus in the Wroxeter Gutter find (Atkinson 1942, pl. 33, G1). *c.* 160–90 AD.

All the window glass was of cast matt/glossy variety, in use to *c*.300 A.D. (Boon 1966).

One melon bead was found (79). These were common, particularly in the first century, becoming less so in the second century

The glass assemblage was therefore fairly unremarkable, consisting largely of bottle fragments, with a few pieces of tableware of reasonably common type. All recognisable pieces fit a first to second century date range.

5 .Copper Alloy (Figure 5:13)

Very little copper alloy was recovered, largely as a result of the soil acidity.

1983 Finds

Brooches *D. Mackreth*

(80) Knee brooch. The spring is housed in an open-backed case with a rounded front by means of an axis bar lodged in the end-plates. The head is plain. The bow is square-sectioned, but otherwise is cabriole-shaped, the upper part of the back being provided with facing cusps. The foot of the bow splays markedly and has a groove along its three main faces. The catch-plate lies in the same plane as the under surface of the foot, but stepped up a little. The return of the slot to hold the pin is broken. The style of this brooch is against it having been made in Britain. Discussion of knee brooches found at Catterick (Mackreth in Wacherm unpublished) reviewed the dating of the broad type and arrived at the conclusion that the period *c*. 150–225 A.D. covered the main manufacturing period and the subsequent time when specimens were survivors in use. Unstratified.

(81) Plate brooch. Very badly preserved, the three fragments only give hints of the original full design. There had clearly been a four-part pattern based on a cross with, most probably, voided circles which touched the adjacent ones. The third fragment, which also has the top of a hinged pin behind, is such that eight of these could be fitted around the edge, the indeterminate ones completing the outer parts of the voided circles. The small projection could then have been mounted on all eight arcs or reserved as a set of four on either the main axies or on the diagonals. The surface of the plate is recessed and contains remains of a mid- to deep blue highly vitrified frit. In the centre of the brooch and rising from the enamel is a damaged stud. Not enough survives for parallels to be sought. In general, however, brooches with voided areas and central studs belong to the second century. They probably occur earlier than the knee brooches, but there is no satisfactory evidence to show that the general class had passed out of use before *c*. 225 A.D. E10.

Other Finds

(82) Fragment of simple buckle, *cf.* Cunliffe, (1971), nos. 85–8. E16. A small number of undiagnostic fragments were also found during the 1983 excavations and three fragments came from the 1984 excavations.

6. Ironwork (Figure 5:14)

The ironwork from both sites was in poor condition. Select pieces were x-rayed and conserved by Sheffield City Museums. The remainder were stored in sealed boxes with silica gel. All the identifiable pieces were of common type and can be parallelled on other military sites

1983 Finds

(83) Spearhead with broken socket and blade, *cf.* Manning, (1976), 18–21. C.

(84) Knife blade with broken tang. Both the tip and the blade edge were broken. E16.

(85) L-shaped staple, used to support drop-hinges, *cf.* at Barhill (Robertson *et. al.*, 1975, 96, no. 2) and Verulamium (Frere, 1972, 180, no. 58). E16.

Three strip fragments, a horseshoe (probably post-Roman), 150 nails (Manning, 1976, type 1) and nine hobnails were also found.

1984 Finds

(86) Ferrule, *cf.* Manning (1976) 21, nos. 24–8. AAB phase 14 hill-wash.

(87) Projectile head. The tip is blunted and bent. The tang is slightly twisted and misshapen. Perhaps a battered or part-made arrowhead, *cf.* Robertson *et. al.* (1975) 99, no. 13 and Manning, (1976), no. 36. AAC phase 14 hill-wash.

(88) L-shaped staple as no. 85. One of the arms has two notches near the corner. These may have been worn by the drop-hinge, or cut in order to lower the hinge. AAC phase 14 hill-wash.

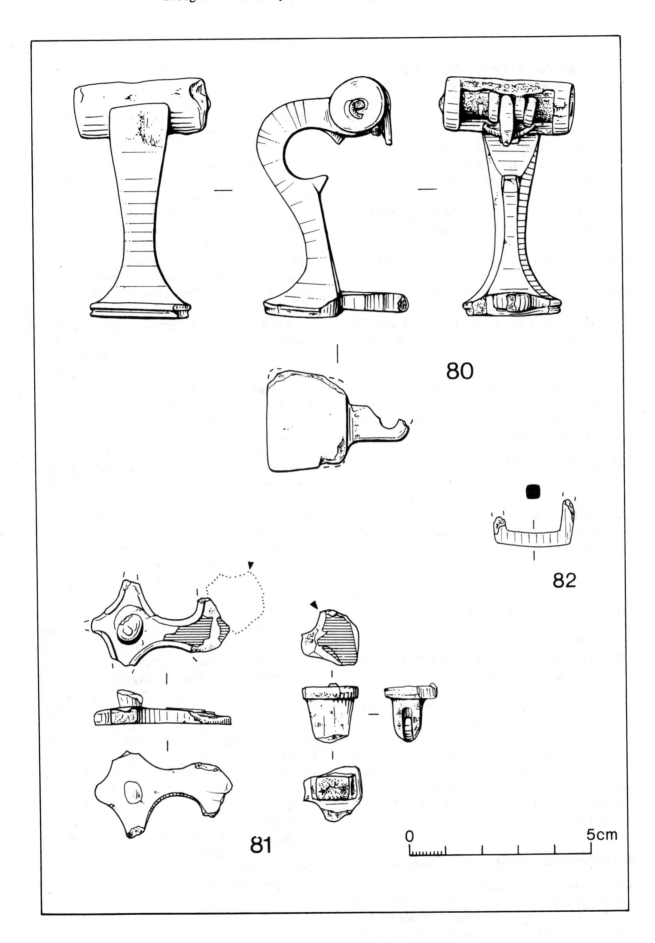

80

82

81

0   5cm

Figure 5:13   Copper Alloy Objects

(89) Square collar, fractured at one corner. A common find on Romano-British sites and used for protecting or binding wooden members, *cf.* Frere (1972) fig. 69 no. 125. Phase 15 ABA cleaning.

(90) Perforated strip, broken at one end, *cf.* bucket handle mount from Barhill, Robertson et al. (1975) 115, no. 72. ACG phase 10 pit.

(91) Knife blade with tang, *cf.* Manning (1976) 37, type II. BBU phase 4 levelling layer.

(92) Knife blade fragment. AAJ phase 11 hill-wash.

(93) Tanged curving blade. The tang is set on the line of the back of the blade and the blade curves backwards. *Cf.* a similar knife from Hod Hill (Brailsford, 1962, G69). ADA phase 11 hill-wash.

The remaining iron fragments comprised unidentifiable lumps, 431 Manning (1976) type I nails, three type II nails and 170 hobnails. These were scattered throughout the contexts.

7. Lead (Figure 5:14)

1983 Finds

(94) Small disc with central perforation. spindle-whorl, *cf.* British Museum Guide (1951) fig. 23, IIId 4, or a lead weight as at Melandra (Bruton, 1907, 106–10). C.

One unidentifiable fragment and a small lump of galena were also found.

1984 Finds

(95) Small disc with central perforation as no. 94. AAC phase 14 hill-wash.

(96) Folded scrap with VO scratched on it. AAE phase 13 hill-wash layer.

10 unidentifiable fragments of lead and 24 small lumps of galena were also found. All the fragments were corroded and most had the appearance of scrap. The lumps of galena were small and none showed any sign of heat treatment.

8. Metalworking Debris *P.M. Barford*

Small quantities of iron slag came from a number of features and these are catalogued in full in the archive. For the typology of slag and other debris noted here see Bayley (1985) and McDonnell (1983).

Justine Bayley examined the possible crucible and her comments are incorporated here.

Some 29 kgs. came from the site. A considerable amount (c. 13 kgs.) came from the floor of Structure 2 (phase 5) and sizeable quantities from the phase 6 layers and the phase 10 enclosure ditch. Little material was recovered from the 1983 excavations.

All of this material was very similar and much of that from phase 7 onwards was possibly redeposited. No slag was found directly associated with hearths ADZ ADY (Phase 8) and AAO (Phase 10).

The debris was almost all iron slag, irregular sub-rounded `lumps' of `smithing' slag predominating. Iron-rich fuel ash slag and denser types of iron slag were very uncommon as were irregular `hearth bottoms'. Only 15 definite examples of the latter were found, but the `lumps' graded into this category. The predominance of slag `lumps' rather than hearth bottoms implies one or perhaps both of two things, firstly that the slag was very viscous or that the operation producing them was not at a high enough temperature to allow the slag to flow to the base of the hearth and form a `hearth bottom'. Most of these `hearth bottoms' were irregular and less than 120mm across. One or two had bellow-blast hollows in the top (eg. one from the phase 6 layers) but there is no reason to doubt that virtually all the slag originated from smithing hearths. No evidence for iron-smelting was found.

A considerable quantity of shapeless iron lumps were also present. Some of these may have been heavily corroded iron objects but some were definitely not. Several seem to have been partially-forged billets of iron bloom. Of particular note was a large, flat sub-rounded piece 80mm x 70mm x 20mm from the floor of Structure 2 (Phase 5). Some of the slag was very porous and iron-rich and is similar to material which would be knocked off a bloom. Some of it contained small, overfired, cindery particles of stone possibly from the hearth or furnace structure or from the coal used as fuel. The nature of the slag implies that blooms were brought to the site, perhaps already partly forged. Whether they were forged into finished objects or into bar-stock for later redistribution cannot be determined. Although no definite forges were identified, the large dump of material in Structure 2 (Phase 5) probably implies the proximity of such a feature. Perhaps a raised forge, of which no other trace now survives, was responsible for this waste.

A small scrap of oxidised fired clay (from the floor of Structure 2) had iron-rich fuel ash slag adhering. This may have been a piece of crucible, but it is more likely to be 'hearth lining'.

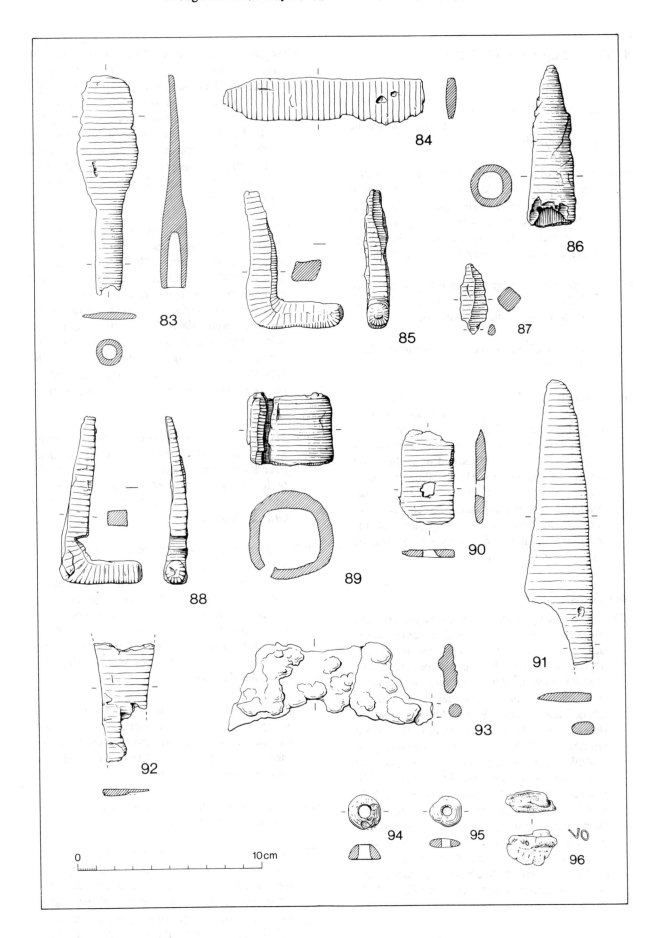

Figure 5:14 Iron and lead Objects

9. Stone (Figures 5:15–5:17)

1983 Finds

(97) three adjoining segments of the upper stone of a flat rotary quern with uneven wear. Millstone Grit. Unstratified.

(98) Segment of upper stone of flat rotary quern, partially perforated halfway down the central socket for the rynd. The upper surface of a handle hole can be seen coming through from the edge but the lower surface has broken away. Unevenly worn. Millstone Grit. Unstratified.

(99) Complete lower stone of flat rotary quern with partially perforated central socket. Unevenly worn. Millstone Grit. Unstratified.

(100–1) Two ballista balls of Millstone Grit. Unstratified.

(102) Naturally rounded, medium-grained Gritstone. The upper surface has a shallow trough of D-shaped section cut into it. The surface of the trough is smooth and it and the surrounding area is scorched and blackened as is the lower surface of the stone. Mould stone for small ingot. X-ray fluorescence analysis at the Ancient Monument laboratory detected traces of copper and lead but the composition of the metal cast in the mould could not be determined with any confidence. C.11.

1984 Finds

(103) Segment of upper stone of flat rotary quern with lip around upper edge and concave upper surface. Around the lip is an inscription SATURNINI. Inscribed quernstones are known from German military sites and on imported lava querns from Binchester and Carlisle (Hassall and Tomlin, 1979, 347 and Wright and Hassall, 1974, 463). Those from Germany are inscribed with the name of a *c(enturia)* or *con(tubernium)* suggesting they denoted the owner (Hassall and Tomlin, 1979, 347). Similarly the Carlisle stone is inscribed CHOV S V (*cohortis* V *centuria* V). An inscribed Sandstone quernstone was found at Chesterholm (Hassall and Tomlin, 1982, 418) indicating British querns were inscribed on occasions, presumably copying the continental practice and giving the owner's name. Millstone Grit. AEN Phase 8 ditch.

(104) Segment of upper stone of flat rotary quern with raised lip around the upper edge. The lower surface is blackened and the upper surface is heat-reddened around the edges and over the lip. There are three grooves, one across and two along the lip, the latter is foreshortened by the break. The central perforation is not circular and, as the stone tapers to only 5mm thick here, may have been enlarged by wear. Millstone Grit. AAT pit.

(105) Upper stone of flat rotary quern, complete except for chipping around the edge. Broken into three segments. The upper surface is concave with a raised lip surrounding a central perforation. The perforation is funnel-shaped with two sockets of semi-circular section for the rynd (Curwen, 1941, 24) running across the grinding surface. A radial groove runs from the outside edge stopping short of the lip around the central perforation. The groove is broken on one side. Millstone Grit. AHA phase 5 floor.

(106) Segment of lower stone of flat rotary quern. The upper surface is smoothed and concave with a low lip surrounding the central, vertical, cylindrical perforation. The walls of the perforation have traces of a ferruginous deposit, perhaps from an iron spindle-sleeve. Millstone Grit. Unstratified.

(107) Segment of a lower stone of a flat rotary quern. The lower surface is slightly heat-reddened. The upper surface has a raised lip around the central perforation. A large chip has been detached at the junction of the lower surface and the central perforation removing most of the wall of the perforation and making it impossible to reconstruct its diameter or length. Millstone Grit. ABA cleaning.

(108) Two adjoining fragments of lower stone of flat rotary quern with central, vertical and cylindrical perforation, splayed towards the base. The lower surface is blackened. Millstone Grit. BEM phase 7 ditch.

(110) Fragment from the edge of a flat rotary quern. Millstone Grit. BEH phase 5 floor.

(111) Segment of upper stone of bun-shaped quern. The lower surface is blackened at the edge and there are traces of a ferruginous deposit. The upper surface is a flattened bun shape with a groove, 3–4mm deep, running around it and a radial handle groove above it. A quern from Leziate, near Lynn, Norfolk, was found with an

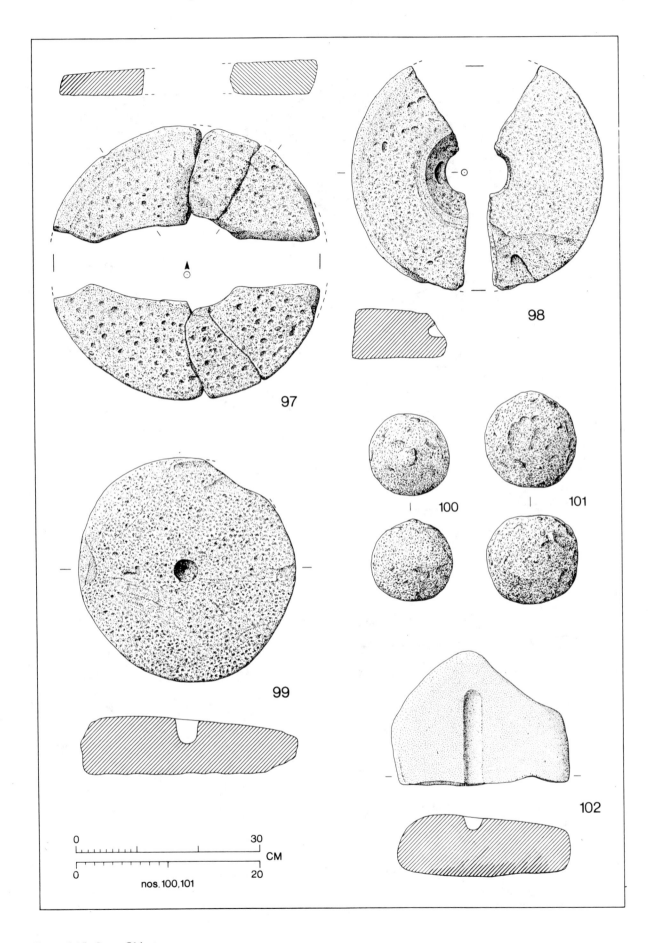

Figure 5:15 Stone Objects

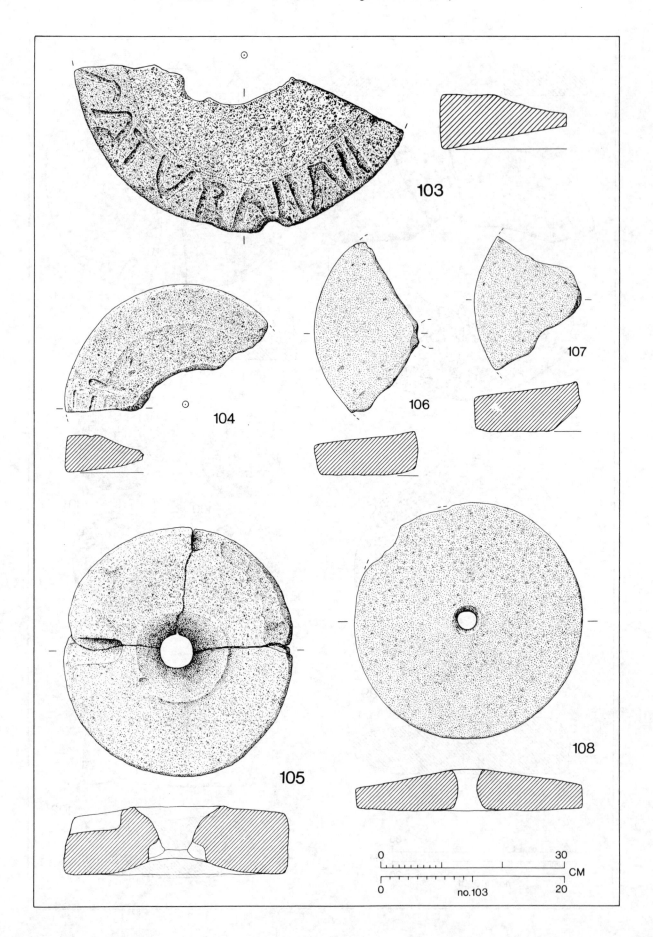

Figure 5:16   Stone Objects

iron hoop in such a groove (see Crummy, 1983, no. 2071). The centre is severely damaged and no central perforation remains. Millstone Grit. AHF phase 5 floor.

(112) Segment of upper stone of bun-shaped quern. The lower surface is smoothed and slightly convex. The upper surface is pecked and bun-shaped, blunted at one end and damaged at the other. There is an off-centre, vertical, cylindrical perforation, for spindle and feed-pipe and a non-perforating, cylindrical handle socket, penetrating laterally. The stone has broken across the off-centre perforation. Millstone Grit. AAF phase 13 hill-wash.

(113) Roundel with ground edge of micaceaous Siltstone. The surfaces are slightly striated. Counter. ABL phase 15 pit.

(114) Rondel with ground edge of fine grained micaceous Sandstone. Rather larger than no. 113. Function unknown. ACN phase 6 levelling layer.

(115) Fragment of oval Limestone tile. The back and one edge are severely flaked. There are three curvilinear notches at the corners which may be broken perforations or accidental breaks. *Cf.* Ling and Courtney (1981) 83 for the use of Sandstone roofing tiles. ABZ phase 12 road patching.

10. Flint

One leaf-shaped arrowhead was found in 1983 and a micro-burin in 1984.

11. Brick and Tile

Some 14kg of brick and tile were recovered from the excavations. An archive catalogue records the material by fabric and form, quantifying by weight. Two fabrics were identified:

A) a relatively soft, orange or red fabric with moderate quantities of fine, well-sorted, clear, angular quartz and medium to very coarse, ill-sorted, rounded or angular brown inclusions, sparse quantities of medium-sized, well-sorted, rounded, soft buff/cream inclusions and coarse, ill-sorted, angular, black inclusions which were hard but friable and very sparse quantities of coarse, very hard, angular black inclusions and coarse Sandstones.

B) a very hard fabric, orange or grey, rather smooth with abundant medium to coarse, ill-sorted, very hard, black, angular or laminar inclusions with conchoidal or laminar fracture, moderate quantities of fine, well-sorted, angular quartz and sparse, medium-size, well-sorted, rounded, soft buff/cream inclusions and brown/black inclusions.

Fabrics A and B were very similar but for the quantity of the very hard, black inclusions in fabric B. These black inclusions resembled shale or chert while those in fabric A resembled iron oxides and soft shales. The buff/cream inclusions resembled siltstones. All these inclusions, as well as the Sandstones and quartz would be common in superficial deposits derived from the Mam Tor beds of the Millstone Grit Series (Stevenson and Gaunt, 1971, 89 and 171) and, therefore, there is no reason to suppose the brick and tile were not manufactured locally. Only 1.5% of the collection was of fabric B suggesting this fabric came from further afield or it was an inferior clay used less often.

Few of the fragments could be classified. Fragments of eight bricks, 11 *tubuli*, one *tegula* and one *imbrex* were identified. Fragments were found throughout the stratigraphic sequence. 40% came from the hill-wash and the only other concentration came from the phase 5 pebble floor. Small quantities were found in the phase 1 and 3 ditches, the levelling layers of phases 4, 6, and 9, some of the phase 7 contexts, the phase 8 road, the phase 10 enclosure ditch and the roads. The presence of small qualities in other contexts and larger concentrations in the are typical of the scatters found on the edge of settlement sites.

12. Fired Clay (Figure 5:17)

13 clay spheres (12 brown and one black), measuring 9–12mm in diameter, were found in 1984 (116–7) and one in 1983 (118). Seven were from phase 14 contexts but six were from phases 4–11. They are thus securely stratified in Roman contexts. Their function is unknown but comparable balls were found at Sewingshields, Northumberland (Haigh and Savage, 1984, 96) and Brough-on-Humber (Wacher, 1969, fig. 47, no. 8).

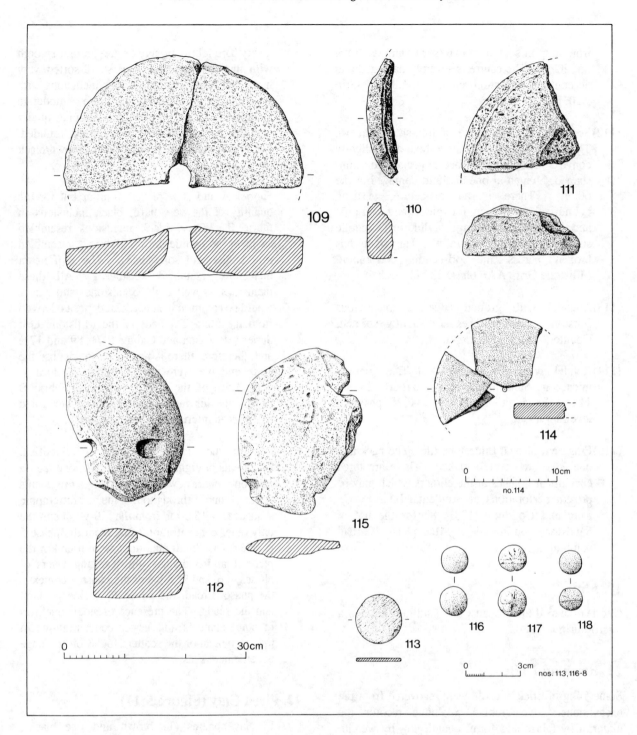

Figure 5:17   Stone and Fired Clay Objects

The Altars

In 1979 two altars were discovered in the course of construction work. The smaller altar was recovered from dumped spoil and its precise point of origin is not known. The larger altar was dug out by hand, a process recorded in a series of photographs. The resulting pit [ABL] lay on the northern limit of the 1984 excavation and thus could be examined archaeologically. The position, approximate level and

In 1979 two altars were discovered in the course of construction work. The smaller altar was recovered from dumped spoil and its precise point of origin is not known. The larger altar was dug out by hand, a process recorded in a series of photographs. The resulting pit [ABL] lay on the northern limit of the 1984 excavation and thus could be examined archaeologically. The position, approximate level and attitude of the altar is known and its stratigraphic location can be suggested. The altar was found lying face down, its long axis west–east and its top to the east, below 0.5m of hill-wash. There was no evidence to suggest that the altar had been deliberately buried in antiquity; it is unlikely that the modern pit would have destroyed all trace of any earlier pit or feature into which the altar had been placed. Rather it would appear that the altar had been deposited upon a contemporary ground surface and subsequently buried by the formation of hill-wash, during phases 11–15 .

The large altar (Plate 5)

The altar is of Gritstone, 0.48m wide, 0.43m thick and 1.09m high. On top of the altar is a shallow, circular, bowl-shaped depression, the focus, to contain offerings or a sacrificial fire. This is flanked by two bolsters or scrolls, which are conventional representations of wooden faggots. The first line of the inscription is cut upon an ansate panel, immediately below. The remaining 7 lines are cut upon a recessed panel, forming the main body of the altar, above a plinth. The altar is weathered. A recent laser enhanced examination of the altar, has not altered the reading suggested by Hassal (1980, 404), which is reproduced below.

The inscription reads:

1 HERCVLI[..]G
2 [..]RESTITVTIONEM
3 PS
4 ACAEP ASC[..]
5 [...]
6 PROCULUS
7 PRAEF POSVIT
8 IDEMQVEDEDICAV
9 VIT

This inscription can in part be restored as : *Herculi [Au]g [ob] restitutionem....Proculus Praef(ectus) posuit idem dedicavit*, and translated 'To Hercules Augustus...Proculus the praefect set this up and dedicated it because of his restoration of...'. The dedication to Hercules Augustus (line 1), the Emperor Commodus 176–192 A.D., has not previously been recorded in Britain, but it occurs in other provinces. The phrase in line 2 occurs in a dedication to the Capitoline Triad set up to record the restoration of a municipal *capitolium* (*CIL* xi 1545=*ILS* 3084) and in a dedication to Fortuna set up to record the restoration of a bath building (*CIL* iii 789). The two letters comprising line 3 appear to be a later insertion. Although the restoration and completion of bath buildings is sometimes recorded upon altars set up within them, these are invariably dedicated to Fortune (e.g. *RIB* 730 and 1212) and it seems impossible to read *Deae Fortunae* in line 1 and a word for shrine or temple should therefore be required as on (*RIB* 1396)

and *Britannia* vii (1976), 378–9, no 2 both recording the restoration of temples. It is tempting to suggest A SO[LO] at the end of line 4. Line 5 will have contained the *praenomen, cognomen* and perhaps filiation of the dedicant, a *praefectus* or commander of an auxiliary cohort, possibly the garrsion of Brough-on-Noe. The altar, dating to the late 2nd century, would appear to belong to the second phase of military occupation at Brough and may commemorate the restoration of a first period structure, possibly a temple.

The small altar (not illustrated)

The top and sides of the small, Gritstone altar (0.55m high and 0.25m wide) are damaged; the damage probably results from its reuse as a building stone. The central panel, which may have formerly contained a painted design or inscription is recessed.

Discussion

From the military zone there are many examples of army officers who, like the *curiales* of the civilian zone, restored temples and dedicated altars (Henig, 1984, 239; Rodwell, 1980, 79–90). Elaborate altars, such as the large altar from Brough-on-Noe, are not infrequently recovered from *vici*, but are rarely *in situ* and few temples have been excavated. The stone packed pit [BAF] on the upper terrace, could have supported such an altar, from which position the altar could have fallen. However, it is probable that the large altar was set up within a temple, but the original location and the processes which removed it and deposited it face down on the lower terrace in the third century or later, are quite unknown. While it is posssible that a temple lay close by the excavated areas , no direct evidence was found. The recovery of the second, smaller altar from close by need not strengthen this possibility; collection and reuse of stone could account for the presence of both.

Environmental Evidence

Charcoal Report *Graham Morgan*

Fourteen samples were submitted for analysis. The charcoals were identified from freshly broken sections under 20x or 100x magnification. The following species were present: Hazel *Corylus avellana*, Oak *Quercus spec.*, Field Maple *Acer campestre*, Poplar-type *Populus spec.*, Gorse-type *Ulex spec.*, Blackthorn *Prunus spinosa*, Hawthorn-type *Crataegus spec.*. It should be noted that it is often impossible to satisfactorily distinguish betwen the following: species: Hazel and Alder, Poplar and Willow, and Broom and Gorse.

Few conclusions can be drawn from this small group of charcoals. The Oak, which was fast grown, probably comes from open and/or damp areas; Gorse (or Broom) is also characterstic of open sites, but the remainder are general woodland species. Such habitats are still represented in the vicinity of Brough-on-Noe.

Charred Plant Remains *Lisa Moffat*

Ten samples were submitted for analysis. Rapid, preliminary assessment confirmed that charred plant material was present, but the quantities were insufficient to warrant exhaustive analysis. The following were represented: Barley (*Hordeum sp.*), Wheat (*Tritium sp.*), Hazel (*Corylus avellana*), Cinquefoil (*Potentilla sp.*), and an unidentifiable *Compositae*.

Animal Bone *Mary Harman*

Only a small amount of bone was recovered, the majority calcined and fragmentary, suggesting that the acidity of the soil had prejudiced survival. No detailed analysis was undertaken, but the bones of cattle, sheep, pig and horse, were identified. Material from the 1983 excavations, which is unstratified and may be recent, includes, calf foot bones, which could represent a hide, and a frontal from a polled sheep; the latter is unusual in the Roman period.

Timber identification *Dr C. R. Salisbury*

The base of a rounded post, 270mm long and 150mm diameter, had been cut level, but there were no identifiable tool marks. The centre of the post had decayed and the top had rotted to a point. The timber was Oak, which was fast-grown. There were 18 rings, insuffient for dendrochronological analysis.

Conclusions

No archaeological features were observed in the exposed strata to the east of the area excavated in 1984 and no Roman material was reported during the extension of the farmyard to the north east; it seems probable that the areas examined in 1983 and 1984, 250m from the fort, are on the edge of the *vicus*. Occupation (phases 1–3) began in the early-to mid-second century with the construction of the upper terrace and road and the east and western enclosures on the lower terrace. There are few finds and little to show how the area was used in the initial phases (1–3); it may have been agricultural. The initial phases of occupation are probably contemporary with the reoccupation and reconstruction of the fort (Period IIa) *c*.154–158 A. D. Evidence of earlier occupation, contemporary with the Flavian (Period I) fort, has been recovered from outside of the south east gate

(Bishop *et al*. this volume) suggesting that a *vicus*, as at Melandra (Webster, 1971, 79–80) and Little Chester, Derby, (Wheeler, 1985b, 300) developed soon after the fort was constructed. It is assumed that *vici* were established at the same time as, or very shortly after, their forts (Sommer,1984, 11) although the evidence is not extensive (Casey, 1982, 124).

The principal occupation of the area excavated in 1984 (Phases 4–11) is dated to the late-second to mid-third century. An assemblage of similar date was recovered from the 1983 excavation. Both sites have structures, either dwellings or outbuildings, and evidence of some metalworking. Some iron smithing, on a minor scale, was carried out; partially forged iron-blooms were brought to the site and forged into bar-stock or objects. The ingot mould (102 in Figure 5:15) suggests some working of non-ferrous metals, again on a minor scale as there is no raw or waste material. There is no evidence that lead was worked. Excavations outside of the south east gate of the fort have also produced evidence of ironworking. Other *vici* (Casey 1982, 129; Sommer, 1984, 35), including Little Chester, Derby (Dool 1985a, 166–175) and Manchester (Jones and Grealey, 1974, 148–50) have produced evidence of iron working and an industry, comprising an 'agglomeration of small workshops...nucleated around a mercantile, semi-urban centre', has been postulated (Cleere, 1982, 128). At Brough-on-Noe there is insufficient evidence to show that iron working served more than immediate domestic requirements. There is little evidence of other activities. Some brick and tile was produced locally, but not pottery; the *vicus* drew on largely the same sources of pottery as Derby and Manchester. Many of the building materials, timber for posts, Limestone, Gritstone and river gravel, for fences, structures and roads, could be got from the immediate environs of the fort. Coal and iron may have travelled a few miles. There is evidence, quernstones and charred seeds, for the consumption of grain and cattle, sheep, pigs and horses were present; it is possible that some of the *vicani* were farmers; it is assumed that the fort had an area of land to be tilled, but evidence of agricultural activity is rarely found in *vici* (Bennet, 1983, 206–7; Casey, 1982, 129). Regarding the arrangement and types of structures located in 1983–4, there is little evidence of overall planning; the development of roads on the lower terrace appears organic and without further excavation it cannot be suggested that iron working was zoned away from other areas.

The principal phases of activity in the areas excavated in 1983–4 belong to the late-second to mid-third century and it is probable that the settlement at Brough-on-Noe attained its full size at this period. Both the date of the settlement, its size and its components, strip buildings, a large (bath/*mansio*) building, a cemetery, minor iron working and such chance finds as an elaborate altar, suggest that the development of Brough-on-Noe is quite typical and can be compared with other *vici* in Northern Britain. The third century has been seen as the heyday of the *vici*, but there is growing evidence of shrinkage and desertion, in the latter part of the century, which increases in the fourth century (Breeze, 1982, 148; Casey, 1982, 124; Jones, R. F., 1984, 41).

There is no evidence of occupation in the areas excavated in 1983-4 after the mid-third century. The abandonment of a peripheral area of the *vicus* in the later-third and fourth century need not necessarily have serious implications for the remainder of the settlement. A minor decline in the population of the *vicus* or a slight shift in the settlement, could account for the desertion of the excavated areas.

Acnowledgments

The Trent & Peak Archaeological Trust is grateful to Mr. Eyre for permission to excavate, to the Historic Buildings and Monuments Commission for England for funding the 1984 excavation, and to the Peak Park Joint Planning Board for funding post excavation analysis of the 1983 excavation. The author is indebted to the excavation team, and in particular to L. Cliffe, A.G. Kinsley and P. Flynn, and to all who have assisted with the project and in particular D.A. Allen, P.M. Barford, P. Beswick, K.S. Brassil, M.J. Dearne, B. Dickinson, M. Harman, D. Kennedy, R.S. Leary, J.A. Lloyd, D. Mackreth, L. Moffat, G. Morgan, K.R. Smith, C.R. Salisbury, and D.F. Williams. The published drawings are by Richard Sheppard. M.J. Dearne, R S Leary and J.A. Lloyd have commented upon an earlier draft of this paper.

6. Geophysical Survey and Excavation in the *Vicus* of Brough-on-Noe (*Navio*) 1986

Keith Branigan and Martin J. Dearne

Introduction

A large scale geophysical survey directed by one of the authors (M.J.D.) and funded by the Peak Park Planning Board and the former Department of Ancient History and Classical Archaeology, University of Sheffield was carried out in April 1986 on land west, north west and south west of the fort at Brough-on-Noe in advance of the afforestation of a number of areas by the land owners, Blue Circle Cement PLC (Figure 6: 1). The results of this survey indicated the desirability of trial excavations which were undertaken by M.J.D. and students of the former Department of Ancient History and Classical Archaeology in June and July 1986 with the kind permission of the land owners and their tennant, Mr. T. J. P. Eyre. This work confirmed the archaeological character and importance of some of the features revealed by the survey and three further weeks of more intensive excavation were directed by both authors for English Heritage in September 1986.

Geophysical Survey

A total of 18, 000 m^2 (1. 8 hectares) were surveyed in 20 X 20m squares representing the majority of the threatened area in the vicinity of the fort and further areas near to the fort not threatened by the afforestation (Figure 6: 1). The most north westerly area to be afforested was not surveyed since the liklihood of archaeological features being present was considered to be low and, especially given that much of the area was covered with very prominent ridge and furrow, several practical problems presented themselves. The survey was undertaken with Digital Impedance Ground Surveying (D. I. G. S.) mark 1 and 2 equipment designed and built by Dr. A. T. Barker of the Department of Medical Physics and Clinical Engineering, University of Sheffield, mounted on rigs built by Mr. M. A. Cruse of the Department of Psychology, University of Sheffield, to both of whom particular thanks are offered. The readings were processed using the 'Geophys' suite of computer programmes designed by Dr. M. C. Bishop to produce dot density and three dimentional images. A general topographic survey was also made to aid the interpretation of the results.

A number of factors made interpretation of the results of the survey difficult. Its execution was hampered by the organisational necessity of carrying it out in April during a period of high rainfall and the saturation of the ground for much of the time is likely to have decreased the potential sensitivity of the resistivity technique used. Further, the nature of the clayey subsoil on the site was less than ideal for the application of the technique. The site is highly variable in its micro-topography, the most important area surveyed (Figure 6: 1 Field 2) representing for the most part a hill slope, and this is likely to have introduced entirely natural variations into the data. Further distortions were caused by known relic field boundaries, pipelines and particularly by relic ridge and furrow ploughing. Given these problems only extensive cross referencing of the data to, in particular topographic information allowed the identification of potential archaeological features. Indeed the probable decrease in sensitivity caused by adverse ground and weather conditions may be reflected by the failure of the survey to identify any fort ditches.

Nevertheless no significant features appeared to be present in fields 1, 3 and 4 (Figure 6: 1) except for an indistinct negative feature later examined by Trench H. Field 2 in contrast yielded a number of possible features. The most important was a long wide band of high readings at the south end of the field (Figure 6: 2 No. 1). Although its continuity was interrupted by relic ridge and furrow and other factors it clearly represented a genuine and significant feature. Excavation (trenches C, K and L) subsequently revealed that it was far wider than the geophysical survey would indicate and was caused by a deep colluvial deposit in a former water course. The apparent southerly edge to it on Figure 6: 2 was not explained by excavation.

Some seven other features were noted from the survey results, mostly indistinct linear groups of unexpectedly high readings. A number of these were subsequently examined by trial trenches, though two (Figure 6: 2 Nos. 3 and 4) lay outside the threatened area and so were not examined. Of those examined Figure 6: 2 No. 2 was the most clearly defined and was demonstrated by trench D to be a two-phase channel. The other features examined (not marked on Figure 6: 2 since they were indistinct) were mainly revealed by trench G as of natural origin. In this eastern part of field 2 the natural included many shale blocks and slabs in linear alignments and these corresponded to the anomalies in the survey data. One other possible feature was demonstrated by excavation

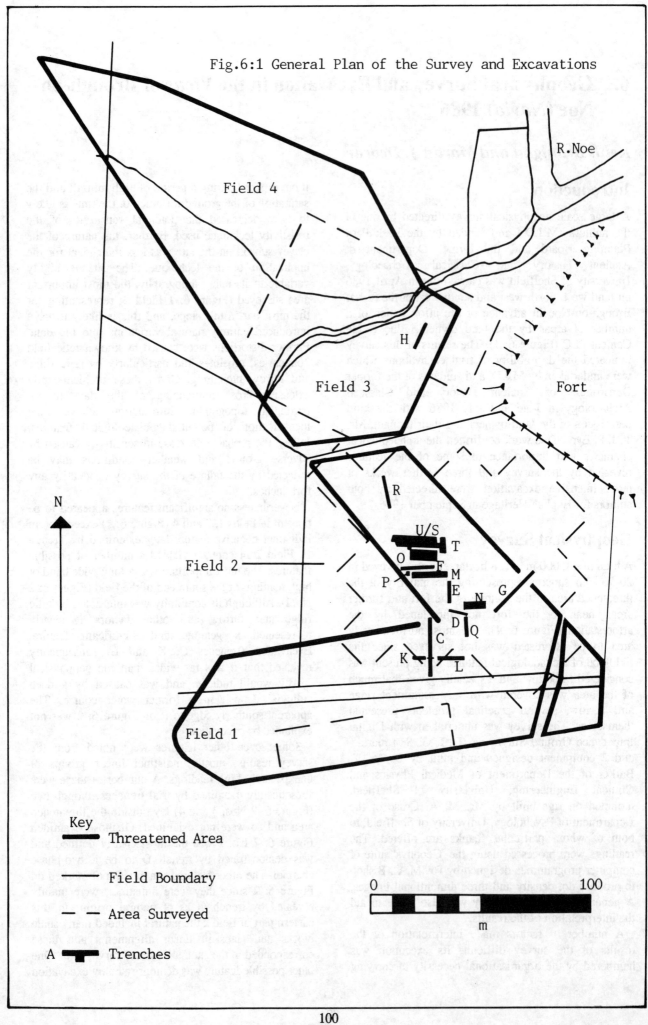

Fig.6:1 General Plan of the Survey and Excavations

R.Noe

Field 4

Field 3

H

Fort

R

U/S

O   T

F
P   M   E   N   G

D   Q
C
K   L

Field 2

Field 1

N

Key

Threatened Area

Field Boundary

Area Surveyed

A   Trenches

0   100

m

Fig.6:2 Field 2:Dot Density Plot of Resistivity Results

Feature 2

Feature 3

Feature 4

Feature 1

N

0   m   40

to be illusory. Although an area of higher readings occured in the region of trench complex F/M/O/P/S/T/U there was no indication that the area was particularly significant, the exploratory trench F being cut in this area only in the hope that Figure 6: 2 no. 3 might continue into the threatened area.

Excavation

The excavations took place in, respectively, early and late summer 1986 during periods of principally fine weather but without the need for extensive or repeated re-wetting and, whilst the nature of the undisturbed subsoil and the fills of many of the cut features were very similar making their differentiation at times problematic only in the case of trenches D and E where excessive drying and cracking occured in the later stages of the trial excavations are any features likely to have been missed. Throughout the topsoil was found to be a thin dark grey-brown humic layer underlain by a thin dark grey-brown subsoil with a zone of small rounded stones. The underlying natural was found in almost all cases to be a heavy, sterile yellow very clayey silt, in some places gleyed to varying shades of grey and blue grey. However, in trenches G and N the natural also contained significant inclusions of slabs of shattered country rock (Limestone Shale), often in lateral alignments. In a number of trenches modern land drains capped with redeposited natural or stiff dark brown clay were identified.

In all cases the topsoil was removed mechanically and in trenches S, T and U the rescue nature of the excavation meant that a limited amount of the upper stratigraphy may have been slightly truncated. However, all features were excavated by hand, though in trenches F and M particularly it was only possible to examine some features by means of areas of sectioning. Time also prevented the excavation of all trenches fully to the natural.

The stratigraphy of trench group C/K/L and of trenches D, E, G, and H cannot be related directly to each other nor to trench group F/M/O/P/S/T/U where most features occured and no significant stratigraphy was encountered in trenches N, Q or R. There are considerable problems in establishing the relative phasing of many features in trench group F/M/O/P/S/T/U. Time did not allow a full area as opposed to multiple trench excavation in this area and this exacerbated the problems of phasing the features, few of which occured in more than one trench and the stratigraphic links between some of which were obscured by modern land drains. The relatively short duration of the site's usage also means that pottery dates are of little use in phasing. Although three broad phases can be established in this trench group the majority of features clearly belong to phase 1. This

phase has been sub-divided into a number of sub-phases and a group of features which cannot be related to this scheme of sub-division. However, in many cases the allocation of features to sub-phases must remain to some extent inferential and which of the features were in use contemporaneously frequently remains unknown.

Trenches F/M/O/P/S/T/U

Phase la (Figure 6: 3)

Three probable clay extraction pits (M27, M28 and O29) may represent the initial usage of the area examined by trenches F/M/O/P/S/T/U. They lay in the east of trenches M and O and, although little of O29 could be examined, all seemed to be very irregular, fairly large cuts into the natural of maximum excavated depth 43cm. All the pits displayed characteristic 'lumpy' irregular bases and were filled with very similar deposits of iron stained clayey silts with frequent charcoal inclusions but few finds (M5, M6, M22, O8 and O9). At least one seems to have been deliberately re-used as a sump, a shallow U-shaped channel (Ml9) typically some 70cm wide, again with a 'lumpy' base, running across the west end of/into M27 from the north. Its fill (M7) was largely indistinguishable from the fill of the pit.

Further west in trench M a rather serpentine, sub-rectangular channel (M18) running obliquely across the trench was cut into the natural. It was 18cm deep and up to 75cm wide and filled with M8, a material very similar to the fills of the clay extraction pits. This also formed a thin spread for at least 70cm to the west suggesting that the channel had silted up and that drainage water had continued to flow along a broader course. The channel was not traced further north in trench F but may have been truncated by later features; it may however have been represented in trench O by O20, an otherwise unphased irregular, slightly narrower channel which deepened as it ran south from a wide, shallow natural gully in the north east corner of the trench. M18 may have been replaced by another channel (M24) further west which was largely removed by later features and was not traced in the south of trench M due to lack of time. However, a truncated fragment of its northern continuation (F21) was recorded in plan. The channel seems likely to have been similarly serpentine to its possible predecessor, some 35cm deep and 47cm+ wide with a flat bottom, vertical western and sloping eastern faces. Its fill (M25) was a light grey silty clay with much charcoal.

A group of confused features partly disturbed by a modern land drain on the south side of trench O seem to represent the primary activity in the rest of the area and limited evidence suggests that they may have heen broadly contemporary with at least parts of an

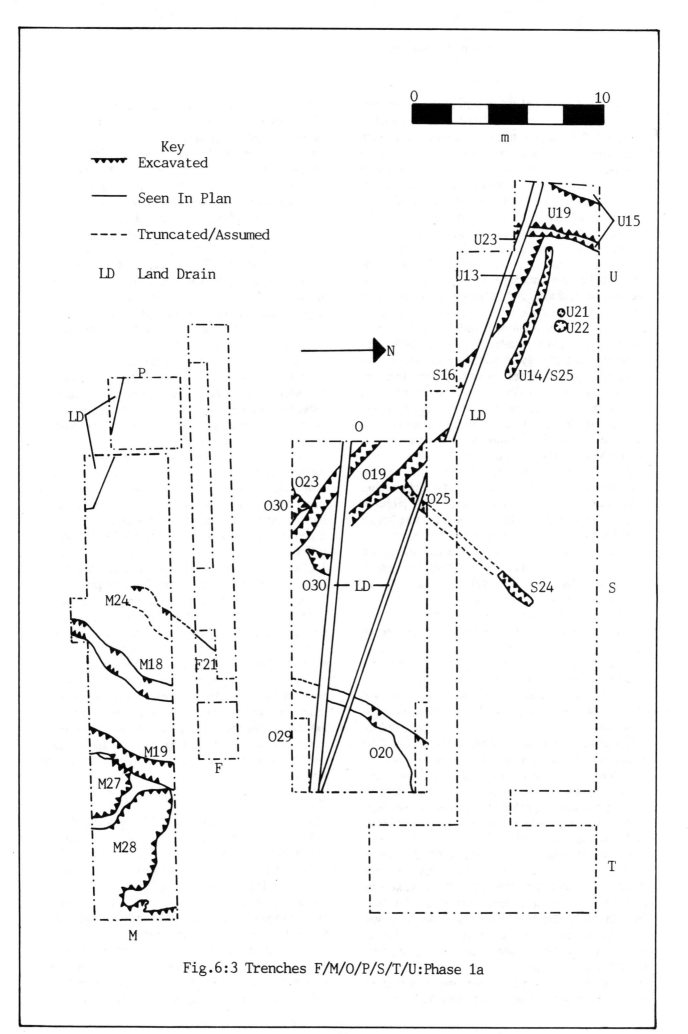

Fig.6:3 Trenches F/M/O/P/S/T/U:Phase 1a

equally confused set of ?beam slots and other features. The earliest and least disturbed feature was O23, a steep sided, U-shaped cut up to 23cm deep and 56cm wide crossing the south west corner of trench O. It was not traced to the south east in trench F but might be represented to the north west in trenches S and U by U13 and/or S16, features very disturbed by a modern land drain. O23 did not appear to be a drainage channel; numbers of large stones occured along its base and it may well have been filled contemporaneously with a number of beam slots (below). Perhaps contemporary with O23 were two definite beam slots at right angles to each other (O19 and 25). Both were rectangular in section, the former *c.* 40cm wide and 14cm deep and the latter *c.* 25cm wide and slightly shallower, though both had probably been slightly truncated by machineing. A vestigal fragment almost certainly of the latter slot considerably to the north east (S24) overlay a filled void probably caused by the grubbing out of a tree root. A very distorted fragment of the former slot was also found immediately north west but its truncation by a modern land drain and removal by later features indicated only that it originally continued for less than another 1. 5m. Little can be said of the building represented by these beam slots. O19 probably represented a main building line of maximum length *c.* 6m while O25/S24 was probably a partition of 6. 5m+ in length. However, beyond the fact that it was of sill beam construction and the probability that it was rectangular little can be said of the building. O23 seems still to have been open when two irregular cuts (O30) were made either side of its south east end. These cuts and the bottom of the south east end of O23 were filled with O28, a distinctive clayey silt of very light grey or even white colour with occasional charcoal flecks and one large, concerted charcoal area (perhaps a hearth rake out). It was also spread over the natural between O23 and O30 and appeared to be a dump, including an almost complete black burnished pie dish base (Figure 6: 10 No. 21). The remainder of O23 and the beam slots O19 and 25 were filled, rather than silted, by the same light grey-brown, slightly olive, fairly sterile clayey silt (O4, 15 and 16) probably immediately after the deposition of O28. The homogeneity of the fills of the beam slots and the main part of O23 represents the main evidence for their being broadly contemporaneous with each other. However, whether they had any functional relationship is unclear. O23 is unlikely to represent any structural component of the building represented by the beam slots, especially if it was identical to U13/S16, but it is possible that it represented a boundary ditch. The nature of the fills of O23 and the beam slots also provides the only evidence for the phasing of other possibly structural features in trenches S and U, for these features were

filled by the same homogeneous dumped material. They were however badly disturbed by a modern land drain in some cases, partly truncated by machineing and form no coherent whole. They included U13/S16 which we have noted might equate to O23; though at the only relatively undisturbed point available for examination it was slightly shallower and much less steep sided. Possibly parallel to it slightly to the south a very small fragment of a ?beam slot (U23) was noted and to the north a roughly parallel but slightly curved slot (U14/S25) was found. It was typically 28cm wide and up to 9cm deep as excavated (though it had probably been truncated by machineing) and of slightly irregular broad U-shaped profile. Butt ends were found at both ends of the feature. North of this were two adjacent possible post holes, again probably truncated. U22 was 50cm in diameter and survived only to 3cm in depth, while U21 was 20cm in diameter and survived to 5cm in depth. In addition to these features the same filling material appeared to have been used to level at least two natural irregularities in the ground surface.

However, the most important of the features linked by this homogeneous fill was U15, a cut up to 67cm deep and over 1. 8m wide which ran nearly north-south at the west end of trench U. In profile it had a steep eastern side and gentler western face with a step or ledge near the top (Figure 6: 9). Whether it fulfilled any structural role was not clear, however U13 may have been cut integrally with it (though this could not be certainly ascertained). Subsequent to the filling of U15 a second, more regularly U-shaped cut (Ul9) was made along its line. This was 1. 35m wide, perhaps broadening to the south, and 41cm deep and was the only feature in the area to contain a different fill (U4). This fill was a dark grey-brown clayey silt with lumps of redeposited natural, occasional charcoal flecks and frequent medium sized stones. A large area of its top was covered by redeposited natural. Again the fill appeared to be a deliberate dump of material not a silting and the cut's function may have been as a large construction trench or similar.

Phase lb (Figure 6: 4)

Stratigraphically later than the 'clay extraction' pits, and the drainage channels in trenches F and M, though not certainly later than features such as O23 and the beam slots etc. in trenches O, S and U was a V-shaped ditch (M23/F25/O21/T9). It was the only feature providing a fixed point in the stratigraphy of more than two trenches and ran in a slightly irregular line north east-south west for at least 16. 5m. It was examined at several points but was best preserved in trench M where it was 57cm deep and up to lm wide with steep sides, a step on the east side and a 30cm wide rectangular ?cleaning slot at its base (Figure 6:

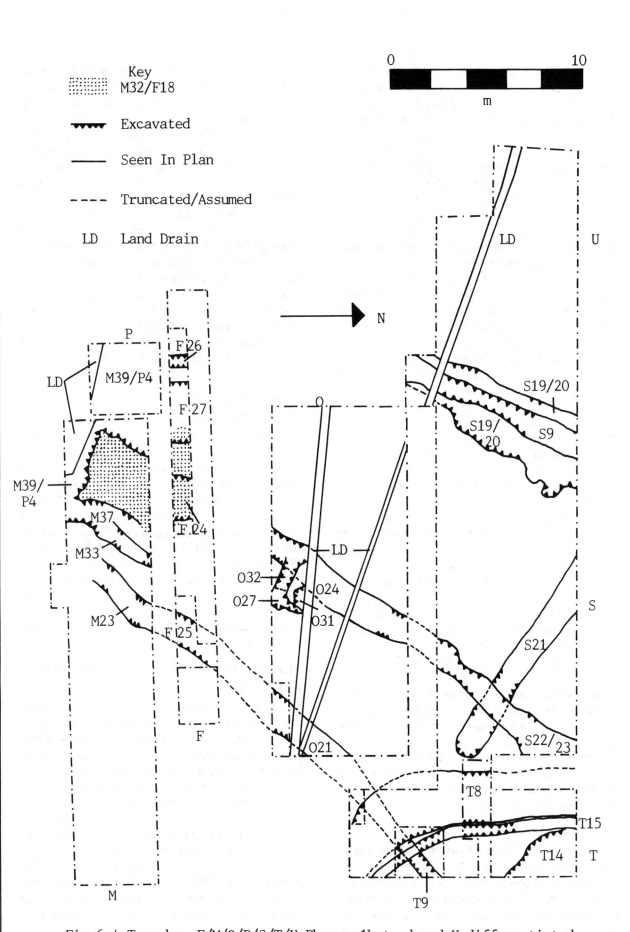

M32/F18

Excavated

Seen In Plan

Truncated/Assumed

LD   Land Drain

0   10

m

Fig.6:4 Trenches F/M/O/P/S/T/U:Phases 1b to d and Undifferentiated
Phase 1 Features

9). Its profile and dimensions were slightly different in other exposures, most notably its width was only *c.* 60cm in trench T, but this was partly accounted for by its course crossing other filled features at some points and its general shape and rectangular slotted base remained constant. However, the step in the eastern side was only noted in trench M, perhaps indicating localised cleaning/recutting. Its fill (M26/F20/O5/T5) was a generally mid grey, silty clay which had gleyed to olive or blue grey in some cases, with few inclusions. In trench T beyond a natural break of slope a second fill (T4) was detected above the main one and included lumps of redeposited natural , caps of which were also found both here and in trench M. The ditch appears to have fulfilled a drainage function but the presence of T4 and the redeposited natural caps may suggest that it was deliberately backfilled once it had become nearly obsolete.

Truncating the phase la beam slot O19, though the point of truncation was partly obscured by a modern land drain, was a later feature S19/20. It was an irregular, lateral feature running north east-south west, from *c.* 1. 5-3m wide with irregular edges, especially on the east and an irregular base superficially similar to the phase la 'clay extraction' pits. Its depth was generally *c.* 17cm but in one area it included a short gully up to 55cm deep. Its fill (S6/14/17) was a mid to dark grey clayey silt, moderately iron stained with charcoal inclusions but its purpose was obscure. Probably very shortly after its cutting a channel (S9) was cut along the same course. It was 55-95cm wide, 7-12cm deep, flat bottomed and with a gentle profile. Its fill was nearly indistinguishable from that of S19/20 suggesting that the latter acted as an overflow for this drainage channel. Irregularities in the bottom of the drainage channel, in contrast to those in the base of S19/20, had the appearance of cattle trample in wet conditions.

Perhaps also belonging to phase lb, though it could equally belong to phase la, was T14, an irregular pit of maximum depth 31cm almost certainly deliberately cut to receive its fill (T6). This was a mid grey or grey-brown clayey silt with patches made up of 50–70% charcoal including identifiable twigs, and elsewhere it included much charcoal, tile/ daub flecks and medium to large stones.

Phase lc (Figure 6: 4)

Subsequent to the filling of the phase lb V-shaped ditch and the deposition of T6 a U-shaped cut (T15), 42cm wide and up to 20cm deep, was made along the middle of trench T, swinging east at its southern end. Stratigraphically after this event, but from the homogeneity of their fills perhaps virtually contemporaneously a very large V-shaped ditch (T8) was cut following its line to its west (Figure 6: 9) and

bordering a natural break of slope immediately west of its edge. It seems likely that T15 acted either as a marking out line, or less likely as a slight construction trench for a pallisade/slight fence, associated with T8. The ditch itself was up to 89cm deep and 1. 85m+ wide, of steep V-shaped profile and may have had a rectangular base (though this was hard to confirm since it penetrated the zone of shattered shale country rock below the natural). Its size, shape and position at a break of slope argues for a land demarcation or even defensive function, although its fill (T2), as with that of T15, was a very clayey, gleyed and ironstained silt in three identifiable horizons with quantities of pottery which had probably resulted from continuous silting.

Perhaps to be allocated to the same phase was a shallower U-shaped ditch (S21) which ran north west from a butt end at the break of slope just west of T8. It was *c.* 95cm wide and up to 40cm deep and filled with S2/5, a dark grey to grey-brown very clayey silt.

Phase ld (Figure 6: 4)

After S21 had silted up, though quite possibly while T8 was still open, a much shallower channel (S22/23/O24) was cut across it and ran north east-south west for at least 13m, truncating some phase la features in trench O. It was flat bottomed and broadened and deepened from *c.* 60-70cm wide and *c.* 3cm deep in much of trench S to lm+ wide and 23cm deep at the southern edge of trench O, but it probably terminated immediately to the south. Like S21 its fill (S3/4/O22) reflected a drainage function.

Few other cut features belong to this phase. O32, a narrow, shallow U-shaped slot or channel that remained open into phase 2, O27, a small ?pit or slot fragment, and O31, a very slight pit were cut but none appeared very significant.

Phase 1 Activity at the West End of Trenches F and M (Figure 6: 4)

Two or three sub-phases of activity were encountered at the west end of trenches F and M which, though certainly earlier than phase two, could not be related to the division of the rest of phase l; except that the latest of the activity occured after phase la. The earliest activity in this area may have been the cutting of two parallel north-south features, F26 and F27, into the natural at the west end of trench F. Both were examined only for half the width of the trench and are presumed to have been removed by later activity to the south; northwards no trench intersected the postulated line of F26 for *c.* 12m but the absence of traces of F27 in trench O suggests that it at least cannot have continued far to the north on the same alignment. In form F26 was a U-shaped ditch or slot 42cm wide and up to 13cm deep filled by redeposited natural contaminated only by charcoal flecks. Just to the east F27 was a much wider feature in all 2. 2m across. It had a very gently sloping western side and a steep eastern one and, although it could not be fully excavated, the indications were that the cut was of ditch or channel, perhaps Vshaped, form in its lower, eastern part. Its full depth could not be guaged but may have been in excess of 50cm. Its fill (F23) was a gleyed clay or clayey silt, perhaps redeposited natural, with very concentrated and compacted areas of charcoal.

A third cut further east in Trench F was F24, a largely unexcavated ?pit with one curved and one straight side. This feature may have belonged to a second sub-phase for it was filled by F18 which formed part of a general layer that also appeared to seal part of the fill of F27. This second sub-phase general layer (M32/F18) covered much of the middle of trench F and west end of trench M and was over 15cm deep in places, though it thinned towards the west. It consisted of light grey silty clay with a browny tinge and moderate, in places frequent, charcoal inclusions and ironstaining. It also contained considerable quantities of pottery including substantial parts of vessels.

Subsequently a large pit (M39/P4) was cut, little of the edges of which were observed but which covered the whole of trench P and part of trench M and clearly continued to the south though not far to the north. Where observed the sides of the pit were sloped and its base was irregular, but at the western side of trench P it was considerably deeper than elsewhere its base having been deepened with a vertical sided cut. In the main area of the pit its depth was up to 33cm but the deeper section and the area near the channels (below) was up to 48cm deep. It appears to have acted as a drainage sump as well probably as a rubbish pit, for a 70cm wide, 48cm deep channel (M37) led into it from the north and was part of the same cut as the pit. This channel was recut (as M33) when it had silted up. The first channel was sub-rectangular, broad and flat bottomed and the recut broadly U-shaped, narrowing from *c*. 70cm to *c*. 45cm as it went north, and some 43cm deep. The pit had two fills, P2 and M38/P3. P2 was a light grey clayey silt with very frequent ironstaining and charcoal inclusions which appeared to have built up rapidly and included few finds except for some large stone slabs lying against the vertical cut. It was found only in the deeper western part of the pit. The main fill (M38/P3) was a mid to dark grey clayey silt with quantities of grit and charcoal. It also produced considerable quantities of pottery, ironwork, slag and other finds. The fill to the initial channel (M36) was identical to this but with few finds. The recut channel, which may have extended the pit slightly to the east as well, was filled with M35/15A, a mid grey brown clayey silt with some charcoal only distinguished from M15 (below)

by its slightly siltier nature, perhaps suggesting that it accrued in phase 2. Neither of the channels into the pit was traced further north.

Phase 2 (Figure 6: 5)

Phase 2 is represented by a group of spreads of material containing few finds in contrast to deposits such as M32/F18 or M38/P3. These deposits occured over the vast majority of trench F (F8, 9, 10 ?and 12), the west end of trench M (M15) and over all but the north west corner of trench O (O4 and 7). Equivalent material was not noted in trench P but is likely to have been missed since the sole function of this trench was to examine pit M39/P4 and to the north of trench O it may have been removed by machineing if it was ever present. The spreads were generally light to mid grey brown silty clays. There was limited variation between them, the main difference being the quantity of charcoal included. In trenches M and F this was significant, particularly in the case of F8 which had large and frequent inclusions along with other possible signs of burning. However, in trench O the deposits were more sterile. Generally they were found to be between 5 and 10cm deep.

Arbitrarily placed in phase 2, though only certainly belonging to some point after phase 1c and before the end of phase 3, is T8A, a shallower V-shaped ditch cut along the line of the earlier T8. This was only recognised in section as its fill (T2A) was almost identical to that of the earlier ditch (Figure 6: 9). It was 71cm wide and 53cm deep and its cutting on the same line as T8 probably suggests that it fulfilled a similar boundary/ ?defensive function at a natural break of slope, though it could not definitely be established that it curved east like its predecessor.

Phase 3 (Figure 6: 6)

The main features of phase 3 were a number of pebble spreads and probably disturbed groups of large stones. The best preserved was F5, a lateral spread of small, rounded, compacted pebbles, in part underlain by F17, a ?foundation spread of rather larger stones and slabs. A line of large stone slabs just under the east edge of F5 may have had some 'kerb' function or at least marked a regular limit to F17. A rather more damaged continuation of F5, or a separate area of pebbling, was O18. The material making up this spread was more variable in size and also included one or two slabs of stone. It may have represented a foundation layer with much of its surfacing lost and its edges were indistinct and disturbed and it had partly sunk into an earlier feature. A third spread (T3) occured in the north east corner of trench T. Again it consisted of small rounded pebbles with a few larger stones and one or two slabs. Though partly damaged by the machine removal of topsoil it appeared to have at least one relatively straight edge.

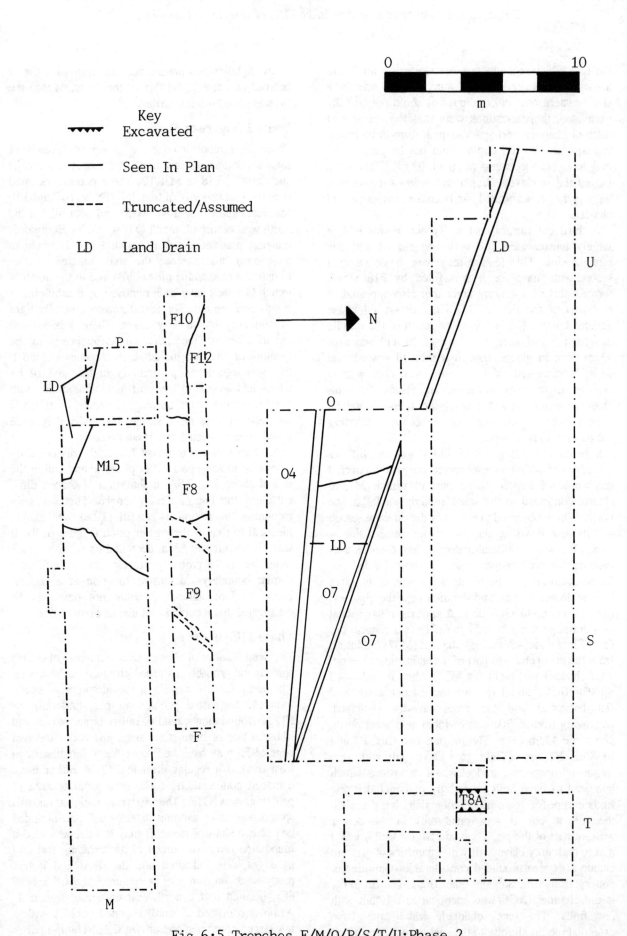

Key
▼▼▼▼ Excavated

——— Seen In Plan

- - - Truncated/Assumed

LD Land Drain

Fig.6:5 Trenches F/M/O/P/S/T/U:Phase 2

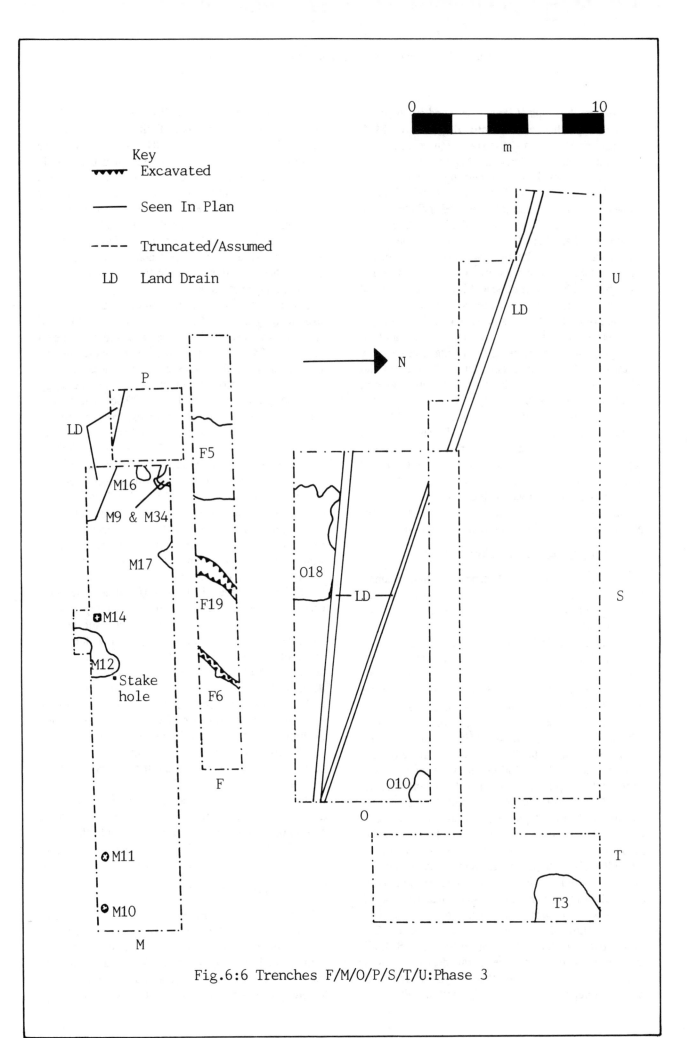

Fig.6:6 Trenches F/M/O/P/S/T/U:Phase 3

Several small groups of large stones and small pebble or rubble patches were identified (M9 over M34; M12; M16; M17; and O10). Their significance if any was not clear. Similarly a shallow and perhaps truncated U-shaped cut (F19) curving across trench F was filled with a silt (F7) which contained many stones and, at its surface, rounded pebbles. Also crossing trench F was an indistinct, ?truncated, shallow U-shaped cut (F6) with a bulge at one point on its eastern side. Its fill (F4) was similar to, but lighter than, the lower topsoil. Its function was not clear but if it had been truncated it might have served as a construction trench for a fence with posts.

Three other late features in trench M (M10, 11 and 14) were truncated, none surviving to more than 6cm in depth, and were disturbed by the machine removal of topsoil. M14 was a rectangular cut 21 x 26cm and M10 and 11 were circular cuts 26cm in diameter. They were on a possible alignment with a possible square stakehole a little further north adjacent to one of the groups of large stones (M12). It was difficult to say, given the truncation, whether these features represented a structure, presumably laying mainly south of the excavated area but the fact that the probable well pit in trench E (below) would have lain immediately to the south and that no traces of other activity were found in trench E argues against it.

Trenches C, K and L (Figure 6: 7)

Excluding a late glacial deposit including small branch fragments retaining bark which was sampled and seperately studied by Dr. Geraint Coles the earliest and principal deposit encountered in trenches C, K and L was C3, a light to mid grey clay probably lain in damp conditions. It was present over the southern 17m of trench C and was filling a natural, probably broadly U-shaped channel running east-west along the south of the field under excavation. This channel seems likely to have been the course of a former tributary of the Bradwell Brook and the same deposit (C3) was established to run for at least 75m along the south of the field by means of trenches and additional test pits. The width of the channel could not be fully established but was probably some 30m and the maximum depth of the post-glacial fill (C3) was *c.* 70cm in the excavated area. The date of the accumulation of this fill, essentially hill-wash, is difficult to fix. Although there were flecks of charcoal in the material at the lowest points examined no artificial material was present at or near its base in the areas that were excavated to natural. The relatively limited number of artifacts from C3, although they included the stamped brick No. 5. 1, all came from near the surface of the deposit or from areas on the channel's northern edge in trench C where the deposits were relatively shallow. Whilst all

the finds recovered were of Roman date it would be unwise to be dogmatic about their date of deposition given that C3 was essentially hillwash and the liklihood that items such as the stamped brick could have derived from structures such as the presumed baths which antiquarian observations suggest may still have been surface features as late as the eighteenth century. However, it is clear that this stream channel would probably have been a significant feature of the topography of the site in the Roman period and it is likely that extensive silting was occuring at the time.

Cut into the top of C3 throughout the 75m examined by trenches C, K, and L and the additional test pits was feature C4. It was a shallow U-shaped cut some 34-36cm wide filled with large stones, fragments of Chalk or fine grained Limestone, *opus signinum* and Roman brick and tile including stamped pieces 5. 2 and 5. 3. The feature ran relatively straight on an east-west course, but in trench K it turned slightly south before continuing again in its east-west course. There was no indication that feature C4 was in any way structural, its fill being randomly placed and its width insufficient for any but the slightest structural function. Rather it was clear that its function was as a land drain, the gaps between the stones being filled by a material identical to C3 and many of the stones showing clear signs of water erosion. Its date is more problematic. Stratigraphically the feature was only later than C3 which we have seen is itself difficult to date with certainty. The land drain included certainly Roman material clearly derived from a substantial, presumably military structure (probably the bath house or a structure within the fort) which had been demolished/ruined. But , especially given the lack of items such as Roman pottery sherds the possibility that the drain was constructed in post-Roman times and utilised material robbed from a Roman structure (or brought to the surface by ploughing) ought to be considered. However, the drain equally included no post-Roman material and the question of its date must remain open.

The only other feature located in this area was C6, a shallow, scooped cut projecting from the western section of trench C for some 50cm and of maximum width 30cm. It was filled with C5, which consisted principally of charcoal and scortched pottery.

Trench E (Figure 6: 8)

With the exception of E11/12, a large circular or pear shaped feature which could not be examined due to a lack of time but which was probably only a variation in the natural, the only important feature in the trench was E7. This was a very large and deep semi-circular feature projecting from the western section at the

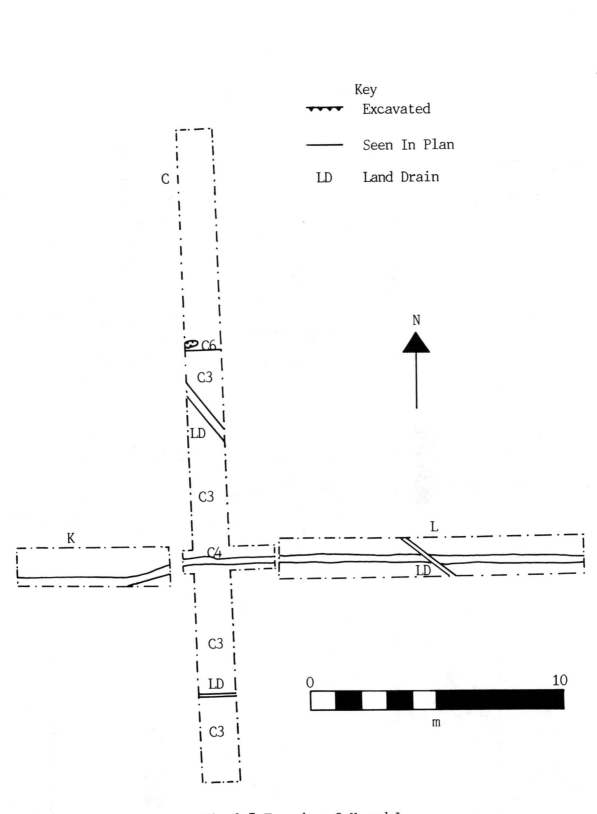

Fig.6:7 Trenches C,K and L

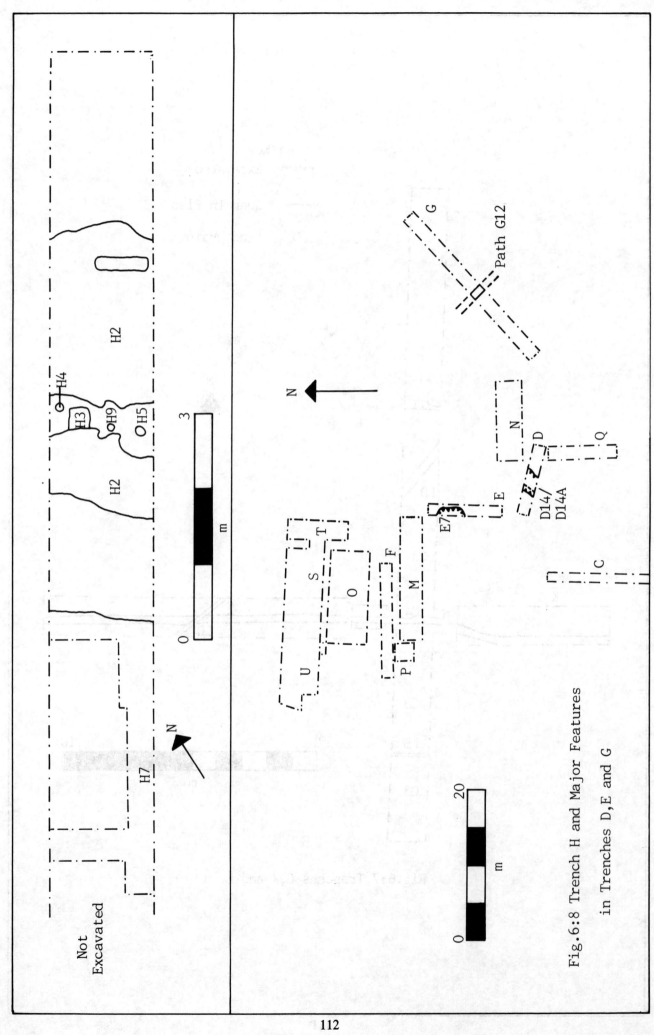

Fig.6:8 Trench H and Major Features

in Trenches D,E and G

northern end of the trench. It seems likely to have continued west of the section to form a circular feature whoes diameter would have been a little over 3. 5m. Its maximum extent east from the section was 1. 35m. It was excavated to a maximum depth of lm but it was far from certain that it had been bottomed at this point when the presence of the water table interfered with excavation. The cut consisted of a relatively steep lip with a possible 'step' some l0 cm from the top and then a gently curving profile, although in the lower parts of the cut the simularity of the natural and the fill made ascertaining the exact profile problematic. The cut was filled with E5A, a mid grey clay or clayey silt with few inclusions distinguished in places from the natural only by the presence of charcoal flecks, pottery and tile sherds. The only variations in the fill were a change to a bluer grey colour due to gleying and a decrease in the number of finds in the lower parts.

The function of this pit does not seem to have been for rubbish disposal, and its fill suggests that it was deliberately backfilled. Its size and probable shape suggest that it may have been a well pit, any well shaft either lying below the level at which excavation was possible or west of the trench edge, or never having been cut. However, this must remain a provisional conclusion.

Trench D (Figure 6: 8)

The principal feature of trench D was a two phase cut, D14/14A (Figure 6: 9). The initial cut (D14) was U-shaped and channel like. It was truncated on the east by D14A but was over 1. 3m wide and filled by D16, a light grey clayey silt. The recut (D14A) probably occured before the origional channel had completely filled and reused the west side of the channel, but extended it to the east making a maximum total width of 3. 15m. This recut was broad and flat bottomed and up to 26cm deep, compared to the first channel which was up to 40cm deep. The main fill of the recut was D6/8, a dark, slightly clayey, grittey silt congruent with a drainage channel function. However, the presence of a group of dumped Limestone blocks at the eastern edge of the cut and of a redeposited natural cap over 1. 2m of the western part of it suggested that it had been deliberately filled in before it had fully silted up.

No other significant features were found in this trench. D12 in the extreme north east corner of the trench was probably a modern land drain cap while D4/18 at the west end initially appeared to be a U-shaped cut with semi-circular projections on the east side. However, the latter proved impossible to follow and may only have represented localised lensing in the natural.

Trench G (Figure 6: 8)

Only one archaeological feature was found in trench G, a path crossing the trench east-west. The path itself (G12) was composed of compacted small rounded pebbles and, though its damaged edges were indistinct, seemed to have a maximum width of *c*. lm. It was underlain by what appeared to be a foundation. This consisted of a dish like lateral cut *c*. 70-80cm wide and l9cm deep filled by G17, redeposited natural with concentrated charcoal lenses and burnt tile and daub, at each side and G18, compacted grit and small stones, which filled the centre of the cut and spread out either side of it.

Trench H (Figure 6: 8)

Lack of time prevented extensive excavation in trench H, the only trench cut to the west north west of the fort, but even so it was clear that few features were present and no dating evidence of any form was encountered here so that even a Roman date for any activity must be uncertain. The main features were two pebbled areas crossing. the trench north-south. Both apparently consisted of unfounded 2-3cm thick layers of stones layed directly onto the natural. H2 was 3. 8m wide and lay some 2. 5m west of the east section. It consisted of small rounded pebbles with occasional larger stones with a mid grey, gritty material between them. H7, some 1. 3m west of it was 3. 6m wide and consisted of flat rounded cobbles up to 12cm in size in places infilled with small pebbles and with a mid grey silty clay matrix between them.

Within H2 two areas seemed to represent accidental or deliberate removal of the pebbling (as opposed to its truncation by later cut features). The first was a rectangular area 20 X 75cm near to its eastern edge. The second was an irregular strip up to 70cm wide nearer to the western end. Four small features were found here and it is possible that the pebbling respected these rather than being removed to allow their insertion. Three of the features (H4, 5 and 9) were circular ?stakeholes of U-shaped cross-section, 10cm wide and deep. The fourth (H3) was a 30cm square setting of stones in heavy mid brown clay. It did not seem to be a post hole packing as such and no post pipe was present. However, it is possible that it served as a small post pad and taken together the features might represent some minor fence line.

Minor and Late Features

Two truncated post holes in trench N (N6 and 7) appeared to be filled with subsoil and may have been post-Roman. They were respectively 45 and 48cm in diameter and of broad U-shaped section. The latest features encountered (except for a number of modern terra cotta land drains) were numbers of stakeholes. A

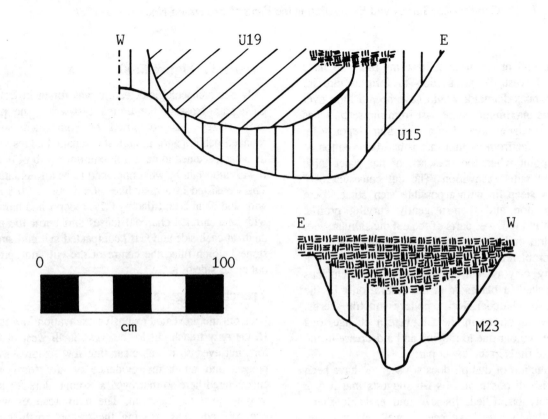

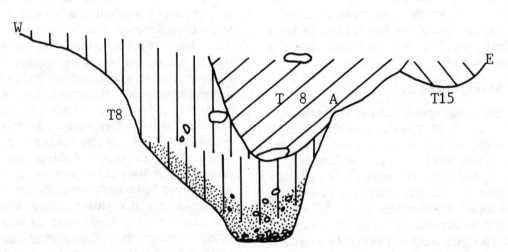

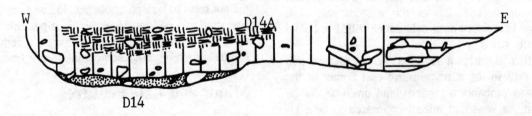

Fig.6:9 Sections

great number of these were found in trenches D, E, F, M, N, O, S, and U. They were 2-7cm in diameter, 5-15cm in depth and of pointed profile. In a few cases a small number of them appeared to form short alignments but most formed no coherent pattern. It seems likely that they represented the repeated repositioning of hurdles or the like in connection with sheep farming in the post–Roman period.

Discussion

With the exception of the cobbled/pebbled surfaces in trench H, whose function and indeed date must remain uncertain, it appears that Roman period activity west of the Brough fort was of limited extent and may have been relatively isolated from the rest of the extra-mural settlement. It is clear that a far more substantial natural channel formerly ran east-west along the south end of the present field west of the fort approximately along the line of the modern field boundary which is still marked by a very minor stream course/ditch. It was presumably a tributary of the Bradwell Brook and, although probably silting at the time, is likely on balance to have been a significant topographical feature in Roman times and to have limited the area available for continuous settlement. However, even the area available for use would not seem to have been taken full advantage of. The negative evidence of trench R and of geophysical data suggests that areas at the top of the present field were not used and this may reflect its relatively exposed position. Equally negative geophysical and excavational evidence suggests that the area towards the bottom of the field saw limited activity. The main feature examined here was clearly a land drain which need not have belonged to the Roman period and even if it did suggests only agricultural activity. Only the two phase drainage channel in trench D suggests other activity and it must be likely that it and many of the other channels partly recorded in trenches F/M/O/P/S/T/U existed in order to drain areas in the centre of the field. The destination of most if not all of these is likely to have been the natural channel at the south end of the field and it is not unlikely that their inputs speeded its rate of silting.

Rather it was the area roughly at the centre of the present field that saw the vast majority of the activity recorded. How far beyond the area excavated such activity extended is not entirely clear. The possible boundary ditch at a natural break of slope in trench T may have marked an eastern limit to activity and this suggestion is strengthened by the lack of features other than the clay extraction pits at the east end of trench M and absence of activity in trench G. The only feature recorded in trench G was a path which seems likely to have acted as a link between the area excavated and the main *vicus* south east of the fort.

This indeed may have been the only formal access to the area since no indications were found in the survey or excavation of a road running toward the fort's west gate. The lack of any features which could be interpreted as structural south of trench O may suggest that the southern limit of the focus of activity lay within the excavated area. However, it is likely that activity continued to the north of trenches S, T and U allbeit for less than 10m while to the west, beyond the area threatened by afforestation, it is entirely likely given the presence of features U15 and Ul9 at the west end of trench U that some form of activity persisted for an indeterminate distance. The site appears to have been used mainly in the Antonine period and, though the dating evidence does not allow of the necessary precision, it is tempting to suggest that it was first extensively used on the re-establishment of the fort 154/8. Whilst some activity, such as the clay mining pits and associated channel (yielding little dating evidence but including Hadrianic/early-Antonine sherds) might be earlier than this the fact that the fort and, as far as is known, the *vicus* were abandoned c. 120-154/8 suggests that considerable caution should be exercised in attributing any activity to the later-Hadrianic or earlier-Antonine periods. Nor is there any evidence for the continuation of usage of the site into the third century although the fort and other parts of the *vicus* remained in opperation. Thus, the site may only have been in use for around 50 years.

The nature of the activity on the site is difficult to assess. There is no indication that it was other than civil but a number of factors suggest that it was unlike the pattern of small residential/craft 'strip buildings' along *vicanal* roads usually found in military *vici*. Firstly the activity appears to have been isolated from the rest of the *vicus*; secondly in the area excavated no roads were found; and thirdly only one building can be confidently identified (though some features in trench U may suggest that others existed, perhaps principally to the west of the area examined). Rather the majority of features encountered in phase 1 related to drainage, probably reflecting a prime disadvantage of the site. On balance it does seem likely that phase 1 saw some residential activity with at least one building, a ?well (if it was open in this phase) and a domestic corpus of pottery and glass including storage, cooking and food preparation vessel forms. However, the nature of the deposits in phase 2, mainly relatively sterile accumulations with possible indications of burning, suggest that the site may have been abandoned or at least little used for a time and it may be that the drainage problems were at least a factor in this abandonment.

In phase 3 the main activity was represented by a number of pebble spreads. There was little to indicate their function(s) but it does seem likely that we are dealing with a number of discrete spreads or areas of hard standing and not one large one. Several possibilities exist as to their function(s) including working surfaces or bases for temporary/moveable structures such as market stalls. An interpretation as damaged floor surfaces of permanent buildings without earth fast foundations is far less likely. Viewing them as bases for stalls may be particularly attractive given the lack of industrial waste in this phase and archaeology's frequent failure to identify areas within *vici* that may have acted as 'market places'. The possibility that *vicanal* markets were held away from the main residential area on residentially or agriculturally unattractive land provided only with areas of hard standing if that is one that has much to commend it. However, in the present instance the general lack of finds from phase 3 may question such an interpretation even if, as is probable, such a market would principally have delt in foodstuffs traces of which would not have survived especially in the hostile pedological conditions of Brough.

Given the apparent isolation of the site from the rest of the *vicus* a variety of other functions either practically or socially incompatable with the rest of the settlement should also be considered both for phase 1 and phase 3. The social ostracism of some group (?such perhaps as prostitutes) might lead to the siting of buildings at some distance from the main settlement. Equally though the possibility that the site had some connection with the lead industry must be considered. Although there remains very little evidence for lead processing or working from the fort or *vicus* at Brough (considering that it lies near to an important lead extraction area) such activity would probably have taken place away from the main residential areas because of the noxious fumes involved. There were a small number of splashes, solidified masses and even two probable casting lugs of lead from the site, notably from the phase 1 pit at the west end of trench M/trench P, as well as one large piece of galena. However, only two possible lead slag fragments were recovered, most slag in fact being ferrous and as with the lead splashes etc. mainly coming from phase 1 features. Thus, there is little to support any suggestion of lead processing on the site and moreover any 'industrial' activity must have been quite minor and have belonged principally to phase 1 and not to phase 3.

The Finds

1 Samian Ware *M.J. Dearne*

Some 216 sherds of Samian ware were recovered but the vast majority were small, abraded and lacking glaze. Only one retained very abraded decoration and only 17 base or rim sherds were present, all small and abraded. In the circumstances the material was not submitted to any specialist but all sherds appeared to be in Central Gaulish fabrics. No forms could certainly be identified.

2 Romano–British Coarse Pottery *R..S. Leary*

Some 1, 728 Romano-British sherds from a minimum of 140 vessels were recovered. The pottery was examined by context and a fully quantified archive is available at Sheffield Museum comprising a catalogue recording fabric, sherd count, form, part, rim diameter, rim percentage, decoration and other conditions; fabric and form type descriptions; tables quantifying the forms and fabrics by phase using sherd counts and rim percentages and summaries of the dating of every context assigned a phase. The fabrics present on the site are described below.

A selection of the pottery has been illustrated to show the range of forms represented and the homogeneity of the assemblages from all phases. Where possible the sherds are from sealed contexts. In order to illustrate as much as possible of the primary evidence all the diagnostic sherds from each assemblage are published regardless of any duplication.

Fabrics

A sample of sherds was examined under a x20 binocular microscope to identify the fabric groups and thereafter identification was carried out by eye except in doubtful cases.

GRA   grey, often sandwich effect with darker grey core. Fairly hard and smooth with laminar fracture. Moderate quantity of very fine, well-sorted quartz; rare, subangular, medium-sized, well-sorted quartz; rare, medium-sized, rounded, well-sorted, grey inclusions (clay pellets?); rare, medium-sized, rounded, well-sorted, brown iron oxides and moderate quantities of medium-sized, rounded, well-sorted, black iron oxides in some examples. Similar to fabrics made at Derby racecourse (Brassington 1971 and 1980).

GRB   grey, sometimes with brown core. Hard, often sandy feel and irregular fracture. Abundant, medium-sized, subangular, well-sorted quartz; moderate, medium-sized, rounded or long and thin, ill-sorted, brown iron oxides; and moderate, medium-sized, rounded, well-sorted, black iron oxides. A general group for sandy grey wares.

OAA   red/orange. Fairly hard with smooth or powdery feel, depending on soil conditions,

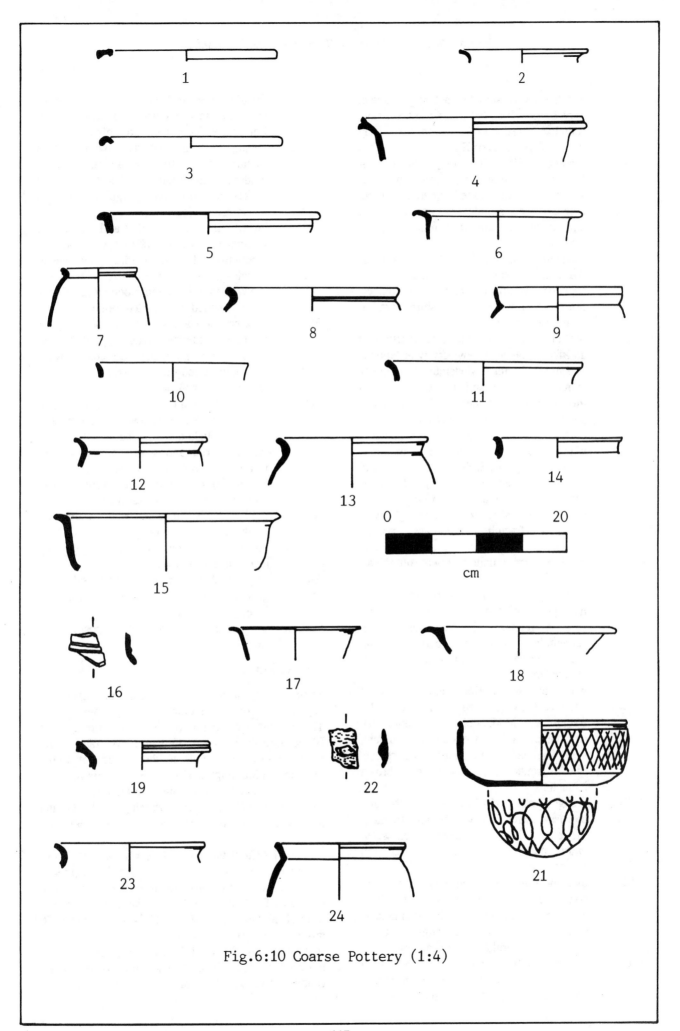

Fig.6:10 Coarse Pottery (1:4)

and laminar or smooth fracture. Moderate, very fine, well-sorted quartz; sparse, fine, rounded, well-sorted red/orange ?clay pellets. As GRA and OBA.

OAB orange/red. Hard often sandy with irregular fracture. Moderate, medium-sized, subangular, well-sorted quartz; sparse, medium-sized, rounded, orange inclusions; and sparse, medium-sized, rounded, black iron oxides.

OAC orange/red. Hard and rough with irregular fracture. Moderate, medium-sized, rounded, well-sorted, brown iron oxides. Softer and finer than Derbyshire ware but otherwise similar.

OBA buff or cream with lighter core. Fairly hard and feels smooth or powdery with laminar or smooth fracture. Moderate, very fine or subvisible, well-sorted quartz and moderate, fine, rounded, well-sorted, black and brown iron oxides. As OAA.

OBB buff, brown or cream. Soft and powdery with irregular fracture. Moderate, medium-sized, subangular, well-sorted quartz; and sparse, medium-sized, rounded, well-sorted, brown or black iron oxides.

OBC buff/brown. Fairly soft and rough with irregular fracture. Moderate, coarse, subangular, well-sorted quartz; and sparse, medium-sized, rounded, brown iron oxides. As OAC.

DBY red/orange/brown/grey. Very hard, feels like petrified gooseflesh and has very irregular fracture. Abundant, very coarse, subangular, ill-sorted quartz; sparse, medium-sized, rounded, brown iron oxides. Derbyshire ware.

FLA white or cream. Hard and smooth, if unaffected by soil, with finely irregular fracture. Moderate, medium-sized, subangular, well-sorted quartz; moderate, very fine, subvisible quartz, and sparse, fine, rounded, well-sorted brown inclusions.

FLB orange with off-white slip. Soft and powdery with fairly smooth fracture. Moderate, fine, sub-rounded, well-sorted quartz, and rare, fine, rounded, black iron oxides.

BB1 black or brown. Hard and sandy. Looks like cod's roe in a clean fracture. Abundant, medium-sized, rounded, well-sorted quartz; and rare, medium-sized, angular, black shale. Black Burnished ware category 1.

GTB1 buff/brown. Fairly hard and smooth with very irregular fracture. Rare, medium-sized, rounded quartz; rare, medium-sized,

rounded grey and red inclusions (?grog); and rare, medium-sized, rounded, brown iron oxides. Very worn, possibly fired clay.

GTB2 cream. Soft and powdery with smooth fracture. Rare, fine, subangular quartz; moderate, fine, rounded, ill-sorted red clay pellets; and rare, coarse, angular, ill-sorted, black iron oxides.

CTB brown with grey core. Soft and rough with laminar fracture. Abundant, very coarse to medium-sized, ill-sorted, plate-shaped vesicles; rare, medium-sized, rounded, brown iron oxides; and moderate, medium-sized, rounded, well-sorted, orange grog.

BSB1 dark brown. Hard and rough with irregular fracture. Moderate, coarse, rounded, well sorted quartz; moderate, very coarse, well-sorted, plate-shaped vesicles; and rare, fine, rounded, brown iron oxides.

CC orange and white paste with dark brown colour coat. Soft and smooth with smooth fracture. Moderate, fine, subangular, well-sorted quartz; and sparse, fine, rounded, well-sorted red inclusions. One Nene Valley type sherd was found. The remainder were rough cast wares.

NSP used for miscellaneous sandy wares not attributable to any other group.

GLAZ green glazed grey ware similar to Derby racecourse glazed ware.

AMP amphora sherds; probably all Dressel 20.

M general group for mortaria (assessed seperately below).

MED/MOD general group for post-Roman sherds.

Discussion

The pottery from phases 1-3 and from the superficial deposits was of a remarkably homogeneous nature. The assemblage comprised four ceramic groups: Black Burnished ware 1 (Gillam 1976), fabrics and forms closely comparable to those made at Derby racecourse (Brassington 1971; 1980; reports in *D. A. J.* 1985), Derbyshire ware and 'pre-Derbyshire' ware (Jones and Webster 1970; Brassington 1971) and non-local wares (colour coated wares, amphorae and mortaria).

Around 22% of the assemblage was of BB1. These types were the best dated coarse ware forms present and even bodysherds provided a *terminus post quem* of 120 A. D. (Gillam 1976, 57). Sherds were present from all phases (nos 5, 7, 10, 12-14 *cf.* Gillam 1976 nos 35 or 58, 21 and 3 or 4 respectively; nos 15, 20 (not illustrated), 23-8, 32, 36 and 39 *cf.* Gillam 1976 nos 60-2, 3, 35, 35, 3 and 4, dated mid- to late-second century). The forms compared well with the Mumrills

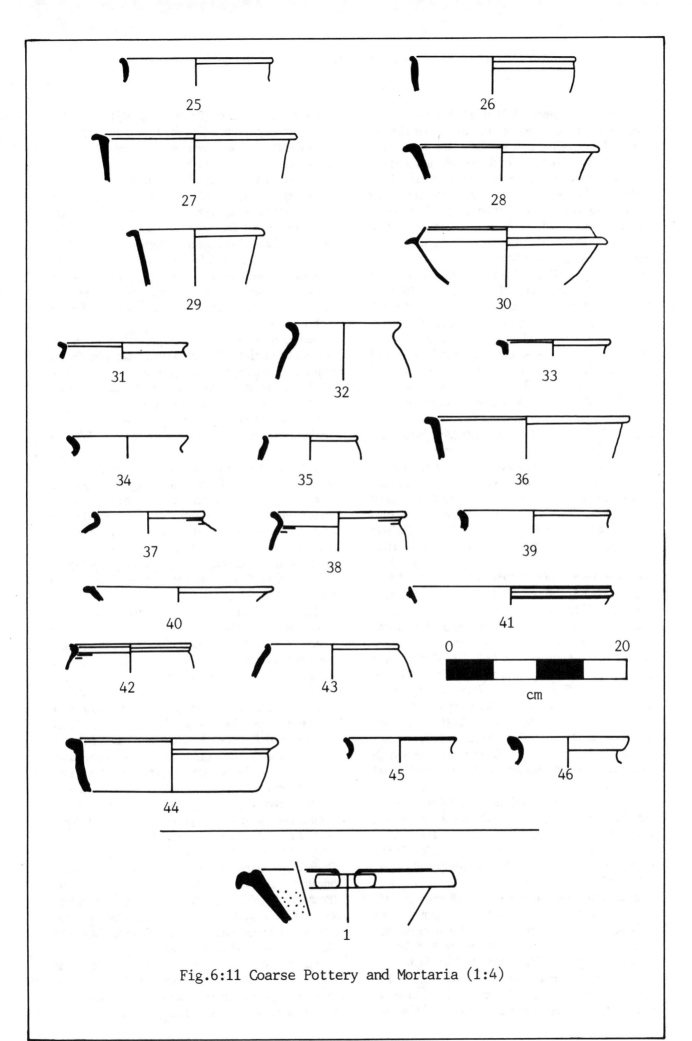

Fig.6:11 Coarse Pottery and Mortaria (1:4)

ditch deposit (Gillam 1963) dated to *c.* 163 A. D. (Gillam 1974, 10). None of the flaring jar rims or flanged bowls of the later-second to fourth centuries were present and only two of the vessels (nos 5 and 7) could be Hadrianic. A grooved rim bowl (no. 21, *cf.* Gillam 1976, no. 52 dated mid- to late-second century) was present and a cordoned sherd (no. 16) in BBl was unusual and no analogues were noted. One small rim sherd (no. 45) from an unsealed and unphased deposit (D6/7/8/9) compared better with a third-century BBl type (Gillam 1976 no. 9, dated mid- to late-third century). However, it is difficult to identify such a small sherd reliably. Thus the BBl wares point to an Antonine date for all the phases.

Vessels in forms and fabrics similar to the products of the Derby Racecourse kilns accounted for 36% of the assemblage (nos 1, 2, 3, 6, 11, 18, 31 and 35 *cf.* Brassington 1980 nos 366, 544, 384, 377, 347, 379, 400, 343 and 344). No. 30 was in a similar fabric and was probably a variant of the flanged bowl series made at Derby. Rather abraded rusticated sherds were found and also a beaker base with a green glaze in a phase 3 deposit (Brassington 1971, 58, 62). The jars (as nos 2, 8 and 11), flanged bowls (no. 18), carinated bowls and rusticated wares were present throughout the life of the Flavian to early-Antonine kilns. Reeded rim bowls (no. 1) were made in the Flavian-Trajanic kilns only, as were the glazed wares (Brassington 1980, 42 and passim). The turned over rim (no. 3) so resembled the rim of a Hadrianic-Antonine bowl form found at Derby (Wheeler 1985a, 120 no. 143) as to make identification certain despite the size of the sherds. This form was found in kiln 5 (Brassington 1980, nos 383-5) dated to the mid-second century and in Hadrianic-Antonine deposits at Derby Little Chester and Racecourse (Wheeler 1985a, 95 no. 28; Dool 1985a, 197 no. 168). The form was copying or influenced by samian forms Dr. 44 and 81 and was also made at Wilderspool (Hartley 1981, 474) where it was dated 110-60 A. D. . Gillam (1970, no. 200) dated it to 140-200 A. D. . These vessels support an Antonine date and also strengthen the possibility of some Hadrianic activity.

The grey ware flat-rim dishes (nos 17 and 29) and the everted-rim jars (no. 34) were almost certainly not from the Derby Racecourse kilns. These were common types in the Antonine kilns at Rossington Bridge, Doncaster, South Yorks. (Buckland *et. al.* 1980, 157 type Ea, Figure 3 nos 7, 8, and 11). This type of everted-rim jar was usually slimmer in body and had longer everted rims than the globular jars with short, everted rims (no. 8) which it superceded in the second half of the second century. The flat-rim dishes clearly copied Black Burnished ware types and continued in production into the fourth century. The narrow-necked jar (no. 19) was heavier than those made at Derby Racecourse during the late-first and early-second centuries (Brassington 1971 nos 151-2) and more like the heavier rims from grey ware kilns associated with the production of Derbyshire ware (Brassington 1980, 45 no. 576).

Flagons in white ware and orange ware with an off-white slip were probably also made at Derby Racecourse (Wheeler 1985a, 91). Simple everted-rim and ring-necked flagons were found at Brough-on-Noe. The latest was a rebated rim flagon (no. 22). It was badly abraded and fragmented but the surviving rim sherds most closely resemble a late-second to early-third century form (Wheeler 1985a, 97 no. 71). However, Antonine parallels were cited by Webster (1961, 105).

Derbyshire ware sherds were present in all phases. The softer fabrics, OAC and OBC, were used for the cupped-rim (no. 9) and rebated-rim jars (Brassington 1971, 60). In the Derby Racecourse kilns only the rebated form was made (Brassington 1971, nos 226-52) and at Derby Little Chester these decline as Derbyshire ware cupped-rim jars appear (Wheeler 1985a, tables 4 and 5). This has led some to conclude that the softer ware was replaced by true Derbyshire ware. At the 1984 Brough site (Drage, this volume) however, the softer fabrics were still common in the late-second to early-third centuries suggesting that they should not be viewed as earlier than Derbyshire ware only but rather overlapping as a variant made at Derby or as a local copy. Derbyshire ware and cupped rim jars in OAC and OBC are therefore dated from the early-Antonine period.

The sources of the grog-tempered and calcite-gritted wares (GTBl and 2, CTB and BSBl) were uncertain. There were only two diagnostic grog-tempered sherds, a flanged bowl (no. 40) and a narrow-necked jar (as no. 46) with undercut rim. The single form in BSBl was a bowl (no. 44, unstratified) which was similar in form and fabric to those from kilns at Bourne, Lincolnshire (Samuels 1983, Figure 214) dated to the late-second and third centuries.

The unstratified material comprised the same range of fabrics and forms with the addition of a single cornice rim beaker (no. 42) and an unusual bead-rim jar in a silver grey ware (no. 43). The former was a common second-century type and the latter was dated to the first and second centuries at Leicester (Kenyon 1948, 102 nos 24-30) and was uncommon in Derbyshire. Amphora sherds were present in small quantities and all resembled Dressel 20 fabricks (Peacock and Williams 1986, 136). One very abraded sherd of Nene Valley type colour coat was recovered from an unsealed and unphased deposit (D6/7/8/9) along with some rough-cast ware.

Thus consideration of the full range of fabrics and forms represented throughout the stratigraphic sequence suggested most of the activity took place in the Antonine period. The relatively small quantity of

Derbyshire ware and the sizeable quantity of Derby Racecourse types point to a period when the Derbyshire ware kilns were only beginning to capture the local market. The assemblage compared well with deposits from Derby Little Chester dated by mid- to late-Antonine samian (Wheeler 1985a, 115 phase 3) and also with the *mansio* deposit at Melandra (Webster 1971, 107) dated early-Antonine. At Derby an increase in the volume of BB1 reaching the site coincided with an increase in the quantity of Derbyshire ware and was associated with a dislocation of local pottery supplies (Wheeler 1985a, 123). At Melandra a high proportion of BB1 ware was noted (Webster 1971, table 2) during the Hadrianic to early-Antonine period and the same trend was also found at Chesterfield, Derbyshire (Ellis 1989, 119). The character of the assemblage at Brough-on-Noe points to a date in the mid-second century when the Derby racecourse kilns were being superceded by those producing Derbyshire ware and the BB1 distributors were able to capture some of the local market, perhaps as a result of these changes.

A small number of contexts yielded Derby Racecourse and other early types only and could date from the Hadrianic period: O6 (no. 1), O9 (nos 2-3), O17 (no. 6), S16 (no. 4, *cf.* Gillam 1970 no. 301 dated 80-130 A. D.), M12, M16, M20, T3 and S6a (no. 41, *cf.* Webster 1971 no. 43 dated to the 120s). However all these contexts contained only two or three diagnostic sherds, often abraded, which could be early-Antonine or residual. Certainly in contexts M12, M16 and T3 (phase 3) these sherds must be seen as residual while S16 was subject to modern disturbance and M20 was redeposited natural.

3 The Mortaria *M.J. Dearne*

Sixty mortaria sherds were recovered representing at least thirty three vessels all of which appeared to date to the second century, although much of the material was very highly abraded. The majority of the vessels appeared to be in Mancetter/Hartshill or Little Chester fabrics (as would be expected given the proximity of those production areas) with a smaller number in a coarser ?local fabric (fabric 6). Severn or eight fabrics were recorded:

Fabric 1 Hard, fine-textured, smooth, white fabric with some well-sorted small red inclusions; small black tituration.

Fabric 2 Hard, fine-textured, white to cream fabric with few small red and black inclusions; grey tituration.

Fabric 3 Hard, fine, cream fabric with frequent small red and black inclusions and traces of a red or brown slip; tituration including quartz.

Fabric 4 Fine-textured, cream fabric often with dark grey core and with some quartz, black and grey and frequent small red inclusions; quartz and perhaps flint tituration.

Fabric 5 Fineish cream to pink fabric often with pale pink core and varying amounts of angular quartz and occasional red and black inclusions; quartz and black tituration.

Fabric 6 Soft, coarse, orange fabric with many quartz inclusions and traces of a cream or white slip; quartz tituration.

Fabric 7 Hard, fine-textured, orange to brown fabric with grey core and frequent quartz and large black and occasional red inclusions; quartz and occasional red and black tituration.

Fabric 8: (N. B. only three small sherds were recovered and were not certainly from mortaria). Soft, white, very sandy fabric with occasional small red inclusions.

Only three vessels call for seperate comment

1 Matching sherds representing half of the rim and upper body of a mortarium in fabric 3. Probably late-second century. From the fill of the re-cut channel in trench D.

2 Rim sherd of a mortarium in fabric 4. Probably mid-second century. From the fill of the phase 1b feature S19/20.

3 Fragmentary rim of a mortarium in fabric 3 with a partial stamp VI[. From the surface of the natural in trench E.

4 The Glass *Jennifer Price*

During the excavations a total of 66 Roman glass fragments were found. Vessel glass accounted for 64 pieces, and the remaining two came from windows; it is noteworthy that no glass objects were found. The range of colours is very limited; virtually all the pieces are blue-green (61 fragments=92. 4%), and the rest are colourless or greenish colourless (4 fragments=6. 1%) and yellow-green (1 fragment=1. 5%). Three groups of fragments have been catalogued in detail:

4. 1 (Figure 6: 15) Contexts F10, M15 and P3

Three body fragments, carinated conical jug or cylindrical bowl. Blue green. Bands of small bubbles. Part of almost straight side curving inwards very strongly to lower body. Short slightly diagonal ribs above carination, continuing onto lower body. Dimensions (largest frag. ; F10) 43 X 52mm; thickness 1-1. 5mm. Also: a) Context M8; blue-green straight body fragment, perhaps conical jug, 2 spiral ribs; b) Context M36; blue-green straight body fragment, perhaps conical jug, 2 vertical ribs; c) Context P2; blue-green straight body fragment, perhaps conical jug, 1 vertical rib.

4. 2 (Figure 6: 15) Context M15

Four joining rim and neck fragments, jar. Pale blue green. Small bubbles. Funnel mouth with everted rim, edge rolled out, up and in, flattened inside; neck tapering inwards. Present height *c.* 40mm; rim diameter *c.* 100mm; thickness 1mm.

4. 3 (Figure 6: 15) Context M15

Base fragment, prismatic vessel, perhaps bottle. Blue green. Concave base, parts of 3 edges extant, apparently with triangular outline. 9 small dimples in underside of base, arranged around central concavity. Patches of wear outside dimples. Dimensions 54 X 60mm; thickness 5+mm.

Number 4.1 and the additional fragments listed appear to come from at least two vessels with nearly vertical ribs, as a considerable difference in the spacing of the ribs can be distinguished. Both are probably jugs with conical carinated bodies, the complete form having a folded rim, long narrow neck and angular handle with central rib, and an open base ring with concave base. Jugs of this form, and very similar jugs with conical bodies without a carination and a simple concave base, were in widespread use in the north west provinces, including Britain, from around A. D. 65 until the early- to mid-second century (Isings 1957 Form 55; Harden 1967). A few complete carinated examples have been found in Britain, as at Colchester, (May 1930, 287-8, pl. XC), and one with two handles from Bayford, Kent (Brailsford 1958, 44, pl. XI. 9), and many fragments are known. They have been discussed in connection with three jugs from a pit dated by samian to A. D. 155-165 at Park Street, Towchester (Price 1980, 66, Figure 15.7-9), and another from a similarly dated pit at Alcester, Warwickshire (Price and Cottam forthcoming).

Number 4.2 is a part of a small jar with rolled rim and funnel mouth, which probably had a convex body and concave base. Small jars are quite common finds in Britain in the first and second centuries. It is usually difficult to establish their precise forms as most of them are very fragmentary; they are rarely included in grave assemblages. A reconstructed example with a similar rim and indented body was found in a pit deposit dated by samian to A. D. 160-70 at Felmongers, Harlow, in Essex (Price 1987, 205, Figure 3. 24), and others are known at Verulamium (Charlesworth 1972, 205, Figure 76. 30) and elsewhere. Small jars are discussed in detail in connection with finds from excavations at Colchester (Cool and Price forthcoming nos 807-30).

Number 4.3 is a base from a prismatic vessel. Such vessels (usually bottles, though some jars are also known) were produced in very large quantities during the first and second centuries for the storage and transport of liquid and semi-liquid substances (Isings 1957 Forms 50, 62 and 90). The commonest form in Britain and elsewhere, is the square bottle, although square jars, and rectangular, hexagonal and octagonal bottles are also found. All the bottles have the same heavy folded rim, short cylindrical neck, wide shoulder and angular ribbon handle (or two on rectangular bottles). Almost invariably, their bodies and bases were blown into a mould, the bases being decorated with designs in relief. This base comes from a vessel which is unusual in two respects. In the first place, the design on the underside of the base consists of circular *impressions* arranged in a convex-sided triangular formation round a central concavity. The surface of the base is pock-marked, indicating that it has been flattened on stone or wood during manufacture, and the circular impressions appear to have been formed after the base was flattened. Hexagonal bottles were occasionally produced without basal designs, as examples with undecorated, pock-marked concave bases are known from Castleford, West Yorkshire and Ribchester, Cumbria (both unpublished), but no parallels have been found for the impressed decoration. The second unusual feature is the shape of the body. The evidence of three sides indicates that this is likely to be a triangular or asymetrical multiangular vessel, rather than one of the usual forms. Triangular bottles have been noted very occasionally; one which appears to have a similar undecorated base with central concavity is known from Pompeii (Morin 1913, 60, Figure 36), and a body fragment from another has been found at High Rochester (unpublished), but they are not at all common. Another highly unusual form is a bottle with one long and eight short sides from Kaloz in Hungary (Barkoczi 1988, 181, pls. XLI, XCVIII. 438), but too little of the Brough-on-Noe vessel has survived for precise identification to be possible.

Most of the remaining fragments are small and their precise forms are not readily identifiable, although it has been possible to establish that the assemblage represents a minimum of seven vessels in addition to the four discussed above, providing a total of at least eleven vessels. Of these at least four are probably tablewares, and at least five appear to be household vessels or containers.

The additional vessel forms represented are a yellowish green vessel with a flat base, perhaps a plate or bowl; a colourless vessel which may be a cylindrical cup; a greenish colourless vessel; a blueish green vessel with indented body and trailed decoration; a blueish green vessel with a thin convex body, perhaps a long necked unguent bottle or flask;

at least one blueish green square or prismatic bottle; and at least one blueish green cylindrical bottle. It is probable, however, that considerably more than two bottles or jars are represented by the 20 fragments of containers from this excavation. These range from the later-first century to the later-second or early-third century at the latest, although few of them are very closely dateable because of the uncertainty concerning their precise forms.

Finally, the fragments of window glass came from at least three blueish green matt-glossy panes, of the kind produced in the first to third centuries by pouring glass into flat trays (Boon 1966).

5 The Brick and Tile *M.J.Dearne*

Some 520 brick and tile fragments were recovered and a fuller archive catalogue is lodged in Sheffield City Museum. Many were abraded, small fragments but numerous large fragments were recovered from the Roman or post-Roman land drain (C4) where they included two fragmentary stamps and occured with blocks of *opus signinum*. The material was sorted by context and, by eye alone, into fabric groups and is quantified by weight in the site archive. It was clear that two or three main fabric groups (one used for tiles and two for bricks) were present although facilities were not available for the detailed analysis of these fabrics. Brick fabric 1, a fine orange fabric similar and perhaps identical to tile fabric 1, occured in a variety of contexts, though the examples from contexts other than C4 showed some firing variations and a greater range of fineness with at least one piece being distinctly sandy. Brick fabric 2 was rather coarser, often with large inclusions and had been fired to varieties of blue grey, mauve, purple and red. It often had two or more colour bands in fracture and was largely restricted to material from C4 and the deposit into which it was cut (C3), though a few chips were noted from other contexts. Tile fabric 1 was a fairly fine orange fabric perhaps identical to brick fabric 1 but in some cases had fired to pink or red and occasionally to grey or to orange/pink/red with grey bands in fracture. This fabric occured throughout the site but showed a greater variability in contexts other than C4. A few fragments had larger inclusions than normal, perhaps reflecting poor clay preparation, but the main variations appeared to be due to firing conditions.

Whilst the bulk of the tile and brick were in these fabrics, and excluding one or two distinctive probably modern pieces found unstratified, some five other brick and tile fabrics appeared to be represented by small groups of material exclusively from contexts other than C4. These were: a) a single brick fragment in a red-orange fabric with frequent small inclusions and mottled black surfaces; b) five small tile sherds in a rather coarse orange fabric; c) eight tile fragments in a medium coarse orange to buff fabric somewhat intermediant between tile fabric 1 and b) above; d) a single tile fragment in a very fine creamy pink fabric; e) up to seven tile fragments perhaps representing a hard fired red fabric of variable fineness, in some cases with a grey 'slagey' interior (though the only two pieces found stratified might have been over fired examples of tile fabric 1 and the remainder could have been modern).

Of the few tiles attributable to a form all but two were *tegulae*. The exceptions were two possible *imbreces* in tile fabric 1. Cross hatching was noted on most tile fragments from C4 and lesser numbers from the rest of the site. A few pieces from C4 also seemed to have had rectangular cut-outs at their edges and many tiles and some bricks from this context retained cement or *opus signinum* on at least one face. The tiles from C4 were 2-5.5cm (and mostly 2. 5-3. 5cm) thick, while the bricks were 5+cm thick.

The only significant pattern of tile/brick distribution was the concentration of material in C4. This seems likely to have been looted from a substantial building (?the military baths) with *opus signinum* ?floors and brick and tile elements for reuse in constructing the feature. The partial stamps on some items probably underline the military origin of the material. However, neither this material or the more general site collection suggests that brick or tile were used in any structures in the area examined.

Three stamps were recorded (previously noted in *Britannia* 18 (1987), 370):

5. 1 (Figure 6: 12) Brick fragment in brick fabric 2 with the fragmentary incuse stamp CO[(the C largely complete, the presumed O incomplete, rectangularised and formed of broken lines). Width 14. 1cm; Length 16. 5cm; Thickness 12. 5cm. From C3, the fill to the natural channel in trench C.

5.2 (Figure 6: 12) Tile fragment in tile fabric 1 but slightly coarser than usual and fired red with the fragmentary incuse stamp C. Width 24cm; Length 26cm; Thickness 6. 2cm. From C4, the Roman or post-Roman land drain.

5.3 (Figure 6: 12) Tile fragment of *tegula* with broken flange in tile fabric 1. Fragmentary incuse stamp C (the letter broken half way down). Width 12. 5cm; Length 18. 4cm; Thickness 14. 7cm. From the same context as 5. 2.

All three stamps are most likely to be expanded CO[H, C(o)[H or similar and to refer to the cohort responsible for manufacture (though not necessarily the cohort in garrison). In addition to the stamps one or two indistinct animal paw and human thumb prints were also recorded.

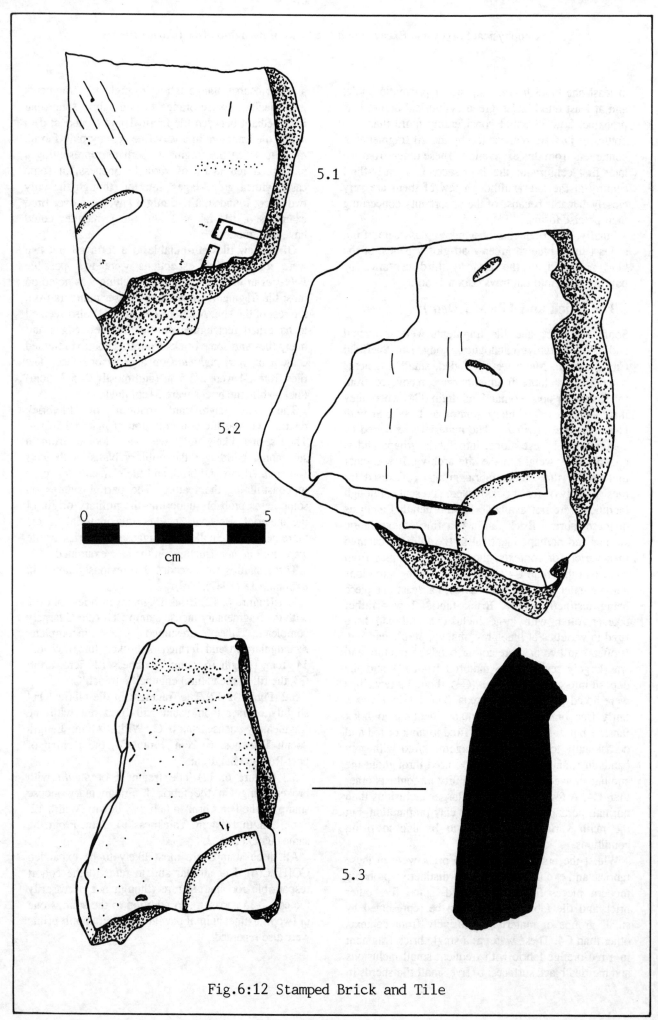

5.1

5.2

0 — 5

cm

5.3

Fig.6:12 Stamped Brick and Tile

6 The Coin *J. F. Drinkwater*

Arg. *Denarius* Obverse: Augustus, bareheaded, r. Reverse: Circular shield, set in square formed by the letters SPQR; above SIGNIS, below RECEPTIS; to the left legionary eagle; to the right normal military standard.
A. D. 19: Spanish mint (*RIC* i (2nd ed. 1984) p. 47, No. 86a). From the fill of the phase lb feature S19/20.

7 The Copper Alloy Brooch *D. F. Mackreth* (Figure 6: 13)

The pin is hinged. The head is a kind of flattened trumpet sweeping out sideways to the ends of the wings. On the head are slight remains of a cast-on loop. The central ornament is a disc with a round cell and a surrounding annulus for enamel, now missing. On one side can be seen a trace of a small boss. Above the disc is a small cross-moulding, while below there are at least three which occupy the upper part of a badly corroded fantail foot. Down the centre of this is a line of lozenge-shaped cells with infilling triangles on each side. Traces of red enamel can be seen in the triangles on the left.

This is the commonest of three designs united by the form of the head, a central motif and a fantail foot, the latter two enamelled. One variant has a circular centre, as here, but divided radially into cells and often with a seperately-made ribbed stud in the middle and three triangular cells on the foot (e. g. Bushe-Fox 1914, 13, Figure 4. 3). The other alternative has the same foot, but has a rectangular panel with a groove top and bottom and a row of rectangular cells for enamel across the middle instead of the disc (e. g. Allason-Jones and Miket 1984, 115, 3. 135). Dating is sparse: Rudston, possibly second century (Stead 1980, 95, Figure 61, 95); Silchester, mid-second century (Boon 1969, 47, Figure 6. 8, poor drawing). The other varieties offer little extra information: Newstead, 80–c. 200 (Curle 1911, 324, pl. LXXXVI, 24; Hartley 1972, 54); Camelon, either late-first or mid-second century (Christison 1901, 406, pl. A, 4; Hartley 1972, 42-4). Taking the form of the head as reflecting the Trumpet type, the second century is indicated, and probably before c. 150/75. From within the surfaceing of the pathway in trench G.

8 Objects of Iron *M.J.Dearne*

Some 78 iron objects were recovered including a modern horseshoe and blade fragment. All except these were highly corroded. Sixty nine were certainly or provisionally identified as nails. Of these few could be more closely classified except No. 8. 13 below, but both round and rectangular headed forms were present. Only the following iron objects were at all identifiable.

8. 1   (Figure 6: 13) Firmer chisel (blade width (max) 12mm; surviving length 59mm). The blade tapers evenly on both sides to a slightly damaged, unsplayed end. The stem is badly corroded and ?broken away and it is impossible to ascertain its cross section. *Cf.* Manning (1985, 22f). From the phase 1 pit fill P3.

8. 2   (Figure 6: 13) ?Punch (surviving length 41. 5mm). Relatively well preserved tip of a ?punch with a square-sectioned rod tapering to a definite point. An alternative interpretation as the end of a tang for a tool (e. g. a file such as Manning (1985, 11 No. 37)) is possible. *Cf.* Manning (1985, l0f Nos. A30-32). From the fill of the phase lb feature S19/20.

8. 3   (Figure 6: 13) Catapult bolt-head (length 67mm). Highly corroded Manning (1985 , 170) type 1 bolt-head with conical (or perhaps origonally diamond-shaped) head and circular neck. X-ray indicates the presence of a socket, though its form is impossible to ascertain. *Cf.* Manning (1985 Nos V252-3). From the phase 3 pebbled surface F5.

8. 4   (Figure 6: 13) ?Latchlifter (or ??bolthead) (surviving length 82. 5mm; width (max) 21. 5mm). Round-sectioned bar, curved in opposite directions at each end and widening at one to a damaged and corroded flat head. There are problems with identifying this as a latchlifter since its 'handle' has no eye and its curvature and length (though incomplete) seem insufficient. An alternative interpretation as a bolt head with bent tang is also problematic. Flat bladed bolt heads are known (Manning 1985 , 175 type II) but none fixed by a tang are known to the author and the bar would be too long for a neck above a socket. *Cf.* a broadly similar piece with a rectangular tang from Kelvedon (Rodwell 1988 Figure 53 No. l0). From T4, the secondary fill of the phase lb V-shaped ditch.

8. 5   (Figure 6: 13) Drop-hinge staple (length 74mm). Corroded and damaged staple of L form. The longer arm is rectangular-sectioned and damaged but appears to be tapering to a point. The shorter has a circular section and is also damaged. Unstratified.

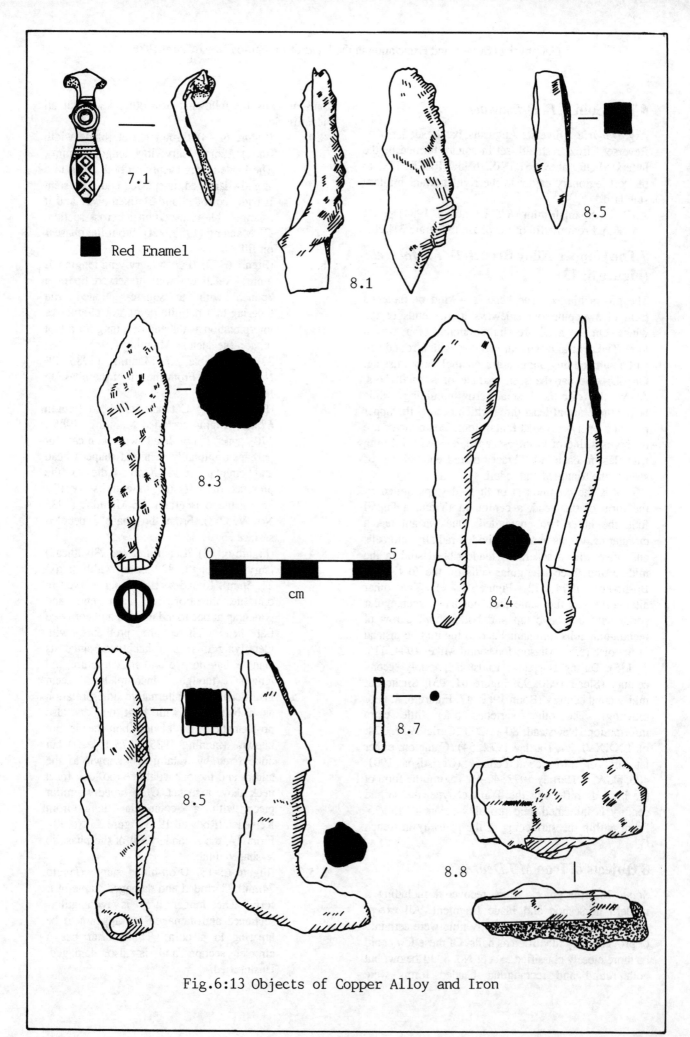

7.1

■ Red Enamel

8.1

8.5

8.3

0   cm   5

8.4

8.5

8.7

8.8

Fig.6:13 Objects of Copper Alloy and Iron

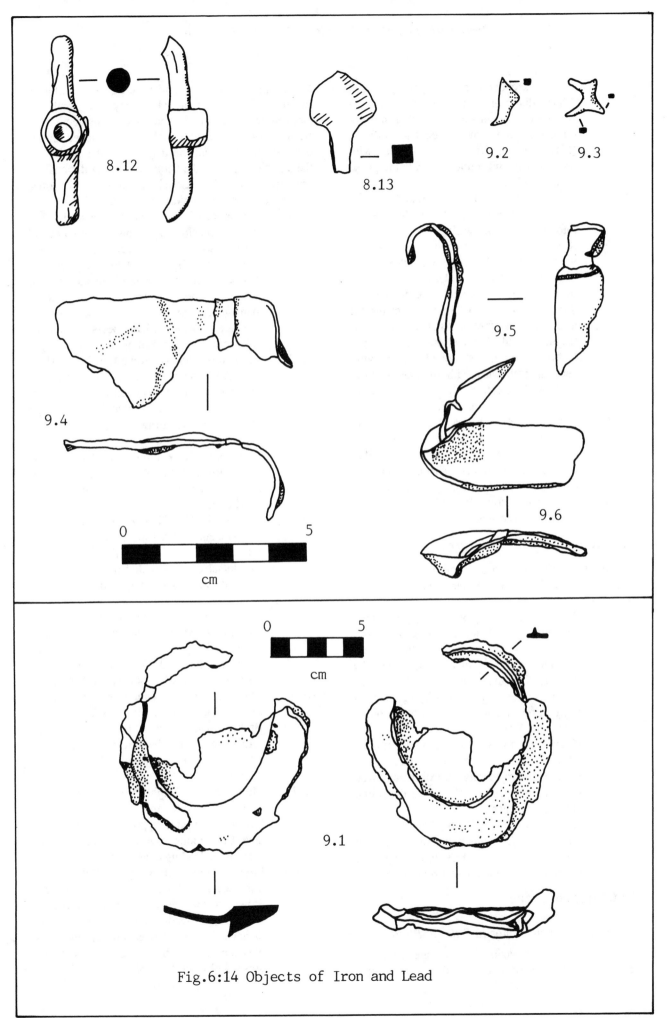

Fig.6:14 Objects of Iron and Lead

8. 6   Circular-sectioned bar fragment (length 30mm; diameter l0mm). Unstratified.

8. 7   (Figure 6: 14) Pin shank (length 17mm) of circular section. Now broken. Unstratified.

8. 8   (Figure 6: 13) Strip (length 48mm) with one rounded end. From the fill to the phase 1 pit M39/P4.

8. 9   Strip (length 49mm) with rounded ends. Now broken. From the fill to the channel into the phase 1 pit M39/P4.

8. 10   Riveted iron strips (length (max) 47mm; width 15mm). Two, or one folded, iron strip(s) riveted together. Unstratified.

8. 11   Round, ?concave object (max diameter *c.* 80mm). Collapsed on lifting. From the fill to the recut channel in trench D.

8. 12   (Figure 6: 14) ?Swivel fragment (length 50mm). Circular sectioned bar curving back at both ends with integral, central, ?hollow projection for ?swivel link. Perhaps modern. Unstratified.

8. 13   (Figure 6: 14) Nail head (surviving length 27mm). Head and part of shank of Manning (1985 , 134ff) type II nail. Flat, rectangular sectioned shank with flat triangular head, slightly rounded by hammering. From the fill to the natural channel in trenches C, K and L.

9 Objects of Lead *M.J.Dearne*

Sixteen lead offcuts, splashes and solidified spills were recovered along with one large lump of galena, including:

9. 1   (Figure 6: 14) Solidified spill (max diameter *c.* 210mm; thickness 8-33mm) now in two pieces. Damaged thin central circular, concave 'plate' surrounded by thicker, irregular border. Probably the result of molten lead solidifying over an object. From the top of the fill of the phase lc channel S21.

9. 2-9. 3   (Figure 6: 14) Casting lugs (lengths *c.* 9mm). Lead blobs with rectangular sectioned projections probably removed from a casting. From the fill to the initial channel in trench D.

9. 4-9. 6   (Figure 6: 14) Offcuts (length up to 60mm). Three offcuts with one straight, cut and one irregular edges found together. From the fill to the phase 1 pit M39/P4.

10 Objects of Stone

a) The Prehistoric Material *Patricia Phillips*

The flint and chert collection from the site consists of retouched and polished tools (9), flakes (16), cores (5), knapping waste (3) and a single bladelet/burin, making 34 artifacts in all. They are made in Derbyshire chert, and in matt and translucent flint from outside the county. All the retouched pieces occur in the flint, and the majority of the cores, and the bladelet, occur in the chert. Maximum dimensions are given for the retouched pieces and cores. Dimensions for broken pieces are prefixed B.

10. 1   (Figure 6: 15) Flint leaf arrowhead. Brown-grey translucent flint. Assymetrical arrowhead, with tip to left of centre. Steep retouch on the ventral (bulbar) surface below the tip on the left indicates that it was rechipped, perhaps after being damaged. The base is also slightly damaged. The arrowhead bears shallow all over retouch. 31 X 18mm.

10. 2   Flint knife. Orangy-brown translucent flint. The flake has been cut in half vertically, leaving part of the facetted butt preserved. The right dorsal edge bears edge retouch/use, including a deep notch in the centre. 45 X 15mm.

10. 3   Flint knife. Dark brown translucent flint. Flake struck off bird's wing butt covered in secondary cortex. Top of knife missing. B 26 X 22mm.

10. 4   (Figure 6: 15) Flint thumbnail scraper. Translucent brown flint. Scraper has steep retouch three-quarters of the way around the dorsal edge. Struck from a broad butt covered with secondary cortex. 21 X 22mm.

10. 5   Flint scraper. Matt light brown flint, white mottling. Steep retouch completely encircles edge of large slightly oval scraper. The bulb has been removed, resulting in a nearly flat base. 50 X 44mm.

10. 6   Flint endscraper. Orangy-brown, white-flecked flint, with highly polished surfaces. Broken distal part of broad blade with scraper end and backed retouch, partly crushed by use, along both edges. B 41 X 23mm.

10. 7   Flint scraper. Bright brown shiny flint, occasional white inclusions. Scraper is broken along edge opposite main scraping area. Continuous even retouch and signs of wear along leading edge. B 21 X 29mm.

10. 8   Flint scraper. Dark grey-black, semi-translucent flint with area of sandy light brown cortex. Scraper bears continuous retouch along leading edge and signs of use damage. There are deep breaks and scars opposite the leading edge on both the dorsal and ventral surfaces. B 22 X 31mm.

10. 9 (Figure 6: 15) Flint axe blade. White flint, matt, with slightly cracked surface. Part of the polished axe blade is preserved, with a broken area beyond, forming a rough triangle. There appears to be use-damage on the blade and on the left dorsal edge of the piece (possible use as scraper). The right dorsal edge has been damaged more recently.

10. 10 Chert core. Striped pale and dark grey chert. Two opposing platforms, one tiny, one larger, and four narrow facets, one showing slight negative bulb. 27 X 13mm.

10. 11 Ditto. Dark grey chert. Tiny. Worn. Two opposing platforms with cortex on both,

and flake scars. 22 X 15mm.

10. 12 Ditto. Pale grey chert. Rectangular. Two similar opposed platforms, one with cortex, one with fossil fragment. Negative bulbs and broad blade scars on two sides. 38 X 18mm.

10. 13 Flint core. Dark grey-orange flint. Area of smooth white secondary cortex. Damaged. One hammered butt. Butt from which most recent flakes removed missing. B 31 X 27mm.

10. 14 ?Ditto. Similar flint. Two areas of sandy cortex. Very damaged.

10. 15 (Figure 6: 15) Chert bladelet/?burin. Dark grey chert. The bladelet or possible burin

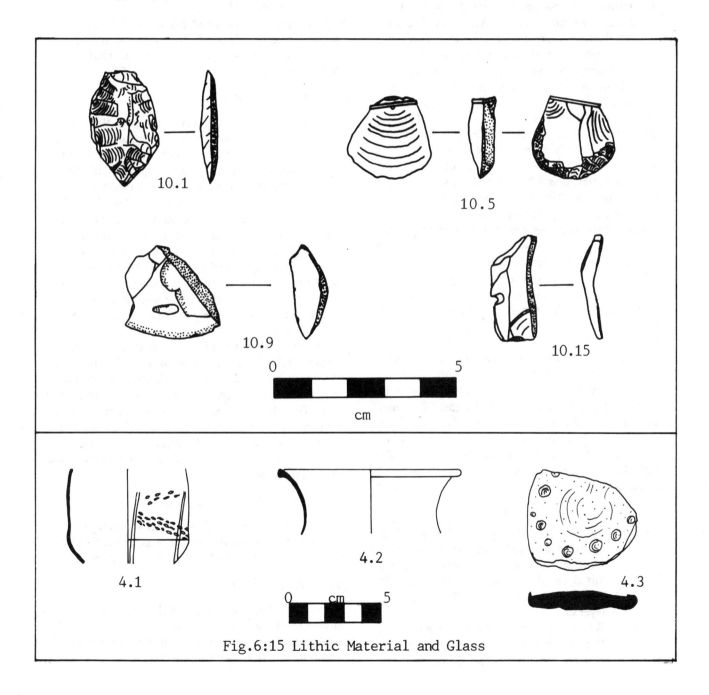

Fig.6:15 Lithic Material and Glass

has a thickened broken tip, with a burin facet down the right edge, and a circular scar or notch in the centre of the left dorsal edge. 27 X 11mm.

Two of the pieces of knapping debitage are of chert, the third piece being in matt flint. Ten of the sixteen flakes are under 20mm in length. Two of the larger flakes are core rejuvenation flakes in matt flint and a third small core rejuvenation flake is in translucent flint. Seven of the ordinary flakes are in translucent flint; three in chert; two in matt flint; and one is in identical material to and was probably struck from the axe fragment 10. 9.

Use-wear or use-damage can be seen on the leading edges of the scrapers, on the broken tip of the arrowhead, and less certainly on the polished axe blade and on the edges of a few flakes. The flint of the retouched artifacts, axe fragment and ten flakes varies widely within the 'matt' and 'translucent' catagories. A whitish-grey matt flint with sandy inclusions, and a translucent brown-grey flint are similar to raw materials found in Lincolnshire and Humberside. More orange matt and shiny flint is more likely to come from the Cheshire plain (I. Brooks pers. comm.). The Cheshire plain tended to be used as a resource area in the Early Neolithic, the Lincolnshire/Humberside tills and coastal resources in the Late Neolithic (Brooks and Garton in prep.). Three cores, two pieces of knapping debris, three flakes and the bladelet/burin are in different types and qualities of chert, known to outcrop in southern Derbyshire, for instance at Bakewell.

The varied typologies and technologies in the collection indicate that there were several periods of frequentation of the area in the prehistoric period. The chert cores, with their bladelet scars, and the bladelet/burin probably date to the Late Mesolithic period. The leaf arrowhead may date to the Early Neolithic, but the form is found throughout the Neolithic period in northern England. Because of its shape and orange shiny flint endscraper 10. 6 may also date to the Early Neolithic. The thumbnail scraper 10. 4 is Late Neolithic–Beaker in date, while the large scraper 10. 5 may have been made in the early Bronze Age, both because of its raw material and its all-round retouch.

b)Other Material *M.J.Dearne*

10. 16 Small ?sculptural fragment (32 X 23mm) in fine grained Limestone, probably broken from the front of a carved stone. Part of a raised circular border with ?soot deposits either side survives. From phase 2 general layer O4.

10. 17 Whetstone fragment (length 115mm; width 50mm; thickness 25-30mm). Fairly fine grained Gritstone. Plano-convex section with rough back and worn upper faces. From the fill of the recut channel in trench D.

10. 18 Ditto (length 90mm; width 26-45mm; thickness 26-30mm). Tapering, square section. Unstratified.

10. 19 Ditto (length 60mm; width 24-26mm; thickness 5-21mm). Tapering rectangular section. Unstratified.

10. 20 Ditto (length 35mm; width 15-20mm). Plano-convex section. Unstratified.

10. 21 Ditto (length 105mm; width 50mm; thickness 30mm) in coarse Gritstone. Irregular form worn on upper surface and two edges. From the fill of the phase la channel M24.

In addition a number of pieces of Gritstone that showed possible signs of working were recovered, notably from the ?well pit in trench E, the phase 1 pit M39/P4 and the recut channel in trench D.

11 Slag *M.J.Dearne*

Seventy fragments of slag were recovered, all but two (which may have been lead slag) relating to iron working. In most contexts finds were only of very small pieces of slag which appeared of little significance. These contexts included representatives of all phases in trench group F/M/O/P/S/T/U. However, slag was not noted stratified in any other trenches. Two contexts produced more significant groups of slag. T6, the phase lb pit fill with charcoal concentrations produced two large and two smaller blocks of slag with some stone inclusions. The slag was black and glassy with purple areas and a mottled cream/ red core and the largest piece was 13 X 8 X 6. 5cm and weighed 723g (25. 5oz).

The largest number of slag fragments (36) came from the fills of the phase 1 pit M39/P4. Much of the slag here appeared to have brick/tile or charcoal inclusions, though none of the pieces were of great size. Two distinct types occured in roughly equal proportions, a black, glassy form and a black to brown cindery form which appeared to be smithing slag. One of the possible lead slag fragments also derived from this pit.

12 Painted Plaster *M.J.Dearne*

Two small fragments of buff plaster retaining traces of red paint were recovered. One was unstratified but the other came from the fill of the phase lc ditch S21.

13 Bone *M.J.Dearne*

No worked bone survived the hostile pedological environment and only eleven very small and unidentifiable pieces of bone were recovered, mostly unstratified or from unsealed contexts.

7. Aerial Reconnaissance at Brough-on-Noe

Martin J. Dearne

The nature of the subsoil and ground cover at Brough-on-Noe is not particularly condusive to the formation of crop marks or other phenomena detectable by aerial photography. The Hope Valley is also a regular venue for glider and hang-glider flights and consequently aerial coverage has in the past been limited. However, a series of oblique views of the site were taken by D. Riley in April 1988 and passed to the author who detected in addition to the known features of the site faint traces of an unrecorded enclosure. The author is most grateful to Dr. Riley for access to these photographs and for allowing him to discuss and reproduce one of them here.

Plate 6 shows the broad outlines of the later fort, together with many of Richmond and Gillam's and Jones's trenches within it and acrosss its defences. The trenches cut in 1980–3 south east of the fort and in 1986 south west of the fort prior to the visible afforestation are also identifiable, together with a water main trench running along the south east edge of the fort and then striking towards the R. Noe. The *agger* of the later track on the line of Batham Gate, visible on the ground and sectioned in 1980-1 (Bishop *et. al.*, this volume), is also clear and shown rectified on Figure 7:1. Two dark lines running parallel to it some distance to the south east appear rather to be tractor tracks leading to the modern field gate.

The newly recognised enclosure (Figure 7:1) appears as faint darker lines adjacent to a bend in the R. Noe in the field of hay grass north east of that in which the fort lies. Parts of all four sides are identifiable and appear to form a rectangular enclosure *c.*47.5 x 50m (0.24 ha) with rounded corners. A single dark line also runs much if not the whole of the length of the enclosure along its centre and continues for a distance beyond its east side. Within the enclosure there are slight traces of a small square feature and of two lines meeting at right angles, none of which seem to have any relationship to the orientation of the enclosure.

The nature of the crop marks suggest that they are caused by negative freatures, presumbly ditches, and the shape of the enclosure would be consistent with a Roman military context. Thus it is possible that the enclosure represents a small military compound such as a fortlet, construction camp, baggage park or detached fort annexe. However, especially if the line along the centre of the enclosure also reflects a ditch rather than a road and the possible (seemingly disorganised) internal features are contemporary with the enclosure such an interpretaion must be highly provisional. Indeed, without at least trial excavation the archaeological character of the features must remain unconfirmed and their date and function conjectoral.

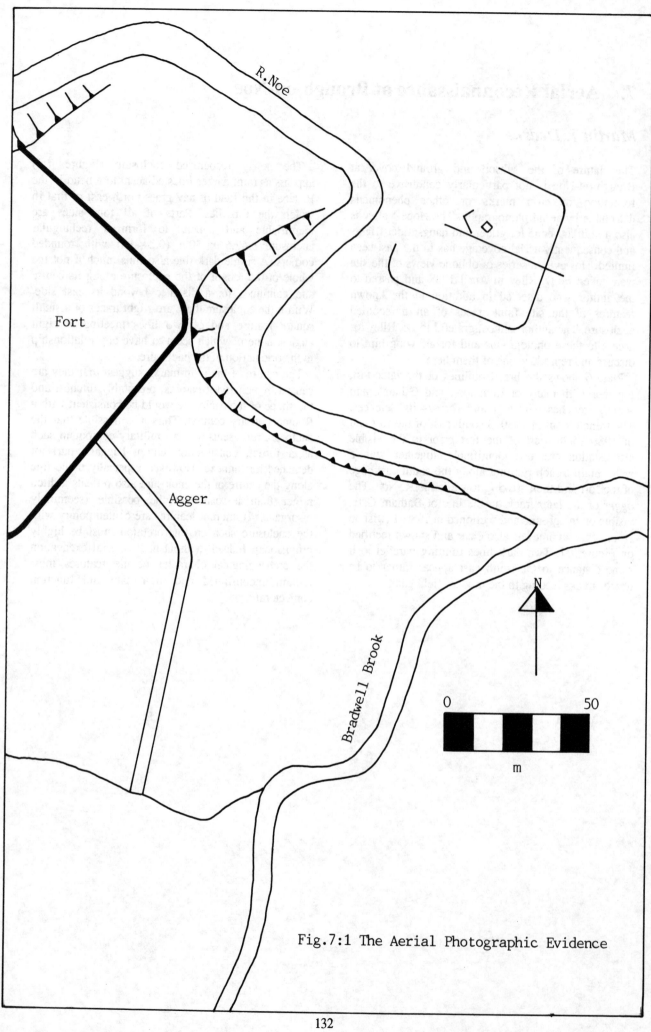

Fig.7:1 The Aerial Photographic Evidence

8. A Stone Ball from Brough-on-Noe (*Navio*), Derbyshire

C.R. Hart

In the 1969 excavations carried out within the fort of *Navio* by G.D.B. Jones and J.P. Wild 'an immense stone ball, 17 inches (43cm) in diameter was found among the debris of period IIB in the inner ditch' (Jones and Wild 1970, 106). A (?) further stone ball has subsequently been recovered 'at a depth of 3½ ft (1m)' by pipeline contractors, *c.* 1972, trenching on behalf of the North Derbyshire Water Board, in the area to the east of the ramparts (SK 18188268). This curious object and a few large animal bones were removed by the contractor to decorate a garden rockery in Chesterfield where they remained unrecorded until 1988, when they were brought to the author's attention.

This latest example of a stone ball is of locally fashioned Millstone Grit, weighing 11 stone (69.854 Kg). It has evenly chisel-pecked surfaces with the exception of two small flat plains lying at right angles to each other, The stone is oval with one axis measuring 42cm long with the other some 35.5cm long (Sheffield City Museum E2921, pending accessioning).

Limited visual comparative studies have been made by the writer with the so-called ballista balls mounted on the High Rochester School House, Northumberland. These stone balls appear to be similar in scale, but are fashioned by flake technique and are of regular spherical form. The High Rochester and Risingham balls are estimated as weighing 'about a hundred weight' (*c.* 50 Kg) (Richmond 1945/6).

The published evidence for such items in the U.K. is plainly inadequate (Campbell 1984). The 1969 Brough stone ball thought to be in the Manchester University Collections is currently not available for examination or weighing (correspondence and pers.comm. G.D.B. Jones 1989; 1990), and may well have been reburied at Brough (pers.comm. G.D.B. Jones via editor 1992). A slightly smaller rounded stone with one flat surface measuring 32cm in diameter from South Shields (S315), with pecked surfaces and weighing 7 stone (44.45 Kg), was recovered from the footings of a 'courtyard building' within the enlarged fort. This also has been tentatively identified by the excavators as a ballista ball (*Arbeia* reports, vol. 2 forthcoming). There are two large stone balls on display in the Roman displays at Tullie House Museum, Carlisle, but these are post-medieval gate pier stones (pers.comm. N. Winterbotham).

The possibility of the Brough-on-Noe and South Shields stone balls being used as stone finials decorating and/or weighing down balls within these military establishments cannot be considered. It is more likely that these rounded stones would have been placed over gateways, or on the ramparts, in readiness to be pushed over and on to any attacking forces. Trajan's column (Lepper and Frere 1988, plate XCVIII/XCIX casts 357–60) depicts the desperate hurling of stones by Roman infantry onto attacking Dacian forces.

Smaller, rounded hand-sized projectiles appear to be much more common than these larger stone balls. Certainly, the larger stone balls' size and weight makes it unlikely that they would have been thrown by a ballista or onager type machine set within these forts. The flat surfaces on the pecked balls would have aided tidy stacking in readiness for an emergency.

9. *Navio*: Synthesis and Discussion

Martin J. Dearne

Introduction

Prior to the publication of the present volume many of the results of the archaeologcial work at Brough-on-Noe over the last 45 years were only accessable through brief notes and interim reports. The full publication of the five major excavations and surveys included in it provides a convenient occasion to assess both what is known of the site and its significance and to examine the priorities for any future work. Although fuller publication of the work of the 1960s would be desirable to clarify details of several known structures much of the fort plan at least in phases 2 and 3 can be outlined, as can at least something of the *vicus*'s plan and development.

In general in the fort synthesis the intention has been to provide some integrated account of what evidence is available rather than to cite extensive parallels for building plans etc. Thus, a good deal of the information and inferences contained in the reports on the fort included in the present volume and previously published in the *Derbyshire Archaeological Journal* have been repeated in the interest of producing one unified account. Indeed, the author's debt to the excavators of the fort from Garstang to G.D.B. Jones will be apparent and only where there seems to be a conflict of evidence have the majority of their conclusions been re-assessed.

For the *vicus* such a narrative account has not been considered appropriate and more emphasis has been placed on attempting to define the plan, extent and chronology of the settlement from the evidence available. Some consideration has also been given to the probable courses of the main roads leaving the site since some of them at least may have affected the siteing of the *vicus*.

A Note on the Fort Plans

As will be apparent from the synthesis there are a number of points of the plans of all four fort phases for which there is either no evidence or for which the evidence is contradictory. In producing Figures 8: 1–8: 4 the intention has been to present as complete as possible a plan for each phase so where it seems reasonable elements such as ditches, rampart lines and internal road courses have been infered from the evidence available (though the reconstruction of building plans from known fragments has less often been found to be justified).However, it should be bourne in mind that such details as the width of the rampart at different points in phases 2 and 3 often

rest on the conclusions reached in the synthesis about the validity of slim or inconsistent evidence and should not be taken as finally established. A number of these problems are treated at some length in the synthesis but it is worth emphasising here that the reconciling of details gleaned over some 90 years and the reliance on incomplete publications and small scale plans has exascerbated the problems. Indeed much has been based on the late Sir Ian Richmond's archive plans held at the Ashmolean Museum which he updated to take account of some later work. Nevertheless the exact course of the phase 2/3 fort wall (and rampart/intervallum road), especially either side of its west corner, has presented particular problems which are unlikely to be fully resolved without further work. Certain features have also had to be omitted or only summarily marked either because they were too small to show (principally the drains and water supply system) or because no satisfactory plans of them have been published (elements of the phase 1 *principia* and granaries and the phase 2a and b barracks).

1) The Fort Chronology

The basic outlines of the fort's chronology were established by Richmond and Gillam (this volume) and confirmed and amplified by Jones, Thompson and Wild (1966) and Jones and Wild (1968). Although the amount of pottery published from the fort remains regretably small no significant revision in these dating conclusions seems necessary.

i) Phase 1 (*c.* 80 – *c.*120)

The phase one fort was clearly founded in the late-first century (e.g. Richmond and Gillam this volume) but its exact foundation date has been little discussed. In common with many forts in northern Britain it has been assumed to be an Aricolan foundation of *c.* 80. However, as noted in the introduction to this volume an earlier foundation date must be a possibility for at least some conventionally 'Agricolan' sites and Jones (1968, 6) has pointed out that Brough is as good a strategic candidate as any for a Frontinian origin, while Hanson (1987, 162) has postulated a post-Agricolan foundation. As yet this question must remain open.

Gillam (Richmond and Gillam this volume) considered the phase 1 occupation to have ended *c.* 125. Jones, Thompson and Wild (1966, 99f) found that the clay dump sealing it contained mainly

Flavian–Trajanic pottery but with a single BB1 sherd dating immediately before 125 and consequently re-dated the evacuation to *c*. 120. Clearly the likely context for the evacuation was the garrisoning of the Hadrian's Wall frontier but it is not possible to establish a precise date for the end of phase one at Brough. A bracket of 120–5 is however clearly indicated.

ii) Phase 2a (154/8–*c*. 200)

The foundation of the phase 2 fort is almost certainly dated to 154/8 by *R.I.B.* 283, an inscription found reused in the later *principia* strongroom recording building work under Julius Verrus. The pottery evidence is less precise (Jones, Thompson and Wild 1966, 100: third-quarter of the second century including much Derbyshire ware now dated *c*. 140+; Jones 1967, 57: late-second century; Richmond and Gillam this volume: mid-second century).However there is nothing here to question the supposition that *R.I.B.* 283 records the construction of the phase two fort.

The end of phase 2a is less secure, resting on the late-second century BBI assemblage found in 1967 (*op cit*). This material, from the *praetentura* barracks suggests a date *c*. 200 for the end of the sub-phase. Some slight support is given by the likelihood that the fort wall was an insertion at the beginning of phase 2b and that it and the ?early-third century *principia* strongroom represent a Severan rebuilding as part of a pattern of such reconstructions in northern Britain (Jones 1967, 157).

iii)Phase 2b (*c*.200–*c*.300)

Phase 2b followed 2a without a gap as is clear from the reconstruction of the *praetenura* barracks on almost exactly the same lines. The end of phase 2b seems from two groups of pottery (Jones, Thompson and Wild 1966, 100; Richmond and Gillam this volume) to have lain in the late-third or early-fourth centuries. A little evidence from phase 3, which again followed without a break, probably suggests that the date in fact lay immediately after 300.

iv) Phase 3 (*c*.300–*c*.350)

The best evidence for the date of the phase 2b/phase 3 interface comes from two coins. A slighly worn coin of 288 was lodged in the phase 3 stable partition wall (Jones and Wild 1968, 93) while a coin of Constantine 1st, perhaps of 310–13 came from below the late causewayed entrance (Bartlett and Dearne this volume).The construction of the latter need not be exactly contemporary with the beginning of phase 3 but, as Jones and Wild (1970, 106) noted, its dating strengthens the case for the changes marking the beginning of phase 3 being essentially Constantinian.

Further evidence is yet required but at the moment a date probably shortly after *c*. 300 seems to be indicated.

The date of the fort's final abandonment at the end of phase 3 is a little more secure. The latest stratified pottery is a hammerhead mortarium of the second-half of the fourth century from the final surface of the *via principalis* which agrees in date with the latest unstratified material (Jones. Thompson and Wild 1966, 101; Richmond and Gillam this volume). Pottery also seems to suggest that the site may have been abandoned by *c*. 360 (Jones and Wild 1968, 93–6) while a coin of Magnentius (350–3) from above the collapsed phase 3 ?*praetorium* (Jones and Wild 1970, 106) offers some corroberation of this. On balance a date immediately after the middle of the fourth century seems to be indicated.

2) The Phase 1 Fort (Figure 8: 1)

Relatively little is known of the phase 1 fort. The defences were found by Richmond and Gillam (this volume) and seen again in 1958/9 (Bartlett and Dearne this volume), while some of the internal buildings are partly known, mainly from incompletely published work in the 1960s. However, much of the size and nature of the fort remains problematic.

i) Size and Defences

The size of the phase 1 fort is still uncertain. At least at the west corner and south west side it had an inner ditch 2.4m wide and 0.6m deep with a rectangular channel at its base which was immediately followed by a 1.5m deep V-shaped ditch probably *c*. 7.3m wide (Richmond and Gillam this volume).The ditches were seen again below the south angle of the later fort in 1958/9 and were probably broadly similar (Bartlett and Dearne this volume). The position, but not form, of the south west gate is known a little north east of the later fort's south west gate. Traces of the rampart were identified by Jones and Thompson (1965) near the later north west gate and given the projected line of the inner ditch it seemed to be some 3.7m (12ft 5in) wide. However, particulary given that rampart material might have been used to seal the phase 1 fort, it might originally have been wider. The rampart was of clay but no further details are available.

The south west and north east defences both lay further north east than those of phase 2/3. The former are known to have been *c*. 10.6m further north east but the latter have not been located. Traces of internal buildings were found below the later north east rampart (Jones and Thompson, 1965) and phase one demolition and tip deposits were located in the vicinity of the later north east ditches, though their exact nature is not clear from the published account (Jones, Thompson and Wild 1966, 101). However,

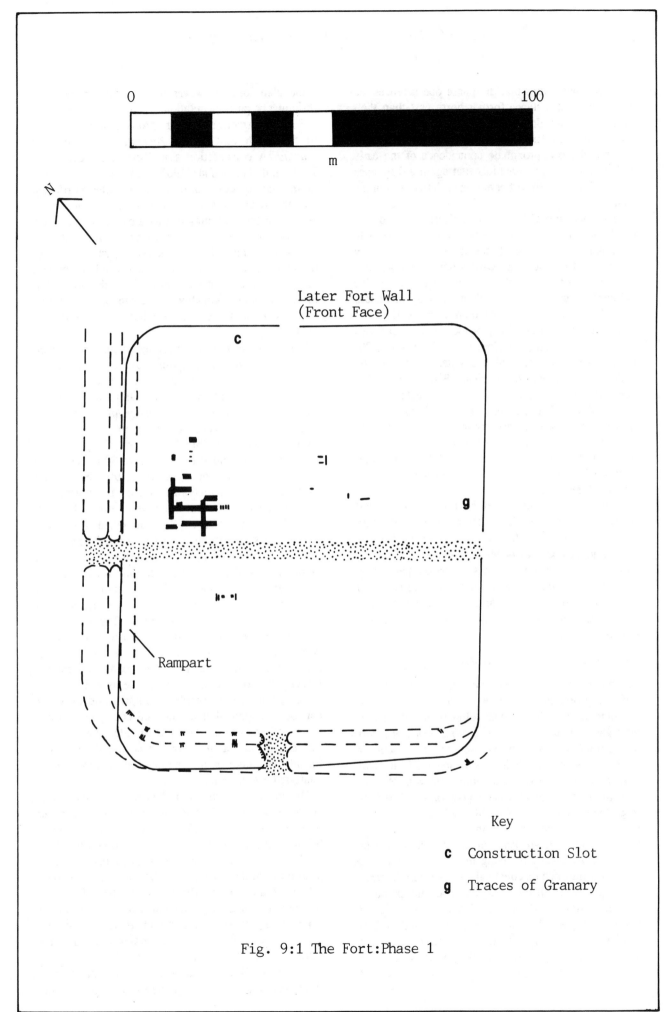

0   100

m

N

Later Fort Wall
(Front Face)

c

g

Rampart

Key

c Construction Slot

g Traces of Granary

Fig. 9:1 The Fort:Phase 1

there are indications that the phase one defences did not lie a great distance further north east than their successors. The relatively steep slope north east of the fort down to the River Noe may have been a limiting factor and the approximate coincidence of the early and later *via principalis* hints that again a difference of 10–12m between earlier and later defences is of the right order.

Richmond and Gillam's work clearly showed that on the north west the phase one defences were only marginally north west of the later fort's. The early fort's extent on the south east is however more of a problem. Bartlett's work (Bartlett and Dearne this volume) suggested that the defences may have lain some 9m further south east than those of the later fort. Certainly the discovery of the phase 1 granaries near the later east gate (Jones and Wild 1968, 90) indicate some greater south east extent. However, the 1980–3 excavations in the *vicus* (Bishop *et al.* this volume) did not reveal any military features. The failure of 1958/9 trench A and a trench cut in 1969 (Bartlett and Dearne this volume; Jones and Wild 1970) to find the early defences may well suggest that the later defences in fact obliterated them and that they did indeed lie only some 9m further south east than the later line.

Given the foregoing, and bearing in mind that further evidence is needed on the north east and south east, a tentative guess for the fort's size may be made at around 104 x 95m or about 1 hectare measuring from the front of the ramparts. Allowing perhaps *c.* 9m for the rampart/intervallum the internal area would be around 0.66 hectares (1.64 acres). Thus, it seems likely that the earlier fort was not greatly larger than its successor.

ii) Plan and Internal Buildings

Richmond recognised that the phase one fort was differently orientated to the later fort. His suggestion (Richmond and Gillam this volume) that the south west gate was the *porta principalis sinistra* of a fort facing north west was superseaded with the discovery of the fort's internal buildings which made it clear that the phase 1 fort faced south west with the *via principalis* in roughly the same position in all periods (e.g. Jones and Wild 1968, 90). Almost nothing is known of the clearly rather small *praetentura* except that the one known gate on the south west was asymetrically placed implying that the *via praetoria* divided it into two disequal halves. The only internal buildings known in the *praetentura* are the probable verandah, drain and hearths of a barracks alligned *per strigas* (sw-ne) found by Richmond and Gillam (this volume). A hypothetical reconstruction might see two barracks (or indeed stables) north west of the *via praetoria* and ? four more to its south east, all

some 28m long. However without further evidence this must be pure speculation.

Further barracks/stables are probably to be expected in the north east of the *raetentura* alligned *per scamna*. A construction slot 76cm wide located by Jones and Thompson (1965, 126) below the later rampart along with a drain *c.* 1.5m further north east probably related to such a structure but little more can be said of the buildings in this area. Even the space available for them is uncertain since the north east defences are unlocated and the north eastern limits of the administrative range are unknown. Four or less likely six barracks of fairly normal width and *c.* 30m in length could probably be accomodated but this must remain no more than speculation without further evidence.

The *latera praetorii* consisting of the *praetorium*, *principia* and granaries laying in the *raetentura* along the *via principalis* are partly known. Excavations by Manchester University in the 1960s revealed the partial plan of the probable *praetorium* at the north west end of the block. It seems to have been an entirely wooden building, as were all phase one structures, represented by beam slots 30–38 cm wide (Jones, Thompson and Wild 1966, 99). No certain external walls were recorded but on the north west side it cannot have extended very much if at all beyond the limits of excavation. Its north west–south east extent seems to have been between 21 and 23m and it was clearly at least 23m south west–north east (Jones and Wild 1970, 100). Certainly it cannot have extended much further south west than the known fragments indicate or it would have encroached on the *via principalis*, though Jones, Thompson and Wild (1966, 99) noted that its construction trenches continued for a short distance under the later *via prinicpalis* suggesting that the road had moved marginally north east of its phase one line. The building's plan is incompletely known and as yet it cannot be certain that the normal courtyard did not exist, perhaps on its north easten side. However, all that can be said at the moment is that the building included a range of rectangular rooms and that no courtyard is evidenced.

The presumed *principia* in the centre of the range is almost unknown. Slots located below the later *via praetoria* by Jones (1967, 155) seem likely to have belonged to it, though they are not shown on Figure 8: 1 since no plan has been published of their positions. Similarly the phase one features exposed by Richmond and Gillam (this volume) included a group of three slots that they speculated at the time might belong to a granary but are in fact probably to be seen as parts of a *principia*. Richmond and Gillam's records are not explicit as to which other features on archive plans belonged to phase one, but three other short wall lines seem more likely to relate to this rather than later phases. Far too little is known of the building to speculate upon its plan or even its size. The granaries were located in 1968 near the later fort's east gate. Their sleeper beam trenches were 35cm wide, aligned north east–south west at 61cm intervals and suggest granaries aligned north west–south east (Jones and Wild 1968, 90). However, too little is known of them to speculate on their number and size.

3) The Later Fort

The later fort is far better known than its predecessor and all excavations at the site have revealed elements of it. Richmond and Gillam (this volume) divined that it encompassed two structural phases and the work of the 1960s established that the first of these in fact consisted of two recognisable sub-phases.

i) The Phase 1/2 interface

The fort was re-established on the same site as its predecessor and most excavations have revealed a layer of clay 23–30cm thick sealing the interior of the earlier fort. This was partly replaced in 1958/9 trench A by yellow gravel (Bartlett and Dearne this volume) and work in 1969 on the site of the phase 2a/b granaries in the same general area indicated that late building activity there had removed phase 1 features and so the clay spread if it had existed (Jones and Wild 1970, 101). Richmond and Gillam (this volume) suggested that the source of the clay was the demolished phase one rampart, no trace of which was found by them. This seems a likely conclusion, though at least a vestige of the rampart is known on the north west (above). The date of this sealing activity has already been shown to be *c*. 120–5. The phase one fort ditches were also filled before the construction of the later fort. Raistrick (in Richmond 1938, 61) suggested that the filling was of stripped turf and Richmond and Gillam (this volume) speculated that this might be from the line of the later ditches. However, whether the ditches would have been left open when the fort was abandoned may be questioned and further evidence is required before accepting that they were only filled at the beginning of phase two.

ii) Size

The later fort faced north east, being layed out in diametrically the oppositie direction to the phase one fort but probably re-using at least the approximate line of the earlier *via prinicipalis* which was presumably still visible. The size of this later fort is better established than that of its predecessor as *c*. 87.5m x 105.5m (0.92 hectares; 2.28 acres) across the walls, the slight revision from Richmond and

Gillam's (this volume) figure being due to the more accurate determination of the position of the south east defences by Bartlett (Bartlett and Dearne, this volume) previously recorded only by Garstang (1904, plate 3). Discounting a slight inturning evident on at least some sides of the fort and allowing for the known, and varying width of the rampart/wall and intervallum road this gives an internal area of *c*. 64 x 85m (0.54 hectares; 1.35 acres). However, these figures cannot be regarded as precise yet. The exact course of the fort wall, especially either side of the south and east corners may yet need revisions since it is based in places on only a few small exposures made over some 90 years which are at times difficult to entirely reconcile.Similarly the width of the rampart seems to have varied from *c*. 10m down to only *c*. 3.4m and indications of the intervallum road width are also variable. Whilst some of these variations may reflect the pressure on space in the fort and the narrowness of the rampart on the north east in particular may be due to the strength of the natural defences here, further evidence is needed before some of the variations can be entirely accepted. This must be especially true of the north east defences where the rampart width, particularly after the insertion of the fort wall, must have been greater than evidence at present indicates.

iii) Phase 2a (Figure 8: 2)

a)The Defences

Although Richmond and Gillam (this volume) presumed the fort wall to be an original phase 2 feature, partly because the lower inner face was undressed, Jones and Wild (1970, 105) expressed the view that it may have been inserted in phase 2b. A further suggestion of this is given by the angle of the rear of the rampart in the 1958/9 section (Bartlett and Dearne, this volume). The evidence is not yet conclusive but points to the wall being a later insertion and it will be discussed below.

The phase 2a ditch system is imperfectly known and the excavated sections suggest irregularities in it. However, it is clear that up to three ditches existed with slighter defence on the north east and north west sides where the River Noe and its unnamed tributary's steep banks provided natural obstacles. Just south west of the north west gate Jones and Thompson (1965, 125; *cf.* also Jones 1967, fig. 3) found that the inner of three ditches was V-shaped, only *c*. 0.7m away from the fort wall and *c*. 6.4m wide. 2.9m further out a second V-shaped ditch was 4.2m wide and 1.4m behind the third, 5.8m wide, ditch. The ditch depths are not published if they were ascertained. Jones (1967, fig. 3) marks traces of a ? road beyond this last ditch. Further south west along the north west side Richmond and Gillam (this

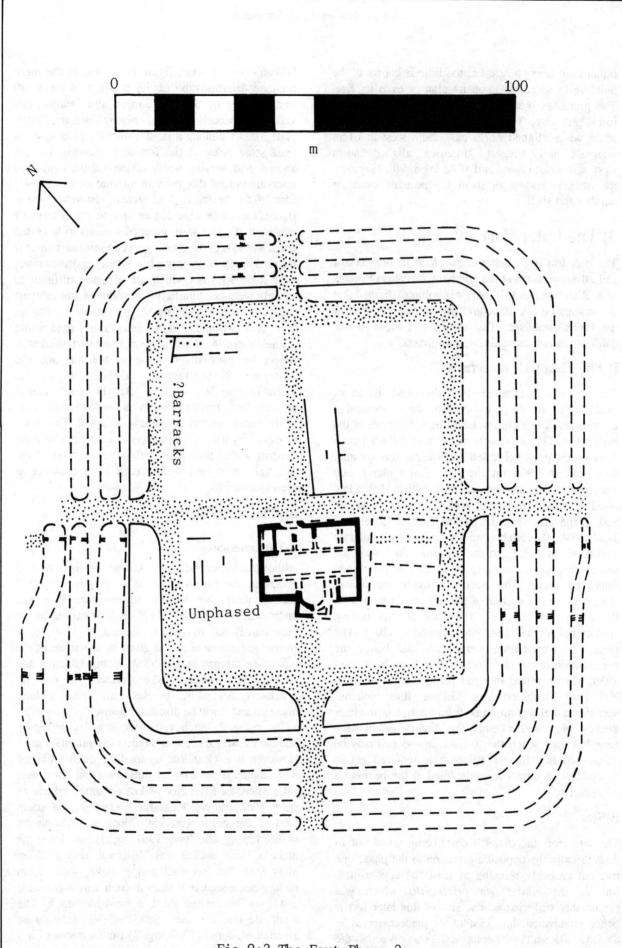

0   100

m

N

?Barracks

Unphased

Fig.9:2 The Fort:Phase 2a

volume, trench 1) found that the inner ditch was 5.6–7.6m wide (on the discrepancy see Richmond and Gillam this volume note 18), 2.1–2.7m deep and now 2.1–2.4m infront of the fort wall. The gap between the inner and middle ditches had dissappeared and the middle ditch had changed to a W profile, being 5.5–6.0m wide in all with elements 0.8 and 0.9m deep. Here the outer ditch was 6m from the middle one, suggesting that it had swung north west, though it had narrowed slighly to 4.9–5.2m having utilised a slight natural gully in its line. Beyond this ditch work in 1986 (Branigan and Dearne, this volume trench H) found some form of hard standing.

Two sections have also been cut on the south east side of the *raetenura*. Jones and Wild (1970, 105) found three ditches near the south east gate, though the size of the gaps between the fort wall and first ditch and it and the middle ditch are not published. The inner was 4.3m wide and 1.8m deep, the middle 3.6m wide and 1.5m deep and the outer, separated by a gap of 7.6m (and so apparently if the other ditches remained on their otherwise established courses, swinging outward) 1.5 m wide and 0.7m deep. Further south west Bartlett (Bartlett and Dearne this volume) found the inner ditch 2.1m in front of the fort wall, to have expanded to 6m wide and well over 2.1m deep. 2.7m in front was the middle ditch, now 4.6m wide and of unknown depth while the outer, here only separated by a gap of 2.7m, was now 2.9m wide and of unknown depth.

Whatever the details the implication is that the defences became more substantial as they ran south west and it is likely that three substantial ditches existed on the uninvestigated south west side of the fort. At least on the north west side the ditch system seems to have become slighter and more compressed as it ran north east. Only one section has been cut through the *praetentura* defences but the encroachment of the River Noe and its unnamed tributary, even allowing for modern erosion, probably meant that less defence was required at least on the north west and north east sides. Two ditches on the north west of the *praetentura* and three on the south east are shown on Figure 8: 2, but this must be conjectoral. The only clear evidence for the defences around this half of the fort is the section cut on the north east side in the 1960s (Jones and Thompson 1965, trench 2; Jones Thompson and Wild 1966, 101; Jones 1967, fig. 3) revealing two ditches, the inner 2.4m in front of the fort wall 2.6m wide but of unpublished depth. The second, 4.3m in front was 2.7m wide and 'shallow'. These slight and widely spaced ditches reinforce the picture of a decreased need for defence on the north east side of the fort, though it is conceivable that a third outer ditch remains to be found. However, triple ditches may be envisaged as far as the east corner of the fort since

modern erosion has probably decreased the width of the neck of land between the fort corner and the River Noe.

Assuming that the fort wall was a later insertion but that its position represents the original front of the base of the phase 2a rampart it appears that the rampart varied in width. It was of clay construction with no signs of timber strapping or stone foundations. If the fort wall was a later insertion its front and rear faces were probably sloping, the rear face at 37° if the 1958/9 section was representative (Bartlett and Dearne, this volume). At this point it was 4.6–4.9m wide.On the north east it was 3.6m thick (Jones and Thompson 1965, trench 2), while, despite some problems with the site records, it was apparently *c.* 7.6m wide on the south west and just north east of the west corner (Richmond and Gillam, this volume). Two sections south west of the north west gate suggest that as the rampart approached it it decreased in width, being 6.4m wide about 15m south west of it and 5.5m wide 3m south west of it (Jones and Thompson 1965, trench1; Richmond and Gillam, this volume note 22). The alignment and position of a phase 2 barracks excavated in the 1960s (below) also suggests that the rampart on the north west side of the *praetentura* may have been around 3.6m wide and may have narrowed even further as it approached the north west gate. As noted above however the narrowness of the rampart around the *praetentura* is a matter to which further attention should be paid before fully accepting the present evidence.

The stone angle towers and gates were presumably phase 2b replacements for timber predecessors, assuming that there were angle towers in phase 2a. No traces of such predecessors are known but little modern work has been done at the fort corners or gates. Richmond and Gillam clearly did not dismantle the stone south west gate and the deep foundations of the stone west angle tower may have removed any timber predecessor while Bartlett did not dismantle the remains of the south angle tower.

b) The Internal Roads

The main roads of the phase 2a fort remained approximately in their positions through to the close of the fort as far as is known.Garstang(1904, plate 3) recorded the *via principalis* at the north west gate and a fragment of the *via decumana* (otherwise unknown) at the south west gate while the course of the former was planned by Jones (1967, fig. 3) based on three seasons of work on its north eastern edge and it is clear that subsequent work also intecepted it. It was *c.* 6m wide. Richmond and Gillam (this volume) identified a side drain along its north east side and the equivalent drain along its south west edge was seen by Garstang (1904, plate3) along the edge of the granaries and again by Jones and Wild (1970, fig. 1) who corrected a planning error making clear that it continued in front of the *principia*. A *via praetoria* drain was found by Richmond and Gillam (this volume) but whether it was a phase 2 south east edge drain or a phase 3 central drain is not clear. Jones (1967, 157f and fig. 3) refers to a central drain 0.8m wide in a 5.2m wide (phase3) *via praetoria* but it is not clear whether he recovered evidence for this or was interpreting Richmond and Gillam's findings.

The *via principalis* clearly lay axially but Richmond and Gillam (this volume) suggested that the *via praetoria* and *decumana* did not. Virtually no evidence bears on the course of the latter but there may be some indications that the *via praetoria* did cross the *praetentura* assymetrically at least in phase 2. The only exposure(s) of the road itself known are those noted above and are of limited use. However, if Richmond's archive plan is accurate the phase 2 barracks on its south eastern edge, its line followed by a phase 2 (south east edge) or phase 3 road drain, ran at an angle to the fort's axis suggesting that the *via praetoria* also ran at an angle across the *praetentura*. On this assumption Richmond on his archive plan placed the uninvestigated north east gate assymetrically and revised the positions of the wall exposures made by Garstang (1904, plate 3) to fit this interpretation. These re-evaluations are followed on Figures 8: 2–8: 4 since the alignment of the barracks seems to be the best evidence bearing on the problem and it is clear that Garstang's plan is often difficult to reconcile with more recent work. Jones (1967, fig. 3) prefered to see the *via praetoria* and north east gate as axial (though his placing of Garstang's wall fragments does not agree with Garstang (1904, plate 3)).This may have been partly dictated by his assessment of the phase 3 barracks/stables, for there is some ambiguity about the subsequent history of the *via praetoria* which it will be more convenient to discuss here rather than below.

If the phase 3 barracks fragments marked by Jones (1967, fig. 3) north west of the road are correctly placed on Figure 8: 4 then they imply that the phase 3 *via praetoria* extended over part of the site of the phase 2 barracks found by Richmond and Gillam, which indeed would explain why they found their phase 3 successors to lie slightly further south east. If this is the case then the *via praetoria* must have moved slightly south east and may have been straightened if it had not been axial in phase 2. However, even if it was straightened it must be the phase 2 line of the *via praetoria* that gives the best indication of the north east gate position. It is these assumptions that are reflected on Figure 8: 4. It should be stressed however that the evidence for the north east gate position and *via praetoria* course remains slim and inferential and whilst fuller publication of the work in the 1960s might throw

some light on the matter only further excavation is likely to resolve it.

The intervallum road is also problematic. On the north east side it was found to be 4.9m wide with the usual side drains whilst just south west of the north west gate it was 5.2m wide (Jones and Thompson 1965, 125). However, there are internal inconsistencies in the archive from 1938/9 which make it uncertain how wide the intervallum road was at the west corner and along the south west side (Richmond and Gillam this volume, note 23). The choice is between 7.6 and *c.* 4.3m and the latter must be much more likely.

A further problem is the road width along the north west side about halfway between the west corner and the north west gate. Richmond and Gillam (this volume, note 38) seem to have found a revetted rampart here separated by only 2.4m from a wall with a 50cm wide drain along its north west side. If the records of the work are correct this suggests that the intervallum road had narrowed from 5.2m near the gate to only 2.4m wide. However, another drain was found further south east and the fact that Richmond did not include the wall on his archive plan may suggest that he doubted its reality. If so the distance from the revetment to the second drain would be about 4.9m which might be a more realistic figure for the intervallum width. An alternative is to see encroachment at some point onto the road (see further below). Apart from a possible gravelled fragment that may or may not have been the road (Richmond and Gillam this volume, editors note) the only exposure of the intervallum road on the south east side is that in 1958/9 trench A. Again this is problematic in that it seems to be far too wide given the known size of the adjacent granary. However, a number of alternative explanations for its apparent width are possible (Bartlett and Dearne this volume) and on balance it seems unlikely that the intervallum here was more than 5.5m wide.

Thus, the intervallum road seems to have varied in width as did the rampart on present evidence. Again pressure on space may have been a fctor and at least one building in the *praetentura* encroached upon the road line after it had been laid out (below).

c) The Main Range of the *Reatentura*

The main administrative buildings, the *principia*, *praetorium* and granaries lay along the south west edge of the *via prinicipalis* in their normal positions in the *raetentura*. The first is well known (Garstang 1904; Richmond and Gillam this volume), and the garanaries have been partly examined (Jones and Wild 1970, 101ff) but the *praetorium* is little known. There is no evidence for any predecessor to the known stone built *principia*. Jones and Wild's (1970, 99) assumption that a wooden predecessor existed cannot be entirely dismissed since the stone building could have removed any traces of it. However, if the strongroom was an insertion in phase 2b as seems likely the balance of probability must be on the stone *principia* being of phase 2a. The only other matter bearing on the question is the presence of a column capital sealing a post hole of a phase 2a or 2b barracks/stable in the *praetentura* (Jones, Thompson and Wild 1966, 100). If the post hole was of phase 2a this might imply the demolition of a structure with stone columns, surely either a *principia* or *praetorium*, at the end of phase 2a. This column capital does not appear to match other column fragments from the *principia* cellar (Garstang 1904, fig. 7 No.2) and built into a modern wall at the site, the former at least presumably being most likely derived from the phase 2b or 3 *principia* or *praetorium* but such an observation is far from proof that it came from a phase 2a building. Moreover even if it did it could come from the *praetorium* where there are no indications of a wooden structure in phase 2a or indeed derive from repairs to a stone phase 2a *principia*. Equally Welsby's (1982, 21f) speculation that the known plan represents conflation of two separate stone phases may be dismissed. Richmond and Gillam (this volume) established that the walls were all of one build and that the insertion of the strongroom in the *sacellum* was the only change before the building went out of use.

The plan of the *principia*, virtually all of which is known, is however atypical. Whilst there is the usual cross hall (internally 23.5 x 5.2m) with a *sacellum* or shrine centrally behind it flanked by offices the usual front courtyard is replaced by a range of rooms. The rear range itself was a little unusual consisting of, from south east to north west (Figure 2: 2), an office 5.2 x 4.0m a narrow ?latrine, the *sacellum* and a room 8.2 x *c.* 3.5m which one suspects may have had a partition of wood. The shrine jutted back up to 3.8m, its rectangular projection at a skew to the line of the building holding the curved and centrally strengthened dias for an imperial statue. The front range consisted of at least three and perhaps four rooms along with a central entrance corridor. The north west pair of rooms were 5.5 x 2.9m and 5.5 x 4.3m while to the south east of the entrance passage one or two rooms occupied an area 9.7 x 5.5m. Richmond and Gillam (this volume) suggested that the area was split in two but the evidence seems to be equivocal (*cf.* Richmond and Gillam this volume, note 29). The building's plan suggests that rather more ?office space was required at Brough than at other forts and that, at a site where space must always have been at a premium, the usual courtyard had to be dispensed with to provide it and this may have implications for the fort's functions.

North west of the *principia* must have lain the *praetorium*. A number of wall fragments and drain lines are known in this area from the work by Garstang (1904, plate 3), Richmond and Gillam (this volume, note 38 and Figure 2: 3) and Jones and Thompson (1965, 125). Two 75cm wide features found by Richmond and Gillam are of unknown form but all well recorded walls are stone built. In the absence of dating evidence little can be said of the features' relationships and only the better established stone wall lines are shown on figs. 8: 2–8: 4. It has been noted already that one wall may imply a narrow or encroached intervallum road to the north west. All but one of the walls seem to be parallel or at right angles to each other but very little can be said with any confidence about the area in any phase.

To the south east of the *prinicipia* lay the granaries, seperated from it by a 3m wide alley with a drain running down the south east side. In phase 2a the granaries were represented mainly by rows of post pits 45cm in diameter spaced at *c.* 1.2m intervals centre to centre, the rows being *c.* 1.2m apart (Jones and Wild 1970, 101ff and fig. 1), implying the support of a ventilated timber floor on a grid of wooden posts. However, at least two post positions at the south east end were replaced by large squared stone blocks 60cm high and 45cm wide which may have supported a loading platform. The granary roof may have been of diamond shaped slates. The open slab drain along the south west edge of the *via prinicipalis* here had a row of upright slabs along its south west edge to stop water reaching the timber posts. Although only the majority of two rows of post pits are known it is clear that the granary was about 17m north west–south east. Its width is unknown but if, as seems likely, the area allotted to the granaries was the same as in phase 2b (about 21.3m) then two buildings each *c.* 17 x10.4m may be likely.

d) The Rear of the *Raetentura*

It seems likely that barracks, stables or the like lay behind the main range of buildings in the *raetentura* but the only building fragments here are probably to be assigned to phase 3.

e) The *Praetentura* (Phases 2a and 2b)

Despite considerable excavation in the north west of the *praetentura* in the 1960s much remains obscure about its form in phases 2a and b. Although it is clear that the relatively poorly preserved traces of barracks/stables in the form of post holes in construction trenches were recovered and that their form in phase 2b was so similar to that in phase 2a that differentiating between the phases was often impossible the interim reports on the work (Jones, Thompson and Wild 1966; Jones 1967; Jones and Wild 1968; 1970) provide little detail and published plans of most of the features are lacking.[1] Consequently only a brief sketch of the buildings may be given. The timber posts on which they were built were in pits up to 45cm in diameter and 30cm deep, packed with heavy stones, in some cases probably re-used, and also probably with hypocaust tiles and *tubuli* fragments. The most north westerly ?barracks had a verandah along the intervallum in one sub-phase and ran north east–south west, that is *per stringas* but its length and width are unknown. A second similar building was apparently detected to its south east and a third beyond it should be presumed. In phase 2a the north westerly building's south west end seems to have had beaten clay floors, a medial dividing wall and at least two partitions at right angles to its axis. Two stone drains, one flowing out towards the intervallum, and a soak-away pit also existed.

Rather better published are traces of a building aligned north west–south east (*per scamna*) along the north east intervallum road which were recovered at the north corner of the *praetentura* (Jones and Wild 1968, 90 and fig. 1). Here postholes representing the ?verandah were found on the north east along with the construction trench for the north east wall some 2.6m further south west and that of the north west end of the building, which seems to have lain at a slight angle to at least the later intervallum road and to have extended as far as the verandah line.

In the south east half of the *praetentura* Richmond and Gillam (this volume) also recovered traces of phase 2 buildings (the existence of sub-phases not being known at the time). Along the south east of the *via praetoria* they recovered the plan of ?barracks aligned north east–south west (*per strigas*) consisiting of 45cm wide construction trenches for post settings packed with blue river cobbles. Two parallel north east–south west walls were traced for a maximum of nearly 23m with traces of a medial wall between them. They met a wall at right angles along the north east edge of the *via principalis* but this wall may have continued south east of its meeting with the south east wall and two further fragments of walls 2.6m apart running south east at right angles to the south east wall were also recovered. The buillding was at least 7.6m wide and either wider than this or adjoined with another to its south east.

Taken together the evidence suggests that the phase 2a and b *praetentura* was, as is anyway to be presumed, occupied by barracks and/or stables. The drains, and particularly soak-away pit in the most north westerly building in phase 2a might hint at the latter in one case but are not sufficient as proof. Whatever their precise function it seems that the arrangement of the buildings was a combination of *per strigas* and *per scamna* (at the north east end). Their length was clearly in excess of *c.* 23m and if the blocks *per scamna* were also of fairly usual width this suggests that they were nearer 29m in length. The blocks *per scamna* themselves will then presumbly have been of a similar length (or if the *via praetoria* did not run axially will have been of disequal lengths), one standing at the front of each side of the *praetentura*.

iv)Phase 2b (Figure 8: 3)

a) The Defences

As discussed above the stone fort wall seems most likely to have been inserted in front of the rampart in phase 2b. The width of the wall seems to have been a little variable though at most places where it has been examined it has been found to be 1.5 to 1.7m thick (Richmond and Gillam this volume, note 21; Jones and Thompson 1965, 125; Bartlett and Dearne this volume). Garstang (1904, 185) gives 1.8m, though he may have been refering to the wall at the west corner which seems to have been thickened. The wall construction was of rubble faced with Gritstone masonry except on the lower inner face and two coping stones and a cornice slab are known from the ditch fills (Jones and Thompson 1965, 125; Jones and Wild 1970, 105).

Of the stone gates two have been excavated while there can be little doubt about the position though not form of the south east gate. The problem of the location of the north east gate has been considered above. Garstang (1904, Plate 3) seems to have cleared the north west gate though there is no detail on his plan. Its fragments shown on Figure 8: 3 are derived from Richmond's archive plan and may suggest that he had access to more detailed records. The gate seems to have been very simple, consisting of fort wall inturns perhaps up to 5.5m long giving a gateway *c.* 4.9m wide. The south west gate is the best known. Richmond and Gillam (this volume) excavated its north west side revealing again a simple inturning of the fort wall 3m long, decreased in width at its internal end. Small fragments of this and the other side of the gate had also been cleared by Garstang (1904, plate3), suggesting again a width of about 4.9m (though there remain some difficulties in entirely reconciling all the work bearing on the fort wall line in this area as is evident from Figures 8: 3

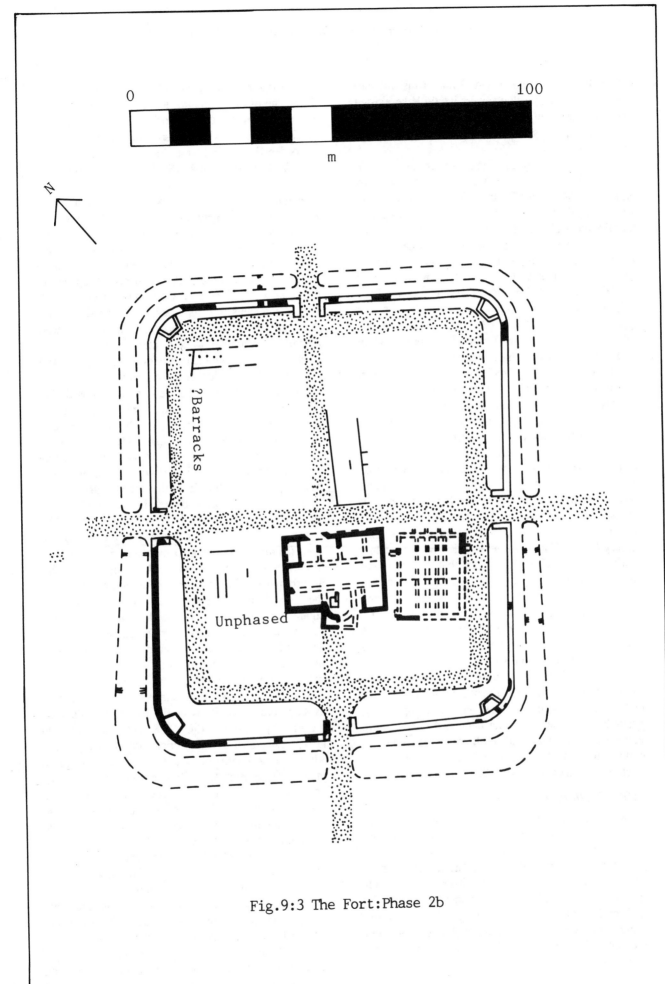

0   100

m

N

?Barracks

Unphased

Fig.9:3 The Fort:Phase 2b

and 8: 4). As Richmond and Gillam (this volume) noted it seems likely that towers would have existed above the gates but there were no guard chambers at the sides and the gates were of simple single portal type.

Two of presumably four angle towers are known. That at the west corner was examined both by Garstang (1904, plate 3) and Richmond and Gillam (this volume). The records of the latter indicate that here the fort wall was thickened to 1.9m and the back wall of the tower lay 5m behind it. It had been carried down to subsoil here because of the presence of the filled phase 1 ditches, the bottom 1.4m being unfaced rubble and the wall 1.3 thick. The length of the back wall was some 2.9m. The south angle tower was apparently a little smaller (Bartlett and Dearne this volume, Figure 3: 1). The fort wall was only slightly thickened here and the back wall lay only some 3.8m behind it, though the latter was only represented by foundations apparently less than a metre thick.

It also seems that the outer fort ditches ceased to exist in or by phase 2b. Richmond and Gilllam (this volume) found that the two outer elements of the ditch system near the west corner contained pottery no later than the late-second century, though Jones and Thompson (1965) did not recover any dating evidence from the same ditches further north east. Of the two ditches known on the north east of the fort, the outer seems to have been closed by the third century (Jones, Thompson and wild 1966, 101) while Jones and Wild (1969, 105) found that the outer, and probably inner, ditches on the south east were closed by the early-fourth century. No significant dating evidence came from the work in 1958/9 except that a wall had been built over the filled inner ditch at some point in phase 3. Although the evidence is less extensive that one would wish it seems likely that all but the inner ditch on the north east and north west sides were filled roughly at the beginning of phase 2b, or more probably had been allowed to silt up late in phase 2a. Whether the same happened on the more vulnerable south west and south east sides cannot be certain but is to be presumed. Thus, only the inner ditch remained open in phase 2b.

b) The *Raetentura*

As with phase 2a nothing is known of the back of the *raetentura* in phase 2b and little can be said of the site of the *praetorium*, though the fact that the granaries were re-built in stone at this time may suggest that the *praetorium* was also now stone built if it had not been before. Again almost nothing can be said of its plan. The main changes known in the *raetentura* were the re-building of the granaries and probably the insertion of a strongroom in the *principia*.

The stone built strongroom lay in the west corner of the shrine of the *principia*, its steps running from its east corner up to a central position in the front of the *sacellum*, and the whole presumably being covered by a wooden floor with a trap door. It was excavated in 1903 by Garstang (1904, 189–92) who found that its stonework was of a different character to that of the *principia* walls (though only the rubble wall foundations are likely to have been preserved for comparison). Internally it was 2.4m long and between 1.5 and 2.1m wide and survived to a depth of 2.4m, though originally it was perhaps nearer 3.3m deep. A rectangular area at the bottom had been deepened by 60cm at some time and Garstang's (1904, fig. 6) section indicates that its sides were sloped and that the stairs overlay it. The steps themselves were assumed by Garstang to be a later insertion but there does not seem any clear evidence to indicate this given that the function of the chamber was clearly as a strongroom and not as a well as he supposed. The deepening at the bottom of the chamber might instead be connected to the construction of the strongroom.

Part of the inscription (*R.I.B.* 283) set up at the beginning of phase 2a was found built into the cellar wall and other fragments of it were found in its fill, having probably fallen from the upper courses of the walls. One fragment was heavily worn (Garstang 1904, 192) and if it too had been re-used in the celllar it seems most likely that it had formed part of the steps (as indeed had another evidently re-used stone). The evidence mitigates against the strongroom being an original feature of the *principia* and the re-use of the inscription suggests a construction date significantly after the mid-second century. However, a date before phase 3 when the *principia* seems to have been of far less substanstial build (below) also seems likely and so the construction of the strongroom seems to fit best into a phase 2b context.

Also in phase 2b the granaries were reconstructed as stone buildings. Parts of the external walls were recorded by Garstang (1904, 188) and Jones and Wild (1970) excavated a full section across one granary while further lengths of external wall were identified in 1958/9 (Bartlett and Dearne this volume). The outer walls were just over 90cm thick, of ashlar masonry with a rubble core and conflation of all known fragments indicates that the building(s) covered an area of 21.3 x16.8m. If Garstang's (1904, plate 3) plan is reliable then the external wall was continuous indicating a single building, perhaps divided in the centre and double roofed. Certainly the external wall was buttressed, parts of the buttresses being found approximately a quarter of the way along the north west and south east walls and at the west corner. The size of the buttress on the north west side, which projected 2.1m from the wall and incorporated a water channel (the continuation of which was found at the west corner in 1958/9) has been suggested as indicating a gable end (Jones and Wild 1969, 104). This would support the presumption that, whether or not the external wall was continuous, two granaries were actually present, orientated north west–south east. The ventilated floors were supported on four north east–south west cross walls about 60 cm wide and 1.2m apart in the centre of the buildings which might have been built in discontinuous lengths. They were not re-located in 1958/9 but this excavation was of limited extent and depth, besides which the walls had clearly been heavily robbed as Jones and Wild (1970, 104) also found. The external wall seems to have been completely robbed out in the vicinity of the south corner where it could not be found in 1958/9 and this may reflect changes connected with the late cavalry exit.

c) The *Praetentura*

As noted above the *praetentura* buildings of phase 2a were reconstructed using the same techniques and with as far as is known substantially the same ground plans in phase 2b. The only published details of identifiable changes in phase 2b relate to the west corner of the most north westerly block where partition wall post holes and a drain of phase 2a were sealed below a new 4 x1.5m floor paved with Gritstone slabs.

v) Phase 3(Figure 8: 4)

Although there is no evidence for a break in occupation between phases 2 and 3 it is clear that the whole interior of the fort underwent a major phase of reconstruction at the time marked by a change to stone or at least half timbered construction over much or all of the fort.

a) The Defences

The evidence of Richmond and Gillam (this volume) and of Jones and Thompson (1965) on the north west and of Jones, Thompson and Wild (1966) on the north east indicates that the inner fort ditch remained open until the abandonment of the fort. However, on the south east even this ditch, where it has been examined south west of the south east gate, was closed, presumably deliberately in or by the early-fourth century. There is no information regarding the fate of the inner ditch to the south west or on the south east north east of the south east gate but it is to be presumed that it remained in existence.

The closure of the inner ditch along at least part of the south east side appears to be connected to changes in the entrance/exit arrangements. There is no evidence for the closure of any of the fort gates but only two have been investigated and it must be possible that the south east gate was closed in phase 3. Certainly on present evidence there was no longer

any *vicus* for it to serve. Either way it was replaced or augmented by the new entrance some 24m further south west which was discovered in 1958/9 (Bartlett and Dearne this volume). Here the fort wall was removed for 6.7m or more and the rampart cut back and probably revetted to form a passageway obliquely through the defences. Roughly parallel to and 1.5m in front of the former fort wall a new wall, 76 cm thick and 13.7m long, was built with a rubble core retained by dressed masonry with an offset on the south east face. It ran along the inner edge of the filled inner fort ditch.

The space between the former line of the fort wall and the new wall was taken up with a pitched stone causeway with a central slab-covered drain. At the north west end of the new wall, opposite one side of the gap in the fort wall the causeway turned south east and continued for a further 7.9m. This section of the causeway was bounded on its north east side by a much rougher wall which was clearly later than the causeway. Subsequent excavation some 9m further north east in 1969 revealed further traces of these late changes (Jones and Wild 1970, 105f). Here a pebble surface lay over the former outer ditches and a pitched stone causeway with central slab covered drain was found over the inner ditch, though it is not clear in what direction it was running. This causeway was up to 2.1m wide compared to the width of 1.5m of the section discovered in 1958/9.Taken together the evidence suggests that the original arrangment was of a causeway passing obliquely through the rampart and the new gap in the fort wall, protected by a new wall in front, then at the end of the wall dividing with one branch turning south east for 7.9m and the other continuing to the north east, presumably to join the road issuing from the south east gate. At some point a rough wall was built sealing off the latter branch, though there is no specific evidence that this happened before the abandonment of the fort.

Jones and Wild's (1970, 105) suggestion that the new entrance would be particularly suited to the known at least partly mounted nature of the late garrison (below) seems a likely one. Moreover the existence of two diverging causeways would allow for the ease of use of the arrangements as both entrance and exit and the presence of a pebbled surface might indicate a parade ground or similar.

b)The *Raetentura*

Little is known of the *raetentura* in phase 3. The *principia* appears to have been rebuilt (Jones and Wild 1970, 104). Only short lengths of the narrow robber trench indicating this are known at the east corner. Similar traces of robber trenches also indicate rebuilding on the site of the phase 2 granaries and the alleyway between the two sites was resurfaced. The construction of both buildings seems likely to have

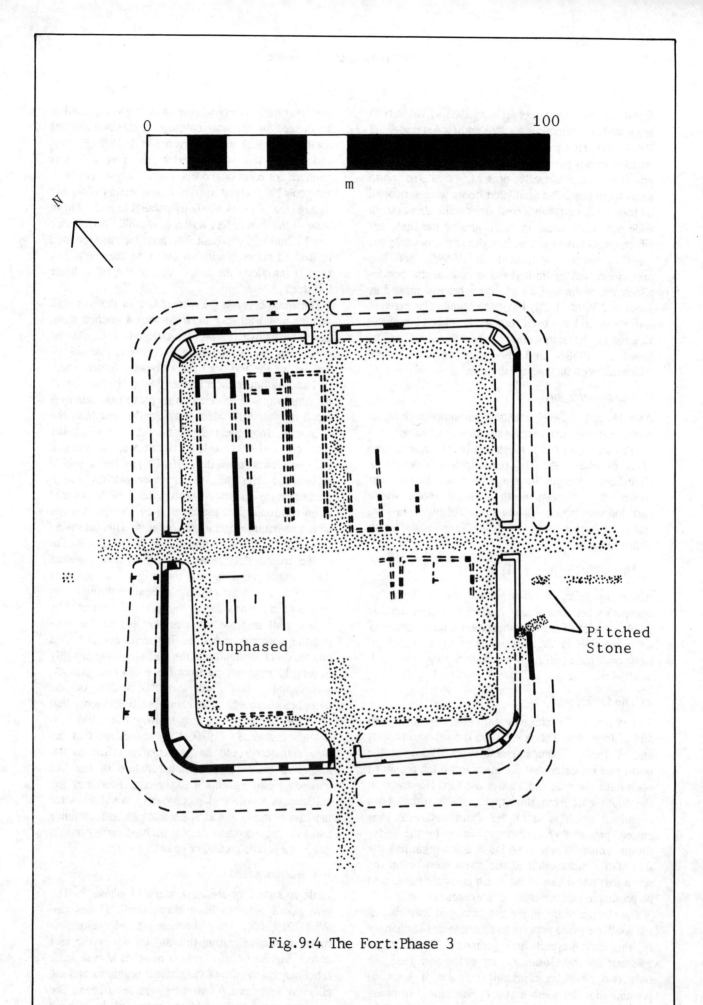

0   100

m

N

Pitched
Stone

Unphased

Fig.9:4 The Fort:Phase 3

been wattle and daub on stone sill walls (Jones and Wild *op cit*). The *principia* site presumably retained its function but nothing is known of the building's plan except that the new structure followed its predecessor's external wall line at least at the east corner. Whether the cellar inserted in phase 2b continued in use is not clear.

The building erected on the former granary site is a little better known. Its robber trenches indicate that it was *c*. 18.3m north west–south east though its north east–south west extent is unknown. Excavations in 1958/9 (Bartlett and Dearne this volume) suggest that at least at the south corner of the former granaries a cobbled area may have existed. This may suggest that in phase 3 the size of the building plot had been decreased, perhaps to allow for a roadway connected to the late entrance/exit to the south east. One partition within the building running north east–south west is known approximately halfway along the building with an offset at right angles to it. This suggests that the building was not now the fort granaries but probably the *praetorium*.

It therefore seems likely that the granaries lay to the north west of the *principia* but yet again very little can be said of this area. Behind the main buildings of the *raetentura* two small fragments of a stone wall, presumably the back of a barracks or stables, are known (Richmond and Gillam this volume). On the basis of the change to stone or half timbered construction in the *praetentura* in phase 3 these fragments are most likely also to be of a north west–south east structure belonging to phase 3 but nothing else is known of the building.

c)The *Praetentura*

The phase 3 *praetentura* is fairly well understood. Six buildings alligned north east–south west (*per strigas*) existed here of which fragments of at least five are known and the best known of which was a stables. This latter, the most north westerly block, was one of the main focuses of work in the 1960s (Jones, Thompson and Wild 1966, 101; Jones 1967, 157f and fig. 3; Jones and Wild 1968, 90ff and fig. 1; 1970, 101).Although little survived at the south west end enough was recovered to define a building internally *c*. 8.5m wide and *c*. 39m long constructed on walls of unmortated roughly cut Gritstone blocks on slightly wider rubble foundations bonded with puddled clay.The walls seem likely to have supported a timber superstructure roofed with diamond shaped stone tiles, many of which were recovered. A single square stone base is known at the south west end of the block and may imply that part of the superstructure was supported on timber uprights. The north east end of the block survived rather better. It was divided by a slightly narrower medial wall which, like the external walls, survived to two to three courses. The north

western half appears to have been a stable. It had a floor of flat cobbles patched with gravel and a mucking out drain whose fill included horses' teeth ran roughly parallel and adjacent to the north west wall, turning north west near the end of the block to pass out under the intervallum road, a triangular gap being left in the wall above the drain's covering stones where it passed through it. To the south east of the partition wall lay a large hearth and this side of the building was clearly not a stables but whether it functioned as living accomodation or alternatively had a workshop role cannot be certain. Nor is it clear whether the whole block was arranged similarly to the north east end or whether other blocks in the *praetentura* were similar. The building seems to have encroached upon the intervallum road to the north west.

Far less is known of the other blocks in the area but it is clear that the north western block was seperated from its neighbour by a 2.7m wide paved alley, that block again being *c*. 8.5m wide and seperated from a third along the *via praetoria* by a 60cm wide gravelled alley. Only fragments of these blocks are known but a trench through the north east end of the middle one revealed an internal stone partition wall 3m south west of the external wall with a stone flagged floor beyond it (Jones and Thompson 1965, 125f). Though scant details are published this appears to be at variance with details of the north east end of the stables block and suggests rather that part at least of this building had a different (?barracks) function.

South east of the *via praetoria* Richmond and Gillam (this volume) found traces of two similar phase 3 barracks/stables though it is a little difficult to be sure which recorded fragments were of phase 3 and which of phase 1 (above). The most likely interpretation of Richmond's archive plan would suggest fragments of two blocks only 7.2m wide internally, though there may be some indication that they widened a little as they went north east, seperated by a 90cm wide alley. Whilst nothing can be said in detail of these two stone/half timbered buildings, and a presumed companion to the south east, it is clear that the buildings here were essentially similar to those north west of the *via praetoria* as further demonstrated by Jones and Wild (1968, 90).

d) The End of the Fort

The end of phase 3 marks as far as is known the end of the utilisation of the fort site, no certain traces of any activity having been recovered post-dating it and no dating evidence post *c*. 350/5 being present. Jones and Wild (1968, 92) suggested that the period closed with deliberate demolition of the fort structures though how far this also applied to the defences is unknown. The only late features which do not seem to be readily explicable in terms of activity in phase 3 are two boulder filled pits revealed in 1958/9 trench A (Bartlett and Dearne this volume) but these may perhaps relate to post-Roman stone robbing.

vi) Miscellaneous Features

One or two miscellaneous features remain to be mentioned. The water supply and drainage systems of the later (phase 2 and 3) fort have been mentioned in passing above. Many of their details are likely to have remained the same throughout the later fort's history, though renewals and repairs doubtless occured and some changes would have been required by the *raetentura* re-organisation in phase 3. The water supply, at least in part, entered the fort through the south west gate where Richmond and Gillam (this volume) excavated a distribution (? and settling/inspection) tank carved from stone linked to a covered water course through the gate. Whether it was a feature of the phase 2a fort or not is debatable. It had two outlets, a hole for a lead pipe near its north corner and a stone conduit near its south corner. The former probably ran towards the phase 2 *praetorium* and the *principia* while the latter perhaps ran south east and then north east towards the *praetentura*. The source of the water can only have been the unnamed tributary of the River Noe to the north west of the fort. Nothing is known of where exactly the aquaduct outside the fort lay and too little is known of the stream's condition in Roman times to speculate on where the take out point would have lain.

The drainage system was as usual based on drains along both sides of the *via principalis* and intervallum roads (known at several points) and central, or in one case possibly side, drains along the *via praetoria* and *via decumana* (seen at the south west gate by Richmond and Gillam). Further drains ran between the phase 2 granaries and *principia* (Jones and Wild 1970, 104; Bartlett and Dearne this volume) and between the *principia* and *praetorium* in phase 2 (Richmond and Gillam this volume) though the former probably went out of use in phase 3. At least two drains seem to have left the *principia*, one from the north corner room and the other from the north west side of the *sacellum* (?having run from the ?latrine to its south east). Others also seem to have run across the site of the phase 2 *praetorium* and phase 3 ?granaries. Clearly also the phase 2 barracks/stables at the north west side of the *praetentura* had drains and the equivalent phase 3 stables had a drain at the north east end which probably ran through the defences to empty into the River Noe. Another drain fragment seen by Garstang (1904, plate 3) curved , probably from between the phase 2 *praetorium*/phase 3 ?granaries and barracks/stables at the back of the *raetentura* towards the fragment found by Richmond and Gillam (this

volume) running out of the fort under the south west gate. A drain also evidently left the north west gate, though the source for this fragment marked by Richmond on his archive plan is unknown, while a central drain also ran along the late causewayed entrance through the south east defences.

One other point requiring attention is the possibility that the defences were equiped with *ballistae*. Even leaving aside the 72cm diameter stone ball found in the inner ditch in 1969 (Jones and Wild 1970, 106) which may be the same as the one reported by Hart (this volume) smaller *ballista* balls are known from the site. One came from the inner fort ditch (Jones 1967, 158), others were found in the *vicus* in 1983/4 (Drage this volume) and further examples are recorded from other parts of the *vicus* and environs (author's records). As Jones (1967, 158) observed there is no evidence for projecting towers on the late defences, though it is perhaps the south east side where they would be most expected and excavation here has been limited.Alternatively there may have been *ballistaria* (catapult platforms) behind the ramparts, but no evidence has been recovered for such structures as yet.

4) The *Vicus* and Roads (8: 5)

Three broad areas of the *vicus* at Brough have so far been investigated by excavation and a large part of it has been subject to resistivity survey (all reported on in the present volume). Taken with antiquarian evidence, minor investigations and limiting topographical and fluvial features a good deal can be said about its general extent. The main area of settlement clearly lay south east of the fort in all periods, extending ultimately across the Bradwell Brook and utilising the available reasonably flat land up to a steeply rising hill. Its south eastern limit was located on the 1984 site. To the east the River Noe probably formed a natural limit but to the west there was no such limitation. However, settlement does not seem to have been continuous as far as the 1986 site and it seems unlikely that the main area of the *vicus* extended much further west than road A (Figure 8: 5). Whether settlement ever spread west along the narrow corridor of flat land either side of the Bradwell Brook is not clear. Batham Gate, the Roman road to Buxton which probably ran in tandem for some distance with a road to ?Carsington, utilised this corridor of land as does the modern road to Bradwell.However, if it is represented by *vicus* road A (Figure 8: 5) and the visible *agger* represents its course (below) the road line will have struck this flatter corridor some distance west of what seems to have been the main settlement concentration probably decreasing the liklihood of road line development.

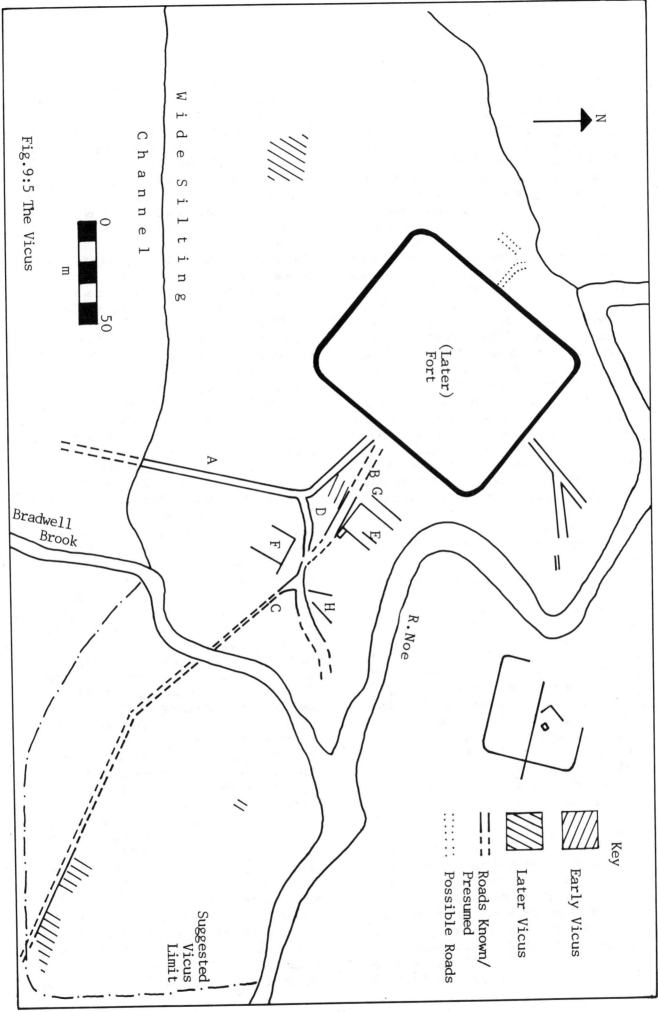

N

Key

Early Vicus

Later Vicus

Roads Known/
Presumed

Possible Roads

Channel

Wide Silting

Bradwell
Brook

(Later)
Fort

R. Noe

A

B
G
D
E
F
C
H

0   50
m

Suggested
Vicus
Limit

Fig. 9:5 The Vicus

151

However, there are some hints of a cemetery lying along this road line. Finds of 'urns etc.' at the Brough Lead Works are marked on early Ordnance Survey maps (e.g.Garstang 1904, plate 1) and a cremation in a Derbyshire ware jar (and so post *c.* 140) was found before 1877 and provenanced as from 'the lead mines of *Navio*' (Bolton Museum Rooke-Pennington Collection 112). Whether the latter's provenance was misrecorded as the *Navio* lead mines rather than works or actually came from a mine in the vicinity of Brough it seems likely to have come from somewhere in the general area of Bradwell. Other discoveries in Bradwell are however less likely to be of relevance. The Grey Ditch, a large linear earthwork running right across Bradwell Dale *c.* 1.25Km from Brough has been seen by some as a post-Roman political boundary (O'Neil 1945) although it might alternatively be an Iron Age stock ranching boundary. Although even if it was in existence by the Roman period it probably had little effect on the settlement at Brough the lack of firm information on its date and the location of a possible cross ditch near its eastern end (unpublished field work by Mr.G.Wilson) emphasizes that further work is required on the feature. An inhumation burial with a spear head, lead spindle whorl, gold inlaid copper 'button' and a coin in a stone cist is known from somewhere at Bradwell as well as a well built stone oven (Ward 1899).The Roman attribution of the latter rests only on contemporary observers' opinions of the style of construction and ought probably on balance to be rejected.The burial seems likely to have been Roman or later since it contained a coin (unfortunately unidentified and lost) but it would be unsafe to speculate further on the date. An uninscribed lead pig from Bradwell is fairly certainly Roman (*Arch.J.* 52 (1895), 33; Dearne 1990, 434 No.52) but as with coin finds from the vicinity noted by Haverfield (1905) need only indicate activity on the road.

Returning to the *vicus* there was clearly limited activity confined to the second half of the second century on the 1986 site south west of the fort (Branigan and Dearne this volume). Its extent was limited and partly dictated by natural features. To its south a fairly steep ridge and what was probably still a wide if silting tributary of the Bradwell Brook must have set a limit. To the north the land rises less steeply to the slight plateau on which the fort sits but the only indication of activity in this area, bounded on the north by an un-named tributary of the River Noe, is the possible hard standing area located in 1986 (Branigan and Dearne this volume, trench H). An extension of activity to the west is possible and probably implied by features recovered in 1986 but no investigation has taken place in this direction.

Across the un-named River Noe tributary the land is exposed and often very damp and presumptions

that it never saw any settlement activity are strengthened by the negative results of extensive geophysical survey here in 1986. The lower, flatter and better drained land north east of the River Noe would have been much more attractive for settlement. Pottery finds are known from the area (author's records) as well as coins but not in quantities which need imply more than casual losses along the ?Templeborough road which seems likely to have crossed it. Some form of rectangular enclosure seems to have existed near to the river at some point (Dearne this volume) but there is no evidence for an extension of the *vicus* here and is seems quite possible that the agricultural potential of this land was not lost on the military and/or *vicani* in a relatively hilly and infertile area.

It is difficult in the present state of knowledge to more exactly define the area of land utilised by the *vicus*. Taking road A, the River Noe, Bradwell Brook and its silted tributary as limits an area of 4.14 heactares (10.23 acres) would have been available immediately south east of the fort (Figure 8:5). Across the Bradwell Brook there is less to indicate the limits of the settlement. It may well be reasonable to see the *vicus* limit located in 1984 as somewhat exceptional since it was adjacent to a major road. Road line situations may well have been regarded as more valuable than other positions in the *vicus* and could have led to the settlement having a greater extent along road lines than between them (though the presence of a minor road leaving the main one on the 1984 site might be cited as evidence against this speculation). The River Noe provides a limit to the north east but we do not know that the settlement ever reached it and there is no evidence for the extent of activity to the south west. Thus, the limit proposed on Figure 8: 5 is very conjectoral. If all of the area enclosed by it was settled an area of 4.37 hectares (10.81 acres) would be added to that immediately south east of the fort making a total of 8.5 hectares (21.04acres). Only around 680m^2 were certainly utilised on the 1986 site south west of the fort and even if activity continued to the west it seems unlikey that the total area of *vicanal* settlement need be raised significantly to take account of its existence.

The development and plan of the *vicus* is like its ultimate extent a matter fraught with problems. However, it does seem reasonable to suggest that the latter was in no small part dictated by the roads that passed through it and it will be as well initially to consider what is known of them. The first point to make is that there is no sign of any attempt to plan the road system in terms of establishing a regular street grid. Rather the indications are of an irregular street system developing based on three major military roads, all ultimately leading to the fort's south east gate. However, these were not the only important roads leading from Brough and those leading to the other fort gates may be outlined first. Records of Cockerton and Heathcote's work drawn on by Hart (1981, fig. 8.4) suggest that a road left the north west gate and tended rather to the north, though even allowing for recent erosion there can have been little room between the fort's north corner and the River Noe. Jones (1967, fig. 1) on the other hand marks a gravelled surface (? a road) beyond the later fort ditches immediately south west of the north west gate and further south west a possible area of hard standing, though not a road, was located in 1986 (Branigan and Dearne this volume). One might expect a road to have left the gate and headed for Melandra Castle, Glossop having crossed the un-named stream to the north west of the fort. However, the first certain traces of this road (Margary 711; 'Doctor Gate') lie 1 3/4 miles away (Wroe 1982, 56) and the evidence at the moment could be equally consistent with just a track running along the north west side of the fort.

An alternative is to see the Melandra road running initially in tandem with that to Templeborough (Margary 710b; Wroe 1982, 59ff; the alternative course suggested by Welsh (1984) seems far less convincing) which is presumed to have left the north east fort gate. Sections cut by Cockerton and Heathcote (*cf.*Hart 1981, fig. 8.4.) do seem to suggest that at least two roads left this gate. One seems to have run nearly straight towards the River Noe while a second branched east and widened and then, to judge from the very poor records of the work, may have continued as one or more narrower roads/carriages. Unless one or other was designed simply for access to the river, which can hardly have been significantly more navigable than today, both presumably crossed the River Noe. Two possible fragments of ?bridge foundations were recorded by Lane (1973, 43) probably approximately on the line of the road running straight from the gate. However, the interpretation of these poorly recorded finds is far from certain and there may be evidence from Cockerton and Heathcote's work that this road stopped short of at least the present edge of the river. If both did cross the river that which branched to the east would be on a better alignment for Templeborough but its river crossing would also be notably close to the rectangular enclosure recognised by aerial photography. Clearly only further work will solve these problems. No road is known leaving the south west gate and given the extensive geophysical survey undertaken on this side of the fort in 1986 it seems unlikely that one existed. Rather the evidence that the fort's water supply entered by this gate may suggest that its main function was not to give access to a roadway. Certainly the area of settlement south

west of the fort does not seem to have been influenced by any road line.

Returning to the south east gate whose roads clearly did influence the *vicus* three major inter-site routes should probably be sought. The most important was probably 'Batham Gate' (Margary 710a) heading for Buxton and it seems likely that another road, probably eventually heading for Carsington (Wroe 1982, 58) diverged from it some way away from Brough. Certainly the roads must have run on much the same line from Brough to Bradwell. There can be little doubt that this unified road line was represented by Road A on the 1980–3 site and that it was primary to the site layout. Excavation in 1980–3 established that the visible *agger* above it was caused by a later track but there seems no reason not to assume that it and so the *agger*, clearly traceable on the 1981–2 resistivity survey (Bishop *et al*. this volume) and aerial photographs (Dearne this volume), followed the Roman road line, itself probably represented by Bishop *et al*. (this volume) Figure 4: 2, feature 10.

If so the road left the south east fort gate, turned south south west a short distance into the *vicus* and ran to the edge of the Halsteads field, thence doubtless crossing the former Bradwell Brook tributary and running over the ridge south of it before turning to follow the Bradwell Brook towards modern Bradwell (Figure 8:6) (Wroe 1982, 54ff). Cockerton and Heathcote seem to have cut a section across this road and probed its width beyond its turn to the south south west (Hart 1981, fig. 8.4), finding a double carriageway in all 6.7m wide. However whether this was the Roman road or the later trackway must remain uncertain and equally whether the whole road line, especially near to the fort continued in use throughout the site's occupation is not certain since only a single re-metalling was found in 1980–3 (and the existence of the late ?calvary exit strengthens the presumption that part of the road may have been superseded after the probable closure of the *vicus*).

The third probable inter-site route from the east side of the fort was a road to ?Chesterfield. Preston (1969) and Richardson (1969) postulated and excavated a road line following a modern lane curving west and then south some 50m from the 1983/4 site (fig. 5: 1) but did not find proof of a Roman date. The possible course was extended by Wroe (1982, 64) but the validity of Preston and Richardson's line in the vicinity of the *vicus* must be questioned by the discovery of the large and clearly important terraced road on the 1983/4 site (Drage this volume). It seems unlikely that two significant Roman roads left the *vicus* in virtually the same direction and by far the most likely explanation is that Preston and Richardson's road line in the vicinity of the *vicus* was in fact a diversion of the original road in post-Roman times. Indeed a route through the 1983/4 site would address the fort far more directly. The exact course of this road through the *vicus* is not known. Its traces were noted for some 40m beyond the 1984 site and its orientation suggests two possibilities. Firstly it may have continued on the same line to cross the Bradwell Brook and join road A or secondly it could have turned at or before a Bradwell Brook crossing so as to run more directly towards the fort. At present the latter option appears to be the most attractive since a road (Figure 8: 5 road C) is known from resistivity survey heading from the centre of the Halsteads field towards the Bradwell Brook on a course that would indeed intercept that of the ?Chesterfield road.

This presumed Chersterfield road was found in 1984 to have been constructed in the early- to mid-second century, and a date close to the re-occupation of the fort 154/8 is a possibility. However, activity of any sort at Chesterfield seems to have terminated in the mid-second century (Ellis 1989, 126) and a military presence may have ceased before this time. If the road did indeed head for Chesterfield, and was an inter-site route not just a link to Ryknild Street, its construction may well have taken place before the first fort at Brough was given up. In any event if the road's continuation is represented by Figure 8: 5 road C it seems that it met a pre-existing road (Figure 8: 5 road B) in the middle of the Halsteads field rather than continuing itself up to the fort gate.

Road B itself, much of whose course was revealed by resistivity survey and excavation from 1981–3 clearly met road A at or near the fort gate having followed a somewhat winding course from the vicinity of the Noe/Bradwell confluence where the military baths were probably situated. It seems to have been constructed fairly early in the site's history, doubtless expressly to provide access to the baths, but may not have been in existence from the very first (Bishop *et al.* this volume) and one wonders whether its slightly wandering course does not reflect the skirting of existing buildings or formalisation of an existing track through the early *vicus*.

Thus, at present there seem to have been initially two important routes running through the *vicus* (roads A and B) and later a third (road C/the Chesterfield road). At least three more minor roads developed at some point. Road D (Figure 8: 5) ran between bends in roads A and B while two small access roads constructed in the late-second to mid-third century were found on the 1984 site. The major roads had clearly dictated the course of at least these roads and the indications are that the later *vicus*'s building orientations were also determined by them (below).For the first fort's *vicus* there is far less evidence. Certainly the activity on the 1980–3 site (Bishop *et al.* this volume) utilised part of a triangular area bounded by roads A and B as they diverged beyond the fort gate and such a position

surely argues that the value of such a restricted and irregular space was in its proximity to the fort with frontages on both early major roads. However, we have nothing to compare the site to since it is the only one to have located traces of the earlier *vicus*. Resistivity survey is of no aid here since the technique given the site conditions is clearly only able to locate stone features and large cut features with fills significantly different to the natural (Bishop *et. al.*; Branigan and Dearne this volume) and even stone founded building is not known in south Pennine *vici* until well into the second century (e.g. Bishop *et al.* this volume). Indeed beyond the fact that activity does not seem to have spread beyond the Bradwell Brook the area occupied by the early *vicus* must remain unknown and could have been very small.

The plan of the later *vicus* is somewhat clearer, though in using the resistivity evidence we should bear in mind that the buildings revealed need not all be contemporaneous, may in some cases represent palimpsests of an area's structural history and at best probably only include the most well built or preserved of structures. The influence of the road network is clearly to be seen though, especially in Figure 8: 5 buildings E and G which lie nearly at right angles to road B, and leave little space between it and themselves (the fragment of building G may have continued towards the road and its apparent end is only due to the limits of the resistivity survey). At least one of the two walls marked H suggests similar orientation and proximity while building F, though set further back seems to straddle the junction of two major and one minor roads. The 1983–4 site also revealed a number of phases of buildings adjacent to a major road and, whilst the area investigated was not large enough to show how reprentative they were, their roadside situation at what was clearly the edge of the *vicus* is unlikely to be accidental. The construction of minor road BAG in site phase 8 (Drage this volume) probably also emphasises the importance placed on access to the main road. Only in the small area south west of the fort excavated in 1986 does there appear to have been no road line influencing the organisation of the *vicus*.

Beyond this basic influence of the road network though it is far harder to define how the *vicus* developed. We have only a glimpse of the first *vicus*. Near the presumed meeting of and between roads A and B timber structures were identified in 1980–3. Their plans could not be fully recovered and even their attribution to civilian not quasi-military activity could be questioned (Bishop *et al.* this volume) though the present author would support a civilian interpretation. However, the site does provide a basic chronology indicating activity from approximately the foundation of the fort to its abandonment *c.* 120. This site, near to the south east gate of the fort (though the exact line of the first fort's south east defences is not established) would perhaps have been part of the core of the earliest *vicus*, its dual road frontages offering obvious attractions to merchants or craftsmen. However, how rapidly the settlement developed and over what area it streached by *c.* 120 is almost unknown. Only the absence of activity on the 1972 and 1983–4 sites (Lane 1973; Drage this volume) gives any evidence for its extent, probably implying that it had not crossed the Bradwell Brook. The somewhat winding course of road B might hint at the presence of pre-established properties between the fort and probable baths at a relatively early date. Certainly the passage of off duty soldiers between the two must have presented an important trading opportunity (and far better explains why a number of *vici* grew up largely between the two than Sommer's (1984, 15) speculations about the placing of the baths deliberately to encourage settlement there).But as yet we can go no further than such speculations.

An occupation break during the fort abandonment *c.* 120–154/8 seems likely on present evidence but that evidence comes exclusively from the small 1980–3 site which does not seem to have been occupied after *c.* 120 and the conclusion must be provisional.Much more extensive excavation would be required to confirm it and it needs to be bourne in mind that even given complete fort and *vicus* desertion a complete absence of pottery at least is not to be expected. Occupied or vacant the site would be a natural stopping place for travelers; though what sort of rate of pottery deposition this might involve it is hard to say. Abandoned or not the *vicus* was probably refounded or revitalised after the re-garrisoning 154/8.

As yet only the 1986 site directly testifys to *de novo* activity that can reasonably be placed at around this date and, whilst it is tempting to connect the clay extraction pits which represent the earliest activity to building work, the site yielded only limited evidence for structures. Certainly if the site implies a re-siting of the *vicus* south west of the fort this was short lived for by the end of the second century activity here had ceased and occupation had already given way by then to ?rubbish dumps and some function utilising areas of hard standing. In contrast at least by the late-second century a sizeable *vicus* was clearly established south east of the fort.

Indeed, the limited extent and duration of occupation on the 1986 site, well away from the fort, connected to the main road lines only by a small path and from the number of drainage ditches cut, probably rather damp, may suggest that it was not part of the normal *vicus*. A number of functional possibilities suggest themselves for the occupational phase. The isolation might indicate civilian, or indeed military, activities not compatible with normal

occupation and one immediately thinks of lead smelting with its noxious fumes. However, there is little evidence even for lead working on any scale. Similary there is no evidence for activities such as tanning (which anyway one would expect to be nearer a river). Alternatively we might be dealing with a group or activity that was ostracised to some extent for social reasons and one wonders whether the deep ditch at the eastern edge of the site does not imply a demarcation between the activity on the 1986 site and the fort. Given that only one building was certainly represented we might indeed be dealing with a single family. Or perhaps with an activity such as prostitution; the image of *vici* as frontier towns with brothels and inns thoroughly intermixed with shops and soldiers' families may be seductive but, especially as forts and settlements became established, must at best be a simplification. One further speculation that might be entertained is that the ocupation on the site was not essentially *vicanal*; that is that it was connected with farming. The possibility that small farms existed, perhaps on land rented out by the military, adjacent to forts and *vici* and supplied them with meat or vegetables should not be discounted.

However, whatever the activity it cannot have been of great duration and was replaced by a probably non-occupational function. Again its remove from the main *vicus* suggests some zoned activity. Metalworking might again be suggested but there is little evidence to support it. Market stall provision is also an attractive suggestion, though the lack of coins and other finds might question it.

Again though it is south east of the fort that seems to have seen most occupation after the mid-second century even if defining its development is problematic.The 1980–3 site never seems to have been occupied despite its position between two major roads near to the fort gate. However, resistivity survey indicates that at some point stone (founded) buildings did occupy areas adjacent to it and the 1983–4 excavations revealed *vicanal* buildings streaching as far as was practicable to the south east by the later-second/mid-third century. Though the latter might represent the extension of activity along a major road line and give an unduely extensive impression of the *vicus*, the buildings do seem to have superseded ditched enclosures which could plausibly be seen as allotments or fields and so may imply the expansion of settlement onto formerly agricultural land. The key question though is whether it would be right to assume that the *vicus* was substantially continuous from the environs of the fort up to this point. We are unable to date the stone (founded) buildings known from resistivity survey but their presence does imply continuous settlement at some point in the later *vicus*'s history. The problem comes in assuming that this was always the case when the one excavated site near to the fort produced no more than probable accumulated rubbish from the fort and/or *vicus* during the later fort's existence. However, that the site was evidently unused at whatever point the stone (founded) buildings in its environs were built seems to indicate that we should be looking for some cause specific to that site and not a general one affecting a wider area. If this conclusion is valid it seems likely that the later *vicus* south east of the fort may well have been large and have grown rapidly in the second half of the second and first half of the third centuries.

The apparent disuse of the 1980–3 site in this context is even more anomalous and a variety of explanations for it ought to be considered. Firstly it is possible that its disuse is an illusion and that it was used for some archaeologically unrecoverable activity. The erection of temporary market stalls might be such an activity and the site, in front of the fort and bounded entirely by roads, might well be an appropriate one for such a market, though there is little in the finds assemblage from the site to support the suggestion. Secondly it is worth pointing out that the land available between roads A and B at this point was limited and formed a triangular plot which may not have been very convenient for building. In addition the desirability of the site may have been reduced by the possible neglect of road A noted by Bishop *et al.* (this volume). Thirdly though we should seriously consider given the site's position between roads leading to the fort gate whether the military may have been responsible for its disuse. At some point buildings appear to have been constructed as close as and closer to the fort than the site in question (Figure 8: 5, E and G) but this could have been long after the mid-second century and an initial military refusal to allow the *vicus* too near to the fort might have been lifted too late to revive the site's fortunes, especially if by then the *vicani* were aspiring to buildings the size of Figure 8: 5, E and F.

The end of the *vicus* presents a further problem. The pottery record from the 1980–3 excavations cannot be used to establish anything of the *vicus*'s later history since it is as likely to be made up of rubbish from the fort as from the *vicus*. Only the 1983–4 site can be used to chart the late fortunes of any part of the settlement and its position at its edge makes it a poor indicator for the *vicus* as a whole.Activity on the site seems to have ended around the middle of the third century (Drage this volume) with some residual pottery of the third/fourth centuries also being found but not necessarily indicating anything other than traffic passing along a road to an occupied fort.The abandonment of the site could be explained by a minor population decline or a shift in the pattern of settlement; or by a more major

vicanal desertion caused by a variety of factors.[2] A hint that it was something more than a minor decline/shift is given by the implied absence of fourth century material on the 1972 site (Lane 1973), though the records of this work are very poor.

If a major decline in , or even complete end to, the *vicus* is involved it would fit a pattern of later-third century *vicanal* decline in the north (e.g. Breeze 1982, 148; Casey 1982, 124; R.Jones 1984, 41). The reasons for such a decline may be several fold and the general trend doubtless disguises factors specific to individual sites but we may note the increasing rate of troop withdrawal and tendency towards smaller garrisons in the later-third and fourth centuries (Breeze and Dobson 1985, 14; James 1984). Equally a tendancy towards payment in kind for the army (e.g. MacMullen 1963, ch.2) may have played a significant role. As far as site specific factors go the most obvious again relates to the garrison. If some decline had begun around the middle of the third century it could have been exascerbated by a garrison change shortly after *c.* 300 with an associated emigration of soldier's dependents. We do not certainly know that such a change in garrison occured but the mid-second century garrison, *Cohors I Aquitanorum*, may have been at Brancaster in the late-third century (Birley 1978) so some change may have occured by the third fort phase when various changes were made to the fort by a mounted or part-mounted unit. However, *Cohors I Aquitanorum* seems to have been *equitata* and we shall see below that the whole unit may not have been at Brough.

Certainly though there is no evidence for either a break in the garrisoning of the fort or for the *vicani* being welcomed to live inside it. The debate about the putative accomodation of soldier's families inside forts supposedly implied by 'chalet' type barracks and numbers of 'female' finds has been explored by several of its supporters and detractors (e.g. Daniels 1980; Bennet 1983, 211; R.Jones 1984, 41; Evans 1984, 43–6; James 1984.165; Dearne 1991, 77) but receives no support at Brough. The anyway small fort shows no late changes which might imply the accomodation of civilians. Nor as yet is there any evidence to suggest that any civilians moved into the fort after its abandonment by the military, though the disturbed nature of the late fort levels make the survival of any such evidence unlikely.

Indeed, whatever the fate of the *vicus* evidence for activity after the closure of the fort is almost non-existent. A single coin shows that someone was still using the roads through the site after *c.* 450 and, as

---

2   The author is most grateful to C. Drage for allowing him to incorporate ideas originally included in drafts of the report on the 1983-4 work in this synthesis and in the broader discussion of the *vicus* functions below.

has already been noted, a thin scatter of material ought to be expected at any major road junction such as Brough whether a fort or settlement was occupied at the time or not at least as long as any form of organised administration persisted in Britain. Subsequently though evidence for activity dissappears until the early modern period on the 1984 site and is represented only by undated stakehole alignments on the 1986 site and by a track replacing Batham Gate on the 1980–3 site.

5) The Function of the Site

There are a number of problems in defining fully the function(s) of the garrison at Brough and uppermost is that the garrisoning units are little known. The size of the fort in all phases suggests either a rather small unit or a detachment of a unit but it is difficult to define exactly what this may imply in terms of actual numbers and types of troops. The only relatively fixed points for the unit type are i) that the phase 2a fort was built 154/8 by *Cohors I Aquitanorum equitata quingenaria* who had previously been at Carrawaburgh at least as builders if not as the garrison (Breeze and Dobson 1978, 244) and in the ?third century were at Brancaster (Birley 1978); and ii) that the phase 3 garrison were at least part mounted. As to the notoriously difficult matter of trying to establish garrison size from fort areas and or barrack size and arrangement there is again little to go on. The internal areas of the phase 1 and phase 2/3 forts at ? 0.66 ha.(1.64 acres) and 0.54 ha. (1.35 acres) respectivley seem unlikely to have been able to hold even a *cohors quingenaria peditata* (Johnson 1983, 292) if the unit was at a probable paper strength of 480 men (on theoretical unit strengths and apparent variations from them see e.g. Breeze and Dobson 1978, 153ff; Keppie 1984, 184).

Barrack accomodation is even less helpful. Nothing useful is known of the phase 1 barracks. In phase 2a and b eight? 10 x 29m barracks may be infered in the *praetentura* with perhaps ?two more in the *raetentura*, while in phase 3 six 8.5 x 39m barracks/stables again with ?two more in the *raetentura* may be likely. Almost nothing is known of their internal arrangements except that at least part of one in phase 3 was a stables. Thus, we cannot say how large the barrack *contubernia* were in most cases. The only hint is given by the dividing wall at the north east end of one phase 3 block which indicates a room *c.* 3m wide, but knowing nothing of the size of the officers' quarters, let alone whether we are dealing with a barracks, stables or even a combination of the two further inference from this slender evidence would be unwise.

Certainly though there is less problem in assuming that a full unit was in garrison in the later phases

when there are indiactions that units were smaller (e.g. Connolly 1981, 253) than in reconciling the size of the fort with the presence of *Cohors I Aquitanorum* in the second half of the second century. Even if the mounted troops' horses were not stabled within the fort , either 488 or 608 men (the strength of such units is debated, e.g. Breeze and Dobson 1978, 153ff) would have to be accomodated. The only reasonable explanations are that the unit was vastly under strength, which is not convincing, or that only part of the unit was in garrison. As noted below a possible role for the garrison would be control of the local lead industry and this might involve the constant absence of detachments (or perhaps even their stationing at some other strategic point such as Carsington from which the lead industry may have been administered; though there is no evidence at the site for a military presence). However, it must be equally likely that we should be looking for a second base for the unit and given this possibility even that the garrison of Brough ceased to be the *Cohors I Aquitanorum* by some point in the third century because it was now based at Brancaster need not be certain[3]. Whether a similarly split garrison should be envisaged in phase 1 we do not know but a slightly depleated *cohors quingernaria peditata*, perhaps in slightly cramped conditions, might well be an alternative since the early fort was clearly a little larger.

Whatever the garrison there can be little doubt that the initial role of the fort was as part of the general garrisoning of the Peak District in the wake of the conquest of the area, as were so many forts in the north conventionally assumed to have been founded under Agricola's governorship. The importance of the Hope Valley as a communications route was clearly not lost on Roman road builders and Brough's prime role would have been the supervision of the roads passing through the valley. The small size of the fort as we have seen probably reflects a small garrison and this in turn might be linked to the fact that , as far as is known, the Peak District was virtually unpopulated on the eve of the conquest and so not considered worthy of a larger presence in the Hope Valley.

There is no inherent reason why this supervisory role, essentially perhaps more policing than anything , should have been superseded or augmented by other functions during the first fort phase. However, there are other roles which the fort could have fulfilled. The transference of administative functions from the

---

[3] Indeed a fort the size of Brough-on-Noe has been provisionally suggested below the saxon shore fort at Brancaster and the tiles recording *Cohors I Aquitanorum* from the site come from an apparently civil area established before the saxon shore fort where much residual material is to be expected in later contexts (Hincliffe and Green 1985, 176–81).

military to the *civitas Brigantium*, the probable but not certain civil *res publica* of the area, is unlikely to have occured before Hadrianic times and some administrative role may have lain with the commander at Brough since no other fort is known in the central Peak District. Yet what administration would have been required before Hadrianic times is debatable. The majority of Peak District rural settlement seems on present evidence to have begun in the early-second century, though the evidence is limited (e.g. Branigan 1991, 62) and never seems to have reached any great density as far north as the Hope Valley (below). However, Buxton may already have been a prosperous spa town and if it did not have its own fort, which is still uncertain, Brough might have played some supervisory role in its affairs.

The most important possible administrative role that the first fort at Brough may have fulfilled however was in the lead (and perhaps silver) extraction industry. The industry cannot be proven to have been in existence before the Hadrianic period but I have argued elsewhere on epigraphic grounds that it was probably active at least as early as the Flavian period (Dearne 1990, 233ff). Even if it was though the nature of its organisation is highly problematic. None of the lead pigs (cast blocks) that can be shown to come from the Derbyshire lead field (*R.I.B.*II i 2404.39–2404.60; Dearne 1990, Appendix 1 Nos. 27–55) has an inscription which need imply military involvement in the industry. It appears that civilian lessees were important in the industry's organisation but it is to be presumed that some imperially sanctioned authority regulated their activities even if, as seems likely , little silver was produced. Such a role may have been fulfilled by a *procurator metallorum* controlling the mining area, which it is clear from pig inscriptions was called, or run from, a site called *Lutudarum*.

Lutudarum, or the settlement within it that provided its administrative functions, seems likely to have been Carsington which comprised a ?small town and a detached ?*villa* type building (Ling and Courtney 1981; Ling 1990; Dearne, Anderson and Branigan forthcoming). The site has produced only unstratified coins and a little pottery dating before the first half of the second century so it is possible that the garrison at Brough, immediately north of the lead field, provided the industry's regulation before the establishment of Carsington. Even if it did not Brough as the nearest fort to the lead field did probably provide any necessary enforcement of mining regulations (although a role for the fort at Derby in both regulation and policing should not be ruled out).

The function(s) of the later fort comprise a similar set of possiblities. Again control of the road lines must have been a function of the garrison, but more specifically a rebellion in Brigantia (which covered

much of northern England and conceivably parts of southern Scotland) in the mid-second century might have resulted in the re-garrisoning 154/8 and would imply that initally the fort was re-established to watch over a potentially troublesome population. However, there are many problems with this interpretation. Firstly the reality of the rebellion rests on a dejected Britannia on the reverse of a coin issue, an inscription whose reading is disputed and a very problematic passage in Pausanias (*Graec. descr.* viii, 43, 4) which might not even relate to Britain (*cf. R.I.B.* 1322; Wilkes 1985; Frere 1987, 133; 1986; Hartley and Fitts 1988, 27f). Secondly the re-occupation of Brough and other sites in northern England might alternatively relate to the withdrawal from Scotland, be it as a result of some rebellion in the rear or not, and the need to find bases for displaced units *c.* 154/8. Thirdly there is no indication that there was any unrest in the Peak District at this time, even if there may have been further north. The fact that the fort was re-established at much the same size tends to reinforce this, though it does not preclude an element of concern for the area's security if there had indeed been trouble elsewhere.

Leaving aside specifically military roles there may have been few potential administrative functions for the fort to fulfill by the time that it was re-established 154/8. The Peak probably passed into care of the *civitas*, most likely the *civitas Brigantium*, in Hadrianic times unless the passage of Pausanias cited above records the return of some part of Brigantia back to military control; and even if it does areas much further north must be seen as more likely candidates for such action. Only the presence of the Derbyshire lead field provides any grounds for not assuming that the Peak District was under civil administration. We have no evidence for the creation of an imperial estate in the area but the existence of one cannot be entirely ruled out. Excepting this possibility though the probably by now increased rural population of the area together with Buxton must have been civil concerns. More importantly the administration of the lead industry must have been vested elsewhere than at Brough between *c.* 120 and 154/8 and Carsington, certainly established before the latter date, is the obvious candidate, probably providing a base for a *Procurator Metallorum*. If so there seems no reason to suppose that the situation changed with the return of the army to Brough.

Again though some connection with the lead industry must still be envisaged for the later fort at Brough. Where-ever the administration was based it is likely that it would have made use of what military resources were available, especially if as seems likely the industry was dispersed and the actual extraction carried out by lessees with opportunities to defraud the exchequer. Be it a policing role, a more direct involvement in supervising production and distribution or just as an armed enforcement of the administrator's authority the Brough garrison must have played some part in the industry. Indeed, that its garrison in phase 2a and phase 3 was at least part mounted would well suit some sort of policing role in the hilly Peak District terrrain and might explain the small size of the fort if patrols were constantly away from it.

One other piece of evidence bears on the later fort's possible connection with lead extraction; the plan of its *principia* in phases 2a and b. It is clear that far more storage or administrative space was provided in the building than in the usual *principia*, especially since the fort was so small. It is conceivable that some of this space was used for the secure storage of lead pigs or for administration connected to the industry. If so we might perhaps envisage that the more northerly parts of the lead field around Castleton and on Bradwell Moor were supervised from here, or indeed that Brough administered some mining purely for military purposes. The lead seal at Leicester recording *Cohors I Aquitanorum* need not come from a time when the unit (?anyway divided) was at Brough and so cannot safely be equated as Birley (1978) suggested with that from the mines (*metalla*) of Alston Moor evidently operated by *Cohors II Nerviorum*. However, the activity of the latter does show that some units might be directly involved in mining in northern Britain. The chemically altered galena (lead ore) samples from the Brough *principia* analysed by Smythe (in Richmond 1938) may provide another hint, though the ore is so plentiful in the area that it would be rash to assert that they had been deliberately heated.

How the role of the fort may have changed by the mid-fourth century when it was abandoned can only be speculated upon. Lead pigs were still being cast in the fourth century (Branigan, Housley and Housley 1986) but their lack of inscriptions may imply some decline in official involvement in the industry; parts of the Carsington settlement certainly seem to have become more agricultural in character (Dearne, Anderson and Branigan forthcoming). Too little is yet known of rural settlement in the area to judge whether there was still a sizable population but single and multiple coin finds suggest that the Peak District was far from abandoned (Dearne 1990, 211k) and Buxton clearly continued in some form until late in the Roman period (Hart 1981, 94). A policing role may therefore still have been thought necessary; certainly supervision of the roads must as ever have been the fort's concern.

On present evidence the Brough *vicus* was founded *c*. 80 at the same time as the fort, probably closed down with the withdrawal of the garrison *c*. 120, reappeared in an eventually at least expanded form in the mid-second century and may have failed or at least contracted a century or more later. This outline requires more confirmation but if it is correct the coincidence of its inception, closure and reappearance with those of the fort emphasise that the initial and probably continuing *raison d'etre* for the Brough *vicus* must have been the presence of the fort. The reliance of *vici* on the military for their existence is a well worked theme and the coincidence of foundation and evacuation dates provides some of the clearest evidence for the phenomenon, nowhere better seen than at nearby Melandra Castle (Webster 1971). Indeed, I have argued elsewhere that, though dating evidence rarely gives the precison that one would like, a similar pattern can be seen at several south Pennine sites which do not subsequently show the features of small towns (Dearne 1991).

That military *vici* in the so-called highland military zone of Britain did not become towns after the withdrawal of the garrisons from the sites as did so many of their southern counterparts has become almost axiomatic, even though a few exceptions occur where special circumstances pertained. Brough lay on the southern edge of this area with towns superseding the *vici* at Little Chester (Derby) and Rocester just south of the Peak District, a 'military town' perhaps developing at Manchester west of it and even two small towns, Buxton and Carsington, becoming established (though without a proven military presence at either) because of the existence of a spa and ?lead mining administration (Dearne 1991). However, Brough would appear to belong with the vast majority of military *vici* in the north where an assumption that they were intimately connected with and even parasitic on the payed garrison must be the starting point for assessing their economies (e.g. Evans 1984). Their effect beyond a relatively limited zone of influence should, without evidence to the contrary, be considered slight (Manning 1975, 115) and indeed they may be seen as 'urban islands in a sea of dispersed settlement' (Jones 1984, 89).

Exactly how this military dependence functioned is more problematic because so few sites, even where excavation has been extensive, have produced convincing evidence for *vicanal* occupations other than metalworking (whose residues are undoubtedly over represented due to their better preservation). Moreover much of the evidence we do have comes from Hadrian's Wall where the concentration of military personal over nearly three centuries at regularly spaced forts and other lesser posts must have produced different conditions to those at intermitently held or rather isolated forts elsewhere in the north. The conventional wisdom is to envisage a mixed population of soldiers' dependents, veterans and often cosmopolitan traders or service providers. Thus, we envisage wives (for unions were surely contracted even before the lifting of the marriage ban on soldiers by Severus), children and other relatives, slaves and freedmen (perhaps not numerous but occasionally recorded), ex-soldiers who chose to remain at their old base, shopkeepers of all sorts, innkeepers, craftsmen in metal, wood and perhaps stone, priests, soothsayers, prostitutes etc. It is almost impossible to cite evidence for the vast majority of these groups from Brough. We have the seemingly ubiquitous metalworking evidence on the 1980–3 and 1983–4 sites; the alter finds on the latter give a hint at the presence of priests; the lead weights found in 1980–3 probably reflect a trader's presence. Beyond this the evidence is increasingly inferential: the alters were carved by a mason, though he need not have been resident at the site; much of the pottery was probably sold by someone at the site, though the trader could again have been peripatetic etc. The paucity of evidence though is partly inevitable for it is hard to see what evidence one would expect to survive of for instance prostitution, while the presence of soldiers wives or veterans is unlikely to be proven except by epigraphy. I have outlined elsewhere some of the complexities of *vicanal* micro-economies that this incomplete evidence may disguise, such as the possiblity of the garrison employing civilian craftsmen to repair or replace a range of gear (Dearne 1990, 123ff; 1991).

One other probable factor in the *vicanal* economy that is too often ignored and for which there may be some evidence at Brough is agriculture. The apparently unoccupied ditched enclosures on the lower terrace on the 1984 site might well be seen as agricultural and , as Drage (this volume) points out, may find a parallel in the ditches preceding the industrial settlement beyond the Little Chester *vicus*. Similarly a possible ?allotment boundary is known at the edge of the Manchester *vicus* (Jones and Reynolds 1978) and Sommer (1984, 36f) lists seven further possible examples of small allotments at the edge of *vici* and ten of more sizeable field systems. At Brough we are probably dealing with allotment/market gardening activity if the enclosures are agricultural and the fact that the ditched boundaries were retained later when the area was built upon probably suggests individual *vicanal* ownership of them. Field systems proper are not known at Brough or apparently any highland zone *vicus* but Sommer's (1984, 38) rejection of the possibility that they existed is perhaps premature given the rarity of archaeological work immediately beyond *vici* and the question of how self sufficient forts and *vici* were is still unresolved.

As far as this assessment goes and despite the lack of evidence in many areas it is probably as satisfactory as one can hope for. But one suspects that it is incomplete for there are hints that some *vici* at least, however central to their existence the continued presence of the military was, may have played other roles at the same time. To any traveller going any great distance in the north of England in the Roman period, be he on official or private business *vici* must have been fairly important. That the *vicani*, especially those at sites on major roads profited from travellers looking to buy provisions, be accomodated for the night, or even just quench their thirsts can hardly be doubted. Structures such as the Melandra *mansio* (Webster 1971) must surely testify to that whatever the exact details of their proprietorship and even if certain official travellers had to be accomodated free. That Brough lies on the same major road as Melandra but outlived it as a *vicus* by at least a hundred years should not be forgotten.

Equally for a *vicus* such as Brough on the margin of a lead mining area there might be profit to be made from other visitors even if the *vicani* themselves were not directly involved in mining. If small scale dispersed mining by lessees was the norm and even if, as is possible, some at least were essentially farmers supplimenting their incomes Brough (along with Buxton, Little Chester ?and Carsington) might have benefited even be it just as somewhere to buy a mule. One has only to look at the Hadrianic Aljustrel tables form Vispasca in Spain (*C.I.L.* ii 5181; Van Nostrand 1937, 167ff; Lewis and Reinhold 1966, 188–94; Edmondson 1987, 244ff) or the early modern parallels from spanish South America (Chevalier 1970; Brading and Cross 1972; Bakewell 1971) to appreciate how diverse the side benfits of mining could be, both for traders and craftsmen and for farmers. However, there is little evidence for any spin off in terms of lead working at Brough. Most metalworking evidence is in fact ferrous and only the lead lamp or lampholder from the 1980–3 site is at all notable as showing a greater use of the metal than in any other Romano-British *vicus*.

Both of these potential stimuli to the economy of the Brough *vicus* must however be seen as very much secondary to the military presence. Only if it developed a market function for the rural population might we be able to begin talking of a role that was significant enough to support numbers of *vicani* on its own. Our knowledge of Romano-British rural settlement in the Peak District is still in its infancy. A pattern of mainly second century cave usage has long been recognised and has recently been reassessed in a national context (Branigan and Dearne 1992) but only recently have numerous open settlements in the river valleys of the White Peak been located by Butcher (Beswick and Merrills 1983), Hart (1981) and Makepeace (1985). Excavation has hardly scratched the surface of this evidence and all too often we can note only second to third or fourth century surface sherds as dating evidence and assume a mixed farming economy probably preponderant in sheep hubandry (Branigan 1991, 62).

Of the few excavated sites Roystone Grange has revealed the fullest picture, that of a probably mixed farm in existence from the early-second century on, and led Hodges and Wildgoose (1980; *cf.* also Hodges 1991) to suggest a deliberate, even forced colonisation of the previoulsy unoccupied Peak in the earlier-second century. Whether this was the case or not, and Branigan (1991, 62) has noted that a third century colonisation is an alternative or complimentary possibility, the present distribution of known sites strongly favours the main lead extraction areas well to the south of Brough, as does the distribution of isolated coin and brooch finds (Dearne 1990, fig. 8; unpublished study of the brooches by the author). That lead mining, either by creating a market for produce or by directly supplementing farmer's incomes, was a key factor in any colonisation seems highly likely. Indeed there are hints from finds at unexcavated sites or in unpublished excavations that some sites such as Rainster Rocks and Robin Hood's Stride in the southern White Peak were quite well to do (e.g. Dool 1976; Price 1985a; unpublished finds in Sheffield Museum).

However, the Hope Valley (Figure 8: 6) seems on present evidence to be very much less densely settled. Only seven rural settlements, three of them in a cluster at Ladybower, have been certainly identified with a few others including the undated series of ?stock enclosures at Dirtlow (Dearne forthcoming) occasionally being suggested as Romano-British and perhaps one or two more being implied by casual finds. None except Dirtlow have been excavated and it would be dangerous to transfer evidence from excavated sites such as Roystone or even the probably mainly pastoral site at Staden near Buxton (Makepeace 1983; 1987; 1989). At present therefore there is little evidence for any clustering of rural sites in the Hope Valley, which we might perhaps speculate formed the fort's *territorium*. Nor is there any noticable concentration of sites near to roads leading to the fort. Indeed it is rather the Wye Valley, at the head of which stood the spa town of Buxton that dominates the rural settlement pattern of the northern White Peak and north of the Hope Valley the Gritsone moors of the Dark Peak are entirely without known settlement. On this evidence it is difficult to see Brough fulfilling a significant market function for the rural community.

It seems therefore that any prosperity at Brough was based on the pay of the military perhaps augmented by the profit made from travellers and the lead industry. A number of approaches might be persued in the hope of guageing the level of this prosperity. The most obvious, the quantity and quality of the artifacts and coins recovered, may be inapproapriate at Brough. The pedology of the site is hostile to many materials and has doubtless decreased the recovery rate especially of copper alloy and bone items, while two of the three excavations carried out have been on rather peripheral areas and the third only encountered activity prior to *c.* 120. This helps to explain why only one coin and three brooches have come from the *vicus* and the eleven coins known from areas entirely beyond the fort and *vicus* suggest that the picture is not representive even of coin survival let alone loss. A better guide is probably given by the size of the *vicus* which suggests a fairly boyant settlement at least in the later-second and early-third century, although the problems in establishing fully the area that it covered at different dates and the possiblity that it included largely unused sites should be bourne in mind.

A third avenue of enquiry is provided by what is known of the plan, construction and fittings of the buildings at the site. Very little can be said of those on the 1980–3 site representing the early *vicus* except that they were of timber perhaps with a stone based frontage beside road B (which would have protected the superstructure from the worst of the water run off from the road). On the 1986 site again little is known of the wooden building(s) belonging to the second half of the second century built on sill beams. On the 1984 site we get slightly more idea of the buildings present at the edge of the *vicus* in the later-second to mid-third centuries. Though they mostly survived only as rubble and cobble floors some of which could alternatively be hard standings, structure 2 at least seems to have been a sub-rectanglular open ended building *c.* 5.75 x 4.5m, probably of timber carried on low stone walls. Similarly structure 5 was probably built on sill walls and sub-divided.

However, it is the building plans revealed by resistivity survey in the Halsteads field near to the fort that are most informative (Figure 4: 2). The buildings' appearance on the survey implies that they were at least stone founded and from this we may infer that they belong to the later *vicus*. Those marked 7 and 9 on Figure 4: 2 provide the most complete plans (and that marked 6 was perhaps similar to No.7) and seem to be buildings around 14.3m wide and over 20.5m and over 19m long respectively. In addition 7 seems to have had a 4.8 x 3.8m annexe to the side of its frontage and the front wall of 9 seems to continue, perhaps suggesting a pair of similar adjoining buildings. In form both may be called strip buildings since their frontages are shorter than their lengths but comparison with Sommer's (1984, fig. 23) analysis of *vicanal* building dimentions suggests that they are considerably wider than most such buildings. Indeed, both fall significantly outside the range of building width/length ratios tabulated by him. Whether, given the still relatively limited numbers of building plans available from *vici* this should be regarded as significant might be questioned. Moreover the image of *vici* as consisting entirely of fairly narrow, long strip buildings with shops/workshops at the front and domestic accomodation behind and/or perhaps on occasions above is doubtless at best a simplification. Yet the width and overall size of the buildings does seem to suggest either a lack of competition for road frontage and/or the presence of comparatively well to do *vicani*.

On balance there does seem to be evidence for a fair degree of prosperity in the later *vicus* given its probable extent and the presence of large stone or stone founded buildings. We are unable to make any reliable estimate of the population so far since so little is known of building density/ contemporanity let alone the function of the buildings. But the presumption at the moment for the later-second and earlier-third centuries must be that a significant number of *vicani* were living at Brough and some probably living quite well.

6) Outstanding Problems and Future Work

There are many outstanding problems with both the fort and *vicus* at Brough. However, given that the fort and a significant part of the *vicus* are scheduled and not at present subject to ploughing or other threats, and that the percentage of the fort so far examined is high compared to that of many fort sites in Britain, excavation over much of the site must be regarded as justifiable only to elucidate well defined and important problems.

With regard to the fort the most important problems still outstanding relate to its first phase. Certain location of the south east and north east defences is required to show the fort's size. However, given the failure of previous work to locate the former especially it seems likely that they may have been partially or wholly obliterated by the later defences. Therefore the south east defences may best be approached either by locating the early south east gate (which should not have been removed since the *via principalis* lay in the same position in all phases) or by fully defining the extent of the early granaries. Further elucidation of the phase 1 internal buildings is also desirable and the presence of the clay sealing layer over the first fort has clearly preserved many of their traces. The recovery of the rest of the plan of the *principia* and *praetorium* are possible objectives but fuller publication of the work of the 1960s would be a prerequisite and the deliniation of at least one barracks might be more useful in indicating the nature of the garrison. Amongst lesser priorities are establishing the course of the *via praetoria* and so the plan of the *praetentura* and similarly further

confirmation of the rampart width (and intervallum road width) would be useful.

The later fort is much better understood and a good number of the disiderata relating to it are matters of detail and not broad plan. Amongst these the definitive establishment of the line and width of the fort wall, rampart and intervallum road is perhaps foremost along with confirmation that the *praetorium* lay to the north west of the *principia* in phase 2 and was replaced by granaries in phase 3. The former would seem to require a number of trenches being cut through the defences but the latter might be at least partially acheived by resisitivity survey. Indeed a resistivity survey of the whole fort would be highly desirable as it might reveal a fairly full plan of the phase 3 fort complicated only by the stone built phase 2 administrative buidings. Amongst other matters of detail a section across the south west fort ditches (beyond the scheduled area) would be useful, especially if it indicated whether or not a major road left the south west gate; and any excavation in the fort should seek to refine the dating of the phase 2a/b and phase 2b/3 interfaces. More important but more problematic than these matters are questions relating to the later fort's barracks and late exit arrangements. The definition of the internal arrangements of the barracks/stables for phase 2a to 3 might considerably advance our understanding of the type(s) of units in garrison and their sizes. The full publication of the work of the 1960s is an essential prerequisite to any such programme of work but it is clear that except at the north east end of the *praetentura* preservation of the evidence is poor and is compounded by the problems of differentiating phases 2a and b. Thus, whether excavation, necessarily in the form of a large open area investigation would be justified may be doubted. The fuller understanding of the late exit arrangements on the south east of the fort is a priority that might more likely be susceptable to excavation but consititutes a major undertaking if they are to be placed in a meaningful context. The main outstanding questions with regard to these late changes are how the pitched stone causeway found in 1958/9 relates to that found along with a pebbled surface in 1969 and whether in phase 3 the rear of the plot formerly occupied by the granaries was left open in connection with the changes. However, in order to place the changes in context it would also be desirable to fully excavate the south east fort gate to establish whether the late exit complimented or replaced it.

In many ways, however, it is the *vicus* or more exactly extra-mural area of the site that is most in need of elucidation in the present state of knowledge. Its chronology, especially the date of its decline/closure is still improperly known and is central to understanding its relationship to the fort and any other role that it may have played. Equally

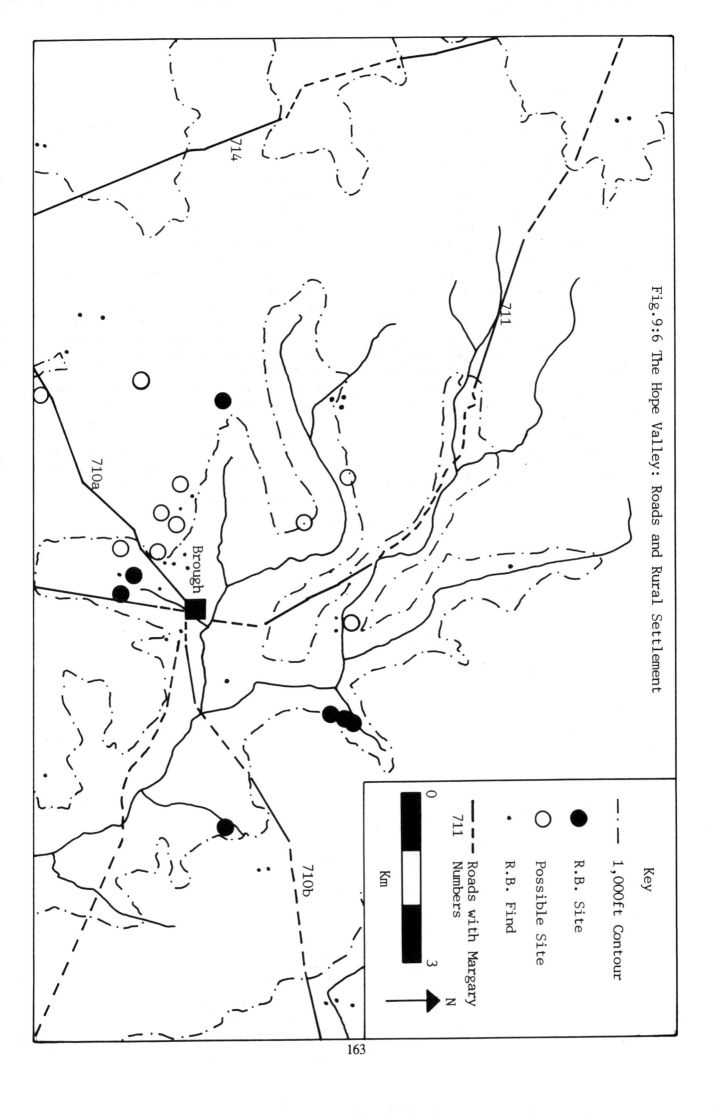

Fig.9:6 The Hope Valley: Roads and Rural Settlement

Key

— — 1,000ft Contour

● R.B. Site

○ Possible Site

· R.B. Find

—— Roads with Margary
711 Numbers

Brough

710a

710b

714

711

N

Km

0   3

163

the range of functions, in as far as they are recoverable archaeologically, that the *vicus* provided can hardly be assessed properly on present evidence. Clearly any threat to areas likely to have lain within the *vicus* but beyond the scheduled area, and especially to any areas that may have held cemeteries which as at so many northern *vici* are entirely unknown, must be closely monitored and rescue excavation must be carried out where necessary. Negative geophysical survey results given what is now known about such techniques' sensitivity at the site cannot be taken as indicating the absence of archaeological features.

As to research work a priority is undoubtedly the investigation of the crop marks revealed by aerial photographs north east of the fort across the River Noe (Dearne this volume). Whilst the field in which they lie is under limited threat at present, though outside the scheduled area, the indications are of an enclosure of some size and quite possibly military character which might have considerable ramifications for the site as a whole. The fact that these are the only crop mark features to have beeen noted at Brough might suggest that they are caused by particularly deep or organic-rich ?ditches and so

might be susceptable to resistivity survey. However, limited excavation at least is required to define the features' date and if possible function; and indeed the traces are faint and certain confirmation that they have an archaeological cause is yet required. Limited excavation, or indeed resistivity survey, in the same field would also be helpful in establishing something of the detailed course of the major roads approaching Brough, at least one of which may have crossed the River Noe near the enclosure.

The majority of dating and functional questions are, however, only likely to be answered by work in the centre of the *vicus*, that is in the Halsteads field. It is clear that resisitivity survey is of use in defining at least the roads and stone (founded) elements of the site and complete coverage of the scheduled area by resistivity and if possible magnetometer survey must be the first reaserch objective here. Subsequently only excavation will advance our knowledge and it is clear from the work to date that this needs to be in the form of a relatively large open area excavation if fully comprehensible information is to be recovered. At present it would seem most appropriate for such an excavation to examine the site of either Figure 8: 5 buildings E or F in its entirety.

Plates

166

Plate 1   The 1980-3 Excavations: general view looking west over trench B. Road B lies in the centre with the stone alignment (context 19) to the left. The south east rampart of the later fort is marked by the bank in the background with the gate and stile marking the approximate position of the fort gate

Plate 2   The 1980-3 Excavations: Hearth B24

Plate 3   The 1984 Excavations: view facing N.E. The figure in the foreground stands at the edge of the modern pit from which the altar was removed; the pit cuts through the edge of the lower terrace road and to the south are the foundations of the linking road. In the middleground machinery and bales overlie the 1983 excavation. In the background the earthwork of the south east wall of the fort, topped by a line of trees, is visible

Plate 4   The 1984 Excavations: view facing S.W. The upper terrace road and in the background hollow-ways and the road
            east to Chesterfield

Plate 5   The inscribed altar

Plate 6 Aerial View of the fort and *Vicus*. The raised platform of the (later) fort, partly edged by trees is at centre in a bend of the River Noe. To the left are the areas afforested in 1986 with traces of the excavation trenches visible. Below the fort the agger of the track superseding Batham Gate is visible with 1980-3 trench B to its right. The 1983-4 site lies across the Bradwell Brook and modern road off the bottom of the photograph. The rectangular enclosure located from the air lies just below the lowest point of the bend in the River Noe

Collected Bibliography

The following abbreviations are used in the bibliography:

Arch.	*Archaeologia*
A.A.	*Archaeologia Aeliana*
Arch.J.	*Archaeological Journal*
Antiq.J.	*Antiquaries Journal*
D.A.J.	*Derbyshire Archaeological Journal*
J.R.S.	*Journal of Roman Studies*
Proc.Soc.Antiq.Scot.	*Proceedings of the Society of Antiquaries of Scotland*
T.C.W.A.A.S.	*Transactions of the Cumberland and Westmorland Antiquarian and Archaeological Society*
T.H.A.S.	*Transactions of the Hunter Archaeological Society*
Y.A.J.	*Yorkshire Archaeological Journal*

Abramson, P. (1988) 'The Search for Roman Castleford', *Current Archaeology* 107, 43–8.

Allason-Jones, L. and Miket, R. (1984) The Catalogue of Small Finds from South Shields Roman Fort *Society of Antiquaries of Newcastle-upon-Tyne Monograph 2*, Newcastle.

Anderson, A.C. (1980) *A Guide to Roman Fine Wares.* Vorda: Highworth .

Atkinson, D. (1942) *Report on Excavations at Wroxeter (The Roman City of Viroconium) in the County of Salop 1923–7*, Oxford: Oxford University Press.

Bakewell, P.J. (1971) *Silver Mining and Society in Colonial Mexico: Zacetecas 1546–1700*, Cambridge: University Press Cambridge.

Barkoczi, L. (1988) *Pannonische Glasfunde in Ungarn.*

Bartlett, J. (1959) Interim Note on Excavations at Brough, *J.R.S.* 49, 108.

Bartlett, J. (1960) Interim Note on Excavations at Brough, *J.R.S.* 50, 216.

Bayley, J. (1985) 'What's What in Ancient Technology:An Introduction to High-Temperature Processes' in P.Phillips (ed) *The Archaeologist and the Laboratory* C.B.A. Research Report 58, 41–4, London: CBA.

Bennet, J. (1983) 'The End of Roman Settlement in Northern England' in J.C.Chapman and H.C.Mytum *Settlement in North Britain 1, 000 B.C.–A.D. 1,000* B.A.R. 118, 205–32, Oxford: British Archaelogical Reports.

Bestwick, P. and Merrills, D. (1983) 'L.H.Butcher's Survey of Early Settlement and Fields in the S.Pennines', *T.H.A.S.* 12, 16–50.

Birley, E. (1978) 'A Note on Cohors I Aquitanorum', *D.A.J.* 98, 59–60.

Birley, E. and Birley, M. (1938) '4th Report on Excavations at Chesterholm-Vindolanda' *A.A.* 4th s.15, 222–41.

Birley, E. and Gillam, J.P. (1948) 'Mortarium Stamps from Corbridge 1906–38', *A.A.* 4th s. 26, 172–201.

Birley, E. and Richmond, I.A. (1938) 'Excavations at Corbridge 1936–1938', *A.A.* 4th s. 15, 243–94.

Bishop, M.C. and Dore, J.N. (1989) *Corbridge:Excavations of the Roman Fort and Town, 1947–80* H.B.M.C.E. Archaeology Report 8, London: H.B.M.C.E.

Boon, G.C. (1966) 'Roman, Window Glass from Wales', *Journal of Glass Studies* 7, 41–5.

Boon, G.C. (1969) 'Belgic and Roman Silchester:the Excavations of 1954–8, with an Excursus on the Early History of Calleva', *Arch.* 102, 1–81.

Brading, D.A. and Cross, H.E. (1972) 'Colonial Silver Mining:Mexico and Peru', *Hispanic American Historical Revue* 52, 545–79.

Brailsford, J. (1958) *Antiquities of Roman Britain* (2nd ed) London: British Museum.

Brailsford, J. (1962) *Hod Hill* vol. 1, London: British Museum.

Branigan, K. (1991) 'Civilian Development in a Military Zone:The Peak A.D.43–400' in R.Hodges and K.Smith (eds) *Recent Developments in the Archaeology of the Peak District*, 57–68, Sheffield Archaeological Monographs 2, Sheffield: J.R. Collis Publications.

Branigan, K. and Dearne, M.J. (1992) *Romano-British Cavemen*, Oxford: Oxbow Books.

Branigan, K., Housley, J. and Housley, C. (1986) 'Two Roman Lead Pigs from Carsington', *D.A.J.* 106, 5–17.

Brassington, M. (1971) 'A Trajanic Kiln Complex near Littlechester, Derby 1968', *Antiq.J.* 51, 36–69.

Brassington, M. (1980) 'Derby Racecourse Kiln Excavations 1972–3', *Antiq.J.* 60, 8–47.

Brassington, M. and Webster, W.A. (1988) 'The Lumb Brook Pottery Kilns', *D.A.J.* 108, 21–33.

Breeze, D.J. (1982) 'Demand and Supply on the Northern Frontier' in P.Clack and S. Haselgrove (eds) *Rural Settlement in the Roman North*, 148–65, CBA Group 3 Occasional Paper, Durham: CBA.

Breeze, D.J. and Dobson, B. (1978) *Hadrian's Wall.*

Breeze, D.J. and Dobson, B. (1985) 'Roman Military Deployment in North England', *Britannia* 16, 1–21.

British Museum (1951) *Guide to the Antiquities of Roman Britain*, London: British Museum.

Brookes, I. and Garton, D. (in.prep.) 'The Characterisation of the Neolithic Flint Resources of the Peak District'.

Bruton, F.A. (1907) 'Excavations at Melandra in 1905', *D.A.J.* 29, 22–63.

Buckland, P.C. and Magilton, J.R. (1986) *The Archaeology of Doncaster:1 The Roman Civil Settlement* B.A.R. 148, Oxford: British Archaeological Reports.

Buckland, P.C., Magilton, J.R. and Dolby, M.J. (1980) 'The Roman Pottery Industries of South Yorkshire', *Britannia* 11, 145–64.

Burnham, B.C. and Wacher, J. (1990) *The Small Towns of Roman Britain,* London: Batsford.

Bushe-Fox, J.P. (1913) *Excavations on the Site of the Roman Town at Wroxeter, Shropshire, in 1912*, Society of Antiquaries of London Research Report, London: Society of Antiquries of London.

Bushe-Fox, J.P. (1914) *Second Report on the Excavations on the Site of the Roman Town at Wroxeter, Shropshire, 1913*, Society of Antiquaries of London Research Report, London: Society of Antiquaries of London.

Bushe-Fox, J.P. (1932) *Third Report on the Excavations of the Roman Fort at Richborough, Kent*, Society of Antiquaries of London Research Report, London: Society of Antiquaries of London.

Bushe-Fox, J.P. (1949) *Fourth Report on the Excavations of the Roman Fort at Richborough, Kent*, Society of Antiquaries of London Research Report, London: Society of Antiquaries of London

Campbell, D.B. (1984) 'Ballistaria in First to Mid-Third Century Britain:A Reappraisal', *Britannia* 15, 75–84.

Carrington, P. (1986) 'The Roman Advance into the North West Midlands Before A.D.71', *Journal of the Chester Archaeological Society* 68, 5–22.

Casey, P.J. (1982) 'Civilians and Soldiers-Friends, Romans, Countrymen?' in P.Clack and S.Haselgrove (eds) *Rural Settlement in the Roman North.* Durham: CBA Group 3 Occasilonal Paper, 123–32.

Charlesworth, D. (1966) 'Roman Square Bottles', *Journal of Glass Studies* 8, 26–40.

Charlesworth, D. (1972) 'The Glass' in S.S.Frere, *Verulamium Excavations Vol.1.* London: Society Ant London Research Report , 196–215.

Charlesworth, D. (1979) 'The Glass' in W.S.Hanson, et al, 'The Agricolan Supply Base at Red Hill, Corbridge', *A.A.* 5th s. 7, 58–61.

Charlesworth, D. (1981) 'The Glass' in J.Wacher and A.McWhirr, *Early Roman Occupation at Cirencester.* Cirencester: Cirencester Excavation Committee, 106–8.

Charlesworth, D. (1984) 'The Glass' in S.S.Frere, *Verulamium Excavations Vol.3*, Oxford Committee for Archaeology Monograph 1. Oxford: Oxford Committee for Archaeology, 145–74.

Chevalier, F. (1970) *Land and Society in Colonial Mexico.* University of California Press.

Christison, D. (1901) 'Account of the Excavation.of the Roman Station of Camelon nr. Falkirk, Stirlingshire Undertaken by the Society in 1900', *Proc.Soc. Antiq.Scot.* 35, 329–417.

Clark, A. (1990) *Seeing Beneath the Soil:Prospecting Methods in Archaeology.* London: Batsford.

Clarke, G. (1979) *The Roman Cemetery at Lankhills.* Oxford: Clarendon Press.

Cleary, S.E. and Ferris, I. (1988) 'Rocester', *Current Archaeology* 10 No.4, 132–3.

Cleere, H. (1982) 'Industry in the Romano-British Countryside' in D.Miles (ed) The *Romano-British Countryside:Studies in Rural Settlement and Economy* B.A.R. 82. Oxford: British Archaeological Reports, 123–35.

Collingwood, R.G. (1916) 'The Exploration of the Roman Fort at Ambleside:Report on the Third Year's Work (1915)', *T.C.W.A.A.S.* 2nd s. 16, 57–90.

Collingwood, R.G. (1928) 'Hardknot Castle', *T.C.W.A.A.S.* 2nd s. 28, 314–52.

Connolly, P.O. (1981) *Greece and Rome at War.* London: MacDonald.

Conway, R.S. (ed)(1906) *Melandra Castle, lst report of the Manchester Branch of the Classical Association.*

Cool, H.E.M. and Price, J. (forthcoming) *Roman Glass from Excavations in Colchester, 19711985,* Colchester Archaeological Report 8. Colchester.

Coombs, D.C. (1977) 'Excavations at Mam Tor, Derbyshire, 1965–1969' in D.W.Harding (ed) *Later Prehistoric Earthworks in Britain and Ireland.* London: Academic Press, 147–52.

Corder, P. (1951) *The Roman Town and Villa at Great Casterton, Rutland.* Nottingham: University of Nottingham.

Crummy, N. (1983) *The Roman Small Finds fron Excavations in Colchester 1971–9*, Colchester Archaeological Report 2. Colchester: Colchester Archaeological Trust.

Cunliffe, B. (1971) *Excavations at Fishbourne 1961–9, Vol.2:The Finds*, Society of Antiquaries of London Research Report. London: Society of Antiquaries of London.

Curle, J. (1911) *A Roman Frontier Post and its People, the Fort of Newstead in the Parish of Melrose.* Glasgow: Maclehose.

Curwen, C.E. (1941) 'More About Querns', *Antiquity* 15, 15–32.

Daniels, C.M. (1980) 'Excavations at Wallsend and the Early Fourth Century Barracks on Hadrian's Wall' in W.S.Hanson and L.J.F.Keppie (eds) *Roman Frontier Studies 1979*, B.A.R. S71i. Oxford: British Archaeological Reports, 173–94.

Dearne, M.J. (1986) *The Military Vici of the South Pennines*, Unpublished M.Phil. Thesis, Sheffield University.

Dearne, M.J. (1990) *The Archaeology of the Economy of the Roman South Pennines with Particular Reference to the Lead Extraction Industry in its National Context*, Unpublished Ph.D. Thesis, Sheffield University.

Dearne, M.J. (1991) 'The Military *Vici* of the South Pennines:Retrospect and Prospect' in R.Hodges and K.Smith (eds) *Recent Developments in the Archaeology of the Peak District,* Sheffield

174

Archaeological Monographs, Vol. 2. Sheffield: J.R. Collis Publications, 69–84.

Dearne, M.J. (forthcoming) 'Survey and Excavation at Dirtlow, Bradwell Moor 1987–8', *D.A.J.*

Dearne, M.J., Anderson, S. and Branigan, K. (forthcoming) 'Excavations at Brough Field, Carsington, 1980', *D.A.J.*.

Dool, J. (1976) 'Roman Material from Rainster Rocks, Brassington', *D.A.J.* 96, 17–22.

Dool, J. (1985) 'Excavations at Strutts Park, Derby 1974', *D.A.J.* 105, 15–32.

Dool, J. (1985a) 'Derby Racecourse:Excavations on the Roman Industrial Settlement, 1970', *D.A.J,* 105, 155–221.

Down, A. (1978) *Chichester Excavations 3*. Chichester: Phillimore.

Down, A. (1979) *Excavations in Chichester 4*. Chichester: Phillimore.

Dressel, H. (1899) *Corpus Inscriptionum Latinarum XV pars 1*. Berlin: Akademie Der Wissenschaften.

Edmondson, J.C. (1987) *Two Industries in Roman Lusitania, Mining and Garum Production*, B.A.R. S362. Oxford: British Archaeological Reports.

Edwardes, W. and Trotter, F .M. (1954) *British Regional Geology:The Pennines and Adjacent Areas*. London: H.M.S.O.

Ellis, P. (1989) 'Roman Chesterfield:Excavations by T.Courtney 1974–78', *D.A.J.* 109, 51–130.

Evans, J. (1984) 'Settlement and Society in N.E.England in the Fourth Century A.D.' in P.R.Wilson, R.F.J.Jones and D.M. Evans (eds) *Settlement and Society in the Roman North*. Bradford: Department of Archaeology, Bradford University, 43–8.

Exner, K. (1939) 'Die Provinzialromischen Emailfibeln der Rheinlande', *Bericht der Romish Germanischen Kommission* 29.

Farrar, R.A.H. (1973) 'The Techniques and Sources of Romano-British Black-Burnished Ware' in A.Detsicas (ed) *Current Research in Romano-British Coarse Pottery*, C.B.A. Research Report 10. London: Council for British Archaeology, 199–227.

Fink, R.O. (1971) *Roman Military Records on Papyrus*. American Philological Association Monograph 26.

Foster, R.H. and Knowles, W.H. (1911) 'Corstopitum:Report on the Excavations in 1911', *A.A.* 3rd s. 8, 137–263.

Foster-Smith, C.H. et al (1984) *A Catalogue of Artifacts and Written Records from Studies of the Roman Fort at Brough-on-Noe (Navio) N. Derbyshire*, Privately Produced by the Dept. Ancient History and Classical Archaeology, University of Sheffield.

Frere, S.S. (1972) Verulamium Excavations 1, *Society of Antiquaries of London Research Report*. London: Society of Antiquaries of London.

Frere, S.S. (1987) *Britannia* (3rd ed.) London: Routledge.

Garstang, J. (1904) 'Roman Brough:Anavio', *D.A.J.* 26, 177–204.

Gibson, J.P. and Simpson, F.G. (1909) 'The Roman Fort on the Stanegate at Haltwhistle Burn', *A.A.* 3rd s. 5, 213–285.

Gillam, J.P. (1957) 'Types of Roman Coarse Pottery Vessels in Northern Britain', *A.A.* 4th s. 35, 180–251.

Gillam, J.P. (1963) 'The Coarse Pottery' in K.A.Steer, 'Excavations at Mumrills Rbman Fort', *Proc.Soc.Antiq.Scot.* 86, 113–30.

Gillam, J.P. (1970) *Types of Roman Coarse Pottery in Northern Britain* (3rd ed.) Newcastle.

Gillam, J.P. (1974) 'The Frontier after Hadrian-a History of the Problem', *A.A.* 5th s. 2, 1–17.

Gillam, J.P. (1976) 'Coarse Fumed Ware in Northern Britain', *Glasgow Archaeological Journal* 4, 57–80.

Gould, J. (1964) 'Excavations at Wall, Staffs. 1961–3', *Trans.Lichfield and S.Staffs. Archaeological and Historical Society* 5, 1–50.

Greene, K. (1984) 'The Roman Fortress at Usk, Wales and the Processing of Roman Pottery for Publication', *Journal of Field Archaeology* 11(4) 405–12.

Guido, M. (1978) *The Glass Beads of the Prehistoric and Roman Periods in Britain and Ireland. Society of Antiquaries of London Research Report* London: Society of Antiquaries of London.

Haigh, D. and Savage, M.J.D. (1984) 'Sewing Shields', *A.A.* 5th s. 12, 33–148.

Hanson, W.S (1987) *Agricola and the Conquest of the North*. London: Batsford.

Hanson, W.S. and Campbell, D.B. (1986) 'The Brigantes:from Clientage to Conquest', . *Britannia* 17, 73–90.

Harden, D.B. (1962) 'Ronan Glass in York' in *R.C.H.M., Eburacum*. London: H.M.S.O., 136–41.

Harden, D.B. (1967) 'The Glass Jug' in M.Biddle, 'Two Flavian Burials at Grange Road, Winchester', *Antiq.J.* 47, 238–40.

Harden, D.B. et al (1968) *Masterpieces of Glass*. London: British Museum.

Harden, D.B. and Price, J. (1971) 'The Glass' in B.Cunliffe, *Excavations at Fishbourne 1961–1969 Vol.2:The Finds. Society Antiquaries London Research Report* London: Society of Antiquaries of London. 317–67.

Hart, C.R. (1981) *The North Derbyshire Archaeological Survey to A.D. 1500*. Chesterfield: North Derbyshire Archaeological Trust.

Hartley, B.R. (1960) 'The Roman Fort at Bainbridge, Excavations of 1957–9', *Proceedings of the Leeds Philosophical and Literary Society* 11, 107–31.

Hartley, B.R. (1972) 'The Roman Occupations of Scotland:The Evidence of Samian Ware', *Britannia* 3, 1–55.

Hartley, B.R. and Fitts, L. (1988) *The Brigantes*. London: Sutton.

Hartley, K. (1977) 'Two Major Potteries Producing Mortaria in the First Century A.D.' in J.Dore and K.Green (eds) *Roman Pottery Studies in Britain and Beyond* B.A.R. S30. Oxford: British Archaeological Reports, 5–17.

Hartley, K. (1981) 'Painted Fine Wares Made in the Raetian Workshops near Wilderspool, Cheshire' in A.C.Anderson and A.S. Anderson (eds) *Roman Pottery Research in Britain and Northwest Europe* B.A.R. S123. Oxford: British Archaeological Reports, 471–80.

Hassal, M.W.C. (1980) 'Altars, Curses and Other Epigraphic Evidence' in W.Rodwell (ed) *Temples, Churches and Religion in Roman Britain* B.A.R. 77i. Oxford: British Archaeological Reports, 79–90.

Hassal, M.W.C. and Tomlin, R.S.O. (1979) 'Roman Britain in 1978;II Inscriptions', *Britannia* 10, 339–56,

Hassal, M.W.C. and Tomlin, R.S.O. (1982) 'Roman Britain in 1981:II Inscriptions', *Britannia* 13, 396–422.

Haverfield, F. (1905) 'Romano-British Remains' in *The Victoria History of the Counties of England:Derbyshire* Vol.2. London: H.M.S.O., 191–264.

Hawkes, C.F.C and Hull, M.R. (1947) *Camulodunum, Society of Antiquaries of London Research Report* London: Society of Antiquaries of London.

Henig, M. (1984) 'Throne, Altar and Sword:Civilian Religion and the Roman Army in Britain' in T.F.C.Blagg and A.C.King (eds) *Military and Civilian in Roman Britain* B.A.R. 136. Oxford: British Archaeological Reports, 227–48.

Hinchcliffe, J. and Green, C.S. (1985) *Excavations at Brancaster 1974 and 1977*, East Anglian Archaeology Report 23. Norwich: Norfolk Archaeological Unit.

Hodges, R. (1991) *Wall-to-Wall History*. London: Duckworth.

Hodges, R. and Wildgoose, M. (1980) 'Roman or Native in the White Peak' in K.Branigan (ed) *Rome and the Brigantes*. Sheffield: Department of Archaeology and Prehistory, 48–53.

Hogg, A.H.A. (1968) 'Pen Llystyn, a Roman Fort and Other Remains', *Arch.J.* 125, 101–92.

Howe, M.D., Perrin, J.R. and Mackreth, D.F. (1980) *Roman Pottery from the Nene Valley:A Guide*. Peterborough: Peterborough Museum.

Hunter, J.K., Manby, T.G. and Spaul, J.E.H. (1967/70) 'Recent Excavations at the Slack Roman Fort near Huddersfield', *Y.A.J.* 42, 74–97.

Isings, C. (1957) *Roman Glass fron Dated Finds*. Groningen: Walters.

James, S. (1984) 'Britain and the Late Roman Army' in T.F.C.Blagg and A.C.King (eds) *Military and Civilian in Roman Britain* B.A.R. 136. Oxford: British Archaeological Reports, 161–87.

Johnson, A. (1983) *Roman Forts of the First and Second Centuries A.D. in Britain and the German Provinces*. London: Black.

Jones, G.D.B. (1967) 'Manchester University Excavations 1967', *D.A.J.* 87, 154–8.

Jones, G.D.B. (1968) 'The Romans in the North West', *Northern History* 3, 1–26.

Jones, G.D.B. (1984) 'Becoming Different Without Knowing It: the Role and Development of Vici' in T.F.C.Blagg and A.C.King (eds) *Military and Civilian in Roman Britain* B.A.R. 136. Oxford: British Archaeological Reports, 75–91.

Jones, G.D.B. and Grealey, S. (1974) *Roman Manchester*. Altrincham: Sherratt.

Jones, G, D.B. and Reynolds, P. (1978) *Roman Manchester:The Deansgate Excavations 1978*. Manchester.

Jones, G.D.B. and Thompson, F.H. (1965) 'Brough-on-Noe (Navio)', *D.A.J.* 85, 125–6.

Jones, G.D.B., Thompson, F.H. and Wild, J.P. (1966) 'Manchester University Excavations at Brough-on-Noe (Navio) 1966', *D.A.J.* 86, 99–101.

Jones, G.D.B. and Webster, P.V. (1970) 'Derbyshire Ware-A Reappraisal', *D.A.J.* 89, 113–30.

Jones, G.D.B. and Wild, J.P. (1968) 'Excavations at Brough-on-Noe (Navio) 1968', *D.A.J.* 88, 89–96.

Jones, G.D.B. and Wild, J.P. (1970) 'Manchester University Excavations at Brough-on-Noe (Navio) 1969', *D.A.J.* 89, 99–106.

Jones, R.F.J. (1984) 'Settlement and Society in N.E.England in the Third Century A.D.' in P.R.Wilson and R.F.J.Jones (eds) *Settlement and Society in the Roman North*. Bradford: Department of Archaeology Bradford University, 39–42.

Kay, S.O. (1962) 'The Romano-British Pottery Kilns at Hazelwood and Holbrook, Derbyshire' *D.A.J.* 82, 21–42.

Kenyon, K.M. (1948) Excavations at the Jewry Wall Site, Leicester, *Society Antiquaries London Research Report* London: Society of Antiquaries of London.

Keppie, L. (1984) *The Making of the Roman Army*. London: Batsford.

Knorr, R. (1910) *Terra Sigillata von Rottenburg*. Stuttgart.

Knorr, R. (1912) *Sudallische-Terrasigillata-Gefasse vo Rottweil*. Stuttgart.

Knorr, R. (1919) *Topfer und Fabriken verzieter Terra-Sigillata der ersten Jahrhunderts*. Stuttgart.

Knorr, R. (1952) *Terra-Sigillata-Gerfasse der ersten Jahrhunderts mit Topfernament*. Stuttgart.

Lane, H.C. (ed) (1973) *Derwent Archaeological Society Research Report No.1*. Chesterfield.

Lepper, F. and Frere, S.S. (1988) *Trajan's Column*. Glouster: Sutton.

Lewis, N. and Reinhold, M. (1966) *Roman Civilisation Sourcebook 2:The Empire*. London: Harper and Row.

Limbrey, S. (1975) *Soil Science and Archaeology*. London: Academic Press.

Ling, R. (1990)'Excavations at Carsington 1983–84', *D.A.J.* 110, 30–55.

Ling, R. and Courtney, T. (1981) 'Excavations at Carsington 1979–80', *D.A.J.* 101, 58–87.

Loughlin, N. (1977) 'Dales Ware:A Contribution to the Study of Roman Coarse Pottery' in D.Peacock (ed) *Pottery and Early Commerce:Trade and Characterisation in Roman and Later Ceramics*. London: Academic Press, 85–146.

MacMullen, R. (1963) *Soldier and Civilian in the Later Roman Empire*. Cambridge, Mass.: Harvard University Press.

Makepeace, G.A. (1983) 'A Romano-British Settlement at Staden near Buxton', *D.A.J.* 103, 75-85.

Makepeace, G.A. (1985) *A Geographical and Systematic Analysis of the Later Prehistoric and Romano-British Settlement of the Upland Limestone and Gritstone Margins of the Peak District and North East Staffordshire* , Unpublished M.A. Thesis, Keele University

Makepeace, G.A. (1987) 'The Romano-British Settlement at Staden near Buxton:the 1983 Excavations', *D.A.J.* 107, 24-34.

Makepeace, G.A. (1989) 'The Romano-British Settlement at Staden near Buxton:the 1984 and 1985/6 Excavations', *D.A.J.* 109, 17-33.

Manacorda, D. (1977) 'Testimonianze sulla Produzione e ol Consumo dell'olio Tripolitano nell'III secolo', *Dialghi di Archaeologia* 9/10, 542-600

Manning, W.H. (1975) 'Economic Influences on Land Use in the Miiitary Areas of the Highland During the Roman Period' in J.Evans, S.Limbrey and H.Cleere (eds) *The Effect of Man on the Landscape:the Highland Zone*, CBA Research Report 11. London: Council for British Archaeology, 112-6.

Manning, W.H. (1976) *Catalogue of Romano-British Ironwork in the Museum of Antiquities, Newcastle-upon-Tyne*. Newcastle: Society Antiquaries Newcastle-upon-Tyne.

Manning, W.H. (1985) *Catalogue of the Romano-British Iron Tools, Fittings and Weapons in the British Museum*. London: British Museum.

Marsh, G. (1978) 'Early Second Century Finewares in the London Area' in P.Arthur and G.Marsh (eds) *Early Fine Wares in Roman Britain* B.A.R. 57. Oxford: British Archaeological Reports, 119–223

May, T. (1903) 'The Lead Weights from Melandra Castle', *D.A.J.* 25, 165–73

May, T. (1922) *The Roman Forts of Templeborough near Rotherham*. Rotherham: Garnett.

May, T. (1930) *Catalogue of the Roman Pottery in the Colchester and Essex Museum*. Cambridge.

Maxwell, G. (1974) 'Objects of Glass' in A.Rae and V.Rae, 'The Roman Fort at Cramond, Edinburgh:Excavations 1954–66', *Britannia* 5, 197–9.

McDonnell, J.G. (1983) *A Survey of the Ironworking Industry in England 700 B.C.–A.D. 600* Dept. Environment Ancient Monuments Lab Report. London.

McNeil, R., Start, D.and Walker, J. (1989) 'Castleshaw', *Current Archaeology* 114, 225–9.

Miller, S.N. (1928) 'Roman York:Excavations of 1926–1927', *J.R.S.* 18, 61–99.

Milne, G. (1986) *The Port of Roman London*. London: Batsford.

Morin, J. (1913) *La Verrerie en Gaule sous L'Empire Romain*. Paris.

Nash-Williams, V.E. (1932) 'The Roman Legionary Fortress in Caerleon in Monmouthshire. Report on the Excavations Carried Out in the Prysg Field 1927–9', *Archaeologia Cambrensis* 87, 48–104.

Olivier, A. (1982) 'The Ribchester *vicus* and its Context-the Results of Recent Excavations' in P.Clack and S.Haselgrove (eds) *Rural Settlement in the Roman North, CBA Group 3 Occasional Paper*. Durham: Council for British Archaeology. 133–47.

O'Neil, B.H.St.J., (1945) 'Grey Ditch, Bradwell, Derbyshire', *Antiquity* 19, 11–19.

Oswald, A. (1937) *The Roman Pottery Kilns at Little London, Torksey, Lincs.*. Shirebrook: G. Marshall.

Parker, A.J. (1973) 'The Evidence Provided by Underwater Archaeology for Roman Trade in the Western Mediterranean' in D.J.Blackman (ed) *Marine Archaeology*. London: Butterworth.

Peacock, D.P.S. (1971) 'Roman Amphorae in Pre-Roman Britain' in D.Hill and M. Jesson (eds) *The Iron Age and Its Hillforts*, University of Southampton Monograph 1. Southampton: University of Southampton, 161–88.

Peacock, D.P.S. (1978) 'The Rhine and the Problem of Gaulish Wine in Roman Britain' in J.du Plat Taylor and H.Cleere (eds) *Roman Shipping and Trade, Britain and the Rhine Provinces*,CBA Research Report 24. London: Council for British Archaeology, 49–51.

Petch, J.A. (1943) 'Recent Work on Melandra Castle.Preliminary Report', *D.A.J.* 17, 49–63.

Petch, J.A. (1949) 'The Date of Melandra Castle:Evidence of the Pottery', *D.A.J.* 22, 1–40.

Ponsich, M. (1974) *Implantation Rurale Antique sur le Bas-Guadalquivir*. Madrid: Casa de Valazquez.

Ponsich, M. (1979) *Implantation Rhrale Antique sur le Bas-Guadalquivir*. Madrid: Casa de Valazquez.

Potter, T.W. (1979) *Romans in the North West*. Cumberland and Westmorland Antiquarian and Archaeology Society Research Vol. 1.

Preston, F.L. (1969) 'The Roman Road Through Hallamshire to Brough-on-Noe', *T.H.A.S.* 9, 235–244.

Price, J. (1977) 'The Roman Glass' in A.Gentry et al, 'Excavations at Lincoln Road, London Borough of Enfield Nov.1974–March 1976', *Transactions of the London and Middlesex Archaeological Society* 28, 154–61.

Price, J. (1980) 'The Roman Glass' in G.Lambrick, 'Excavations in Park Street, Towcester', *Northamptonshire Archaeology* 15, 63–9.

Price, J. (1983) 'Roman Vessel Glass' in C.Heighway, *The East and North Gates of Gloucester*. Bristol: Western Archaeological Trust, 168–70.

Price, J. (1985) 'The Roman Glass' in L.Pilts and J.K.St.Joseph, *Inchtuthil:The Roman Legionary Fortress*. London, 303–12.

Price, J. (1985a) 'Two Pieces of Polychrome Mosaic Glass Table-Ware from Roman Britain', *Antiq.J.* 65, 468–70.

Price, J. (1987) 'Glass from Felmongers, Harlow in Essex.A Dated Deposit of Vessel Glass - Found in an Antonine Pit', *Annales du 10th Congres de l'Association Internationale pour l'Histoire du Verre, Madrid-Segovie 23–28 Septembre 1985*, 185–206.

Price, J. and Cool, H.E.M. (1985) 'The Glass' in H.R.Hurst, *Kingsholm*. Cambridge: Gloucester Archaeological Publications, 41–54.

Price, J. and Cottam, S. (forthcoming) 'The Roman Glass' in S.Cracknell (ed) *Excavations at Birch Abbey Alcester*. London: Council for British Archaeology.

R.I.B.= Collingwood, R.G. and Wright, R.P. (1965) *The Roman Inscriptions of Britain Vol.l.* Gloucester: Sutton.

R.I.B. IIi = Frere, S.S., Roxan, M. and Tonlin, R.S.O. (1990) *The Roman Inscriptions of Britain Vol.2: Instrumentum Domesticum, Fasicule i.* Gloucester: Sutton.

Richardson, G.G.S. (1969) 'Excavations on Early Roads East from Brough-on-Noe', *T.H.A.S.* 10, 245–51.

Richmond, I.A. (1925) *Huddersfield in Roman Times.* Huddersfield: Tolsen Memorial Museum.

Richmond, I.A. (1938) 'Interim Report on Excavations at the Roman Fort at Brough, Derbyshire', *D.A.J.* 59, 53–65.

Richmond, I.A. (1943) 'Roman Legionaries at Corbridge, their Supply Base, Temples and Religious Cults', *A.A.* 4th s. 21, 127–224.

Richmond, I.A. (1945/6) 'Roman Artillery', *Durham University Journal* 38, 60–3.

Richmond, I.A. and Birley, E. (19303, 'Excavations on Hadrian's Wall in the Birdoswald-Pike Hill Sector 1929', *T.C.W.A.A.S.* 2nd s. 30, 169–205.

Richmond, I.A. and Birley, E. (1940) 'Excavations at Corbridge 1938–9', *A.A.* 4th s. 17, 85–115.

Richmond, I.A., Hodgson, K.S. and St.Joseph, K. (1938) 'The Roman Fort at Bewcastle' *T.C.W.A.A.S.* 2nd s. 38, 195–237.

Richmond, I.A. and Gillam, J.P. (1950) 'Excavations on the Roman Site at Corbridge 1946–49', *A.A.* 4th s. 28, 152–201.

Richmond, I.A. and Gillam, J.P. (1952) 'Further Exploration of the Antonine Fort at Corbridge', *A.A.* 4th s. 30, 239–66.

Richmond, I.A. and Gillam, J.P. with Birley, E. (1951) 'The Temple of Mithras at Carrawburgh' *A.A.* 4th s. 29, 1–92.

Riley, J.A. (1979) 'The Coarse Pottery from Berenice' in J.A.Lloyd (ed) *Excavations at Sidi Khrebish Benghazi (Berenice) Vol.3.* Tripoli: Deprtment of Antiquities of Libya, 113–232.

Rivet, A.L.F. (1964) *Town and Country in Roman Britain* (2nd ed.) London: Hutchinson..

Rivet, A.L.F. and Smith, C. (1981) *The Place Names of Roman Britain* (3rd ed.) London: Batsford.

Robertson, A.S., Scott, M. and Keppie, L. (1975) *Bar Hill* B.A.R. 16. Oxford: British Archaeological Reports.

Rodwell, K.A. (1988) *The Prehistoric and Roman Settlement at Kelvedon, Essex.* London: Chelmsford Archaeological Trust Report 16/CBA Research Report 63.

Rogers, G.B. (1974) *Poteries Sigillees de la Gaule Centrale, Gallia supplement 28.*

Salway, P. (1981) *Roman Britain.* Oxford: Oxford University Press.

Samuels, J. (1983) *The Production of Roman Pottery in the East Midlands,* Unpublished Ph.D. Thesis, Nottingham University.

Simpson, F.G. (1913) 'Excavations on the Line of the Roman Wall in Cumberland During the Years 1909–12', *T.C.W.A.A.S.* 13, 297–397.

Simpson, G. (1973) 'Roman Manchester and Templeborough:the Forts and Dates Reviewed' in C.Hawkes and S.Hawkes (eds) *Greeks, Celts and Romans.* London: Dent.

Smith, A.H.V. and Butterworth, M.A. (1967) *Miospores in the Coal Seams of the Carboniferous of Great Britain* Pal. Assoc.Special Paper No.l. London: Palaeontological Association.

Smithard, W. (1911) 'The Roman Camp near Coneygrey House, Pentrich', *D.A.J.* 33, 111–14.

Sommer, C.S. (1984) *The Military Vici in Roman Britain* B.A.R. 129. Oxford: British Archaeological Reports.

Speidel, M. (1973) 'The Pay of the Auxilia', *J.R.S.* 63, 141–7.

Start, D. (1985) 'Survey and Conservation Work at Castleshaw Roman Forts, 1984–5', *Greater Manchester Archaeological Journal* 1, 13–18.

Stead, I.M. (1976) *Excavations at Winteringham Roman Villa, and Other Roman Sites in N.Lincolnshire, 1958–1969.* London: H.M.S.O..

Stead, I.M. (1980) *Rudston Roman Villa.* Leeds: Yorkshire Archaeological Soceity.

Steer, K.A. (1951) 'The Roman Fort and Temporary Camp at Oakwood, Selkirkshire', *Proc.Soc.Antiq.Scot.* 86, 81–105.

Stevenson, L.P. and Gaunt, G.D. (1971) *Geology of the Country Around Chapel en le Frith,* Memoirs of the Geological Survey of Great Britain. London: H.M.S.O..

Tchernia, A. (1967) 'Les Amphores Romaines et L'Histoire Economique', *Journal des Savantes* 224 (Oct.–Dec.).

Thompson, F.H. (1976) 'The Excavation of the Roman Ampitheatre at Chester', *Arch.* 105, 127–239.

Thompson-Watkin, W. (1885) 'The Roman Stations of Derhyshire', *D.A.J.* 7, 70–91.

Todd, M. (1969) 'The Roman Settlement at Margidunum.The Excavations of 1966–8', *.Transactions of the Thoroton Society* 73, 6–111.

Tylecoate, R.F. (1986) *The Prehistory of Metallurgy in the British Isles.*

Van Nostrand, J.J. (1937) 'Roman Spain' in T.Frank (ed) *An Economic Survey of Ancient Rome Vol.3.* Paterson, N.J.: Pageant. 119–224.

Wacher, J.S.O. (1969) *Excavations at Brough on Humber 1958–61,* Society of Antiquaries of London Research Report. London: Society of Antiquaries of London.

Walker, J.S.F. (1986) *Roman Manchester, A Fronstier Settlement.* Manchester: Greater Manchester Archaeology Unit.

Walters, H.B. (1914) *Catalogue of Greek and Roman Lamps in the British Museum.* London: British Museum.

Ward, J. (1899) 'Roman Remains at Bradwell', *D.A.J.* 21, 1–4.

Webster, G. (1961) 'An Excavation on the Roman Site at Little Chester, Derby', *D.A.J.* 81, 85–110.

Webster, G. (ed) (1976) *Romano-British Coarse Pottery: A Student's Guide* (3rd ed.) CBA Research Report 6. London: Council for British Archaeology.

Webster, P.V. (1971) 'Melandra Castle Roman Fort:Excavations in the Civil Settlement', *D.A.J.* 91, 58–117.

Wedlake, W.J. (1982) *The Excavation of the Shrine of Apollo at Nettleton, Wiltshire, 1956–71*, Society of Antiquaries of London Research Report. London: Society of Antiquaries of London.

Welsby, D.A. (1982) *The Roman Military Defence of the British Provinces its Later Phases* B.A.R. 101. Oxford: British Archaeological Reports.

Welsh, T.C. (1984) 'Road Remains at Burbage and Houndkirk Moors, Sheffield–A Possible Roman Road', *Y.A.J.* 56, 27–31.

Wheeler, H. (1985) 'Conclusion:The Development of Roman Derby', *D.A.J.* 105, 300–4.

Wheeler, H. (1985a) 'North-West Sector Excavations 1979–1980', *D.A.J.* 105, 38–153.

Wheeler, R.E.M. and Wheeler, T.V. (1928) 'The Roman Ampitheatre at Caerleon, Monmouthshire', *Arch.* 78, 111–218.

Wilkes, J.J. (1985) 'R.I.B. 1322:A Note', *Zeitschrift fur Papyrologie und Epigraphik* 59.

Wright, R.P. and Hassal, M.W.C. (1974) 'Roman Britain in 1973:II Inscriptions', *Britannia* 5, 461–470.

Wroe, P. (1982) 'Roman Roads in the Peak District', *D.A.J.*102, 49–73.

Wroe, P. and Mellor, P. (1971) 'A Roman Road Between Buxton and Melandra Castle, Glossop', *D.A.J.* 91, 40–57.

Young, .C.J. (1980) *Guidelines for the Processing and Publication of Roman Pottery from Excavations.* DoE Occasional Paper No. 4. London: HMSO.

Zevi, F. (1967) 'A Review of Callender Roman Amphorae', *J.R.S.* 57, 234–8.

ENGLISH HERITAGE
CENTRAL ARCHAEOLOGY SERVICE
FORT CUMBERLAND
FORT CUMBERLAND ROAD
EASTNEY, PORTSMOUTH
HANTS.
PO4 9LD